Will the Nazi Eagle Rise Again?

What the Church Needs to Know about BDS and Other Forms of Anti-Semitism

"Christian activism in the Middle East too often bears fruit that contradicts basic Christian values. If we Christians want to be relevant in a region drenched by strife and bloodshed, we'll have to overcome introspection, look beyond the pink colored mirror, and listen to Jewish voices as well. David Friedman is such a voice, living for many years in the region, observing, listening, researching and thinking thoroughly."

— Johannes Gerloff, Journalist, Theologian, Lecturer and Author; Jerusalem, Israel

"This book lays out the issues clearly. Anti-Semitism is not what we should expect from the Church and from Evangelicals, in particular. We are in a war and David Friedman's book has the essential information for us to stand firm with Israel–God's forever chosen people–for their God-given task to bless the world."

— Roger Walkwitz, President, Asia Pacific Messianic Fellowship, Florida, USA

"I greatly appreciate this book. We ought to listen carefully to its message; it is the right book at the right time.

Dr. Friedman exposes the roots of Anti-Semitism being resurrected in our days, especially in our Christian Church. This is clearly visible for all who want to see, particularly in political and religious attitudes and activities which discriminate against the modern State of Israel.

I strongly recommend this book and I hope that it will find many open minds and hearts to receive its truths in love and faith."

— Dr. H. Kägi, Teacher and Theologian, Basle, Switzerland

"David Friedman is like 'the sons of Issachar–men who understood the times, with knowledge of what Israel should do,' (1 Chron. 12:32). *Will the Nazi Eagle Rise Again?* is a timely and important response to the dangerous hatred of the State of Israel that is growing in society and in the Church. Read it to learn what is happening and to get the truth."

— Michael Rydelnik, Professor of Jewish Studies, Moody Bible Institute, Chicago, IL

Will the Nazi Eagle Rise Again?

What the Church Needs to Know about BDS and Other Forms of Anti-Semitism

David Friedman, Ph.D.

Lederer Books
A division of
Messianic Jewish Publishers
Clarksville, MD 21029

Unless otherwise noted, all Scripture quotations are taken from the *Complete Jewish Bible.* Copyright by David H. Stern, Jewish New Testament Publications, Inc., 1998.

Also quoted is the NASB, used by permission of The Lockman Foundation.

Printed in the United States of America
Cover design by Lisa Rubin,
Messianic Jewish Publishers
Graphic Design by Yvonne Vermillion,
Magic Graphix, Westfork, Arkansas

2017 1

ISBN 978-1-936716-87-6
Library of Congress Control Number: 2016961728

Published by:
Lederer Books
A Division of Messianic Jewish Publishers & Resources
6120 Day Long Lane
Clarksville, MD 21029

Distributed by:
Messianic Jewish Publishers & Resources
Order line: (800) 410-7367
lederer@messianicjewish.net
www.MessianicJewish.net

Dedication

I dedicate this book, with gratefulness, to my wife.

"May *Adonai* lift up His face upon you, and give you shalom."

Table of Contents

Foreword

by L. Mayekiso

There is no simple answer to the rise of anti-Semitism within the Church, since several factors converge to produce this disturbing outcome. Nevertheless, it is difficult to understand how believers in the God of Abraham, Isaac, and Jacob can choose to stand in solidarity with those who deny Jewish history and its connection to the land of Israel. How is it fathomable that a person, on the one hand, can lay claim to believe the Bible and yet, on the other hand, staunchly refute the Scriptural truth that Israel is the Land promised to the Jewish people? This only can be attributed to spiritual blindness, as the commands and prophecies relating to Israel are found in both testaments of the Bible.

The passage of time has seen various theologies infused with political agendas and creative modern narratives that have led to increased hostility towards the Jewish state of Israel. Chief amongst these is Replacement or Fulfillment Theology that, sadly, is almost as old as the Church itself. Clearly, Paul's message in Romans–which cautions the Church to avoid arrogance and to remember that it is a grafted branch–continues to fall on deaf ears. Liberation Theology is its contemporary evolution.

This theology is motivated by revolutionary political activism and interprets Scripture from the perspective of the poor or oppressed in their quest for justice and protection of human rights. While its origins may have been noble, its application today seems to have morphed into something far removed from Scripture. This theology found its way to South Africa and into the expression known as South African Black Theology.

In seeking to emulate South African Black Theology and seize the opportunity to make an emotional connection with the struggle of the Black people against the apartheid government, a segment of the Church in Israel has developed Palestinian Liberation Theology. Stemming from this, the Kairos Palestine Document–mimicking the South African Kairos document of the mid-1980's–was released in 2009. It was addressed to the global Church as an appeal for their support against what was termed "Israeli apartheid" and "occupation." Consistent with Liberation Theology, it is extraordinary that a document–which purports to be Christian in nature–can dismiss all Scripture relating to God's covenants with Israel and prophecy, and finally seek to endorse Palestinian political attempts to expunge Jewish history in Israel. Terms such as "oppression," "settlement" and "colonialism," in relation to Israel, are used to pervert history.

The groundwork was laid in South Africa in 2001 and 2009 for labeling Israel as an "apartheid state." The BDS (Boycott, Divestment and Sanctions) has exploited the historical links between the African National Congress (ANC) and the Palestine Liberation Organization (PLO) by making South Africa the center of its delegitimization campaign. Apartheid took place in South Africa, so who could be better placed to lend credibility to the apartheid libel against Israel than we Black South Africans? We in South Africa are rightfully viewed by the world as the moral arbiters of what constitutes apartheid.

The sad reality is that most South Africans, as with the majority of people around the world, are largely uninformed about the situation in Israel. The BDS seduces Black South Africans to see themselves in the shoes of Palestinians and to relive their apartheid experiences. As a Black South African who has endured apartheid, and made several visits to Israel, I can with a clear conscience state that Israel is not an apartheid state and bears absolutely no resemblance to the institutionalized racial oppression that I lived under in South Africa. As a Black South African, who was born in an apartheid homeland and experienced the cruelties of such an oppressive racial system, I am deeply offended by this comparison.

Although apartheid was repealed more than two decades ago in South Africa, the legacy still lingers as many individuals in our country still display racist attitudes. I have experienced racism in some of the world's democratic capitals, including Washington, D.C., London, and Paris. In Israel, I have felt the complete freedom of being to which all people aspire–where neither my skin color nor my religion determined how those around me related to me.

If anything, as an African, I can readily identify with the quest of the Jewish people for their ancestral homeland. The great strides that are evident in their nation's development not only confirm that there is a God and his Word comes to pass, but also gives the people of Africa hope that we, too, can emulate them.

Therefore, the only substitute for those who are not acquainted with the facts first-hand, is factual and actual literature that provides an authentic perspective which goes beyond 1948 in dealing with the full history of the Jewish people and their prophetic destiny. Ignorance of scripture, history and facts cannot be an excuse, and the Israel-Palestine conflict is one where no person who believes in God can afford to be an innocent bystander. There is a duty upon each one of us to acquaint ourselves with the truth without fear or favor. I have spent several years speaking, teaching, lobbying and engaging different audiences in a quest to present an accurate portrayal of Israel. In this time, I have come to appreciate the need for a reliable resource that encompasses issues of faith, history and politics into one book.

This is it. I encourage you to read, be informed, inspired and challenged; but, most of all, go out there and speak the truth.

Luba Mayekiso
Africa for Israel Christian Coalition
Republic of South Africa

Foreword

by H. Raysman

There is growing and widespread concern among Jews in Israel and in the diaspora, and among friends of Israel everywhere, about the increasing threat posed by the BDS (Boycott, Divestment and Sanctions) movement. The BDS movement has become the spearhead and rallying cry for those who wish to demonize and delegitimize the Jewish State. While the BDS rhetoric purports that Israel must be pressured through boycotts, economic divestment and sanctions to change their policies towards the Palestinians–allowing them their own freedom and independence–the real intention of BDS is much different.

In spite of this campaign, Israel is feeling very little economic pressure from the BDS movement. Almost every major hi-tech giant today has a Research and Development center in Israel. Trade with booming developing countries like India and China is at record levels. The State of Illinois recently unanimously passed a bill which would prevent the State's pension fund from investing in companies that boycott Israel. At this point, the BDS movement is not an economic threat to Israel. The real threat posed by BDS is in its success in poisoning hearts and minds against Israel.

BDS gives haters of Israel a tangible campaign around which to focus their efforts. Instead of just spewing hatred against Israel, the BDS movement allows them to spew their hatred while targeting a purpose with which people can identify and join. "Human rights" has become the proverbial magician's cloak that, while sounding ethical, actually conceals the truth from others. As is already evident, the fight against the BDS movement will not be easy. Nevertheless, it is a fight that must be fought, not only for the sake of the Jewish people and for the sake of the Land God granted to them, but for the sake of biblical truth.

BDS supporters who claim to be motivated by Israel's human rights record deliberately choose to ignore the horrific human rights abuses of every single one of the surrounding Arab nations. They are silent in their condemnation of these and other tyrannical states and dictatorships, yet not hesitant to castigate Israel. The double standards and hypocrisy of this movement must be examined.

Second Kings 6:15-18 describes the incident of Elisha and a city under attack:

> 15 When the servant of the man of God got up and went out early the next morning, an army with horses and chariots had surrounded the city. "Oh, my lord, what shall we do?" the servant asked.
>
> 16 "Don't be afraid," the prophet answered. "Those who are with us are more than those who are with them."
>
> 17 And Elisha prayed, "O LORD, open his eyes so he may see." Then the LORD opened the servant's eyes, and he looked and saw the hills full of horses and chariots of fire all around Elisha.

> 18 As the enemy came down toward him, Elisha prayed to the LORD, "Strike these people with blindness." So he struck them with blindness, as Elisha had asked.

It is possible that current supporters of the BDS movement are doing so out of fear and ignorance. If we truly desire to be effective in our opposition to BDS, both we and those who have been blinded by BDS propaganda have to be informed. Dr. David Friedman's book is timely as it exposes the spirit behind the BDS campaign, the false allegation of apartheid, and the theological push toward supercessionism. May the God of Israel open the eyes of all who call upon the Name of the LORD; we ask and pray in Yeshua's name!

Herschel Raysman, Rabbi
Cape Town, RSA, June 2015

Introduction

In 2004, I was visiting a friend in Switzerland. We went hiking in the Alps on a crisp winter day. After a tiring uphill climb of an icy, narrow, winding metal staircase, we reached our destination. We were thoroughly exhausted from the forty-five minute, steep walk through two Swiss mountain villages, and up onto the top of the 900-meter high "hill." From every direction, we could see snowy mountain peaks; toward Lucerne to the southwest, there was simply a stunningly breathtaking view of the Swiss Alps. My friend and guide–Gunter–then informed me that we were seeing some 40 kilometers into the distance. When we looked north, the view into Germany was clear.

Gunter remarked that he had been climbing this hill to enjoy the views for over twenty years and had never seen a winter day with such a clear panorama. Out came the cameras, and as we set up to take shots of the Alps, I saw something that utterly amazed me. There was a metal bench on the antenna's gallery porch for climbers to rest on. It was just in front of me. On the bench was an engraving right into the silver metal. It was a caricature of a man who was hanging at the end of a rope, with a caption that said in German, *Sharon must die!* [1]

Gunter shook his head. "I am ashamed that any Swiss person would think this," he told me. "You know, we Swiss weren't as innocent and neutral during the Holocaust as people think we were. You know the story of the Nazi gold, right?" he asked me. "Unfortunately I do," I answered. "And you know that although Swiss Jews were safe here, our government turned back many German Jews who fled here for refuge, insuring their death. People here are terribly naïve," he continued. We both sat on the bench, and the thrill of the view was interrupted for a short while.

My friend continued:

> We have learned nothing from what happened. Anti-Semitism in Europe hasn't been this intense since the Holocaust. Too many of us think that they can support the claims of the PA but not be anti-Semitic. They believe that there is a difference between hating Israelis and hating Jews. No, my friend, in Europe today we see Hitler's ideas being recycled, and the problem is that young people, even our young politicians here in Switzerland, can't remember the lessons of the Holocaust. Not one Swiss person should pretend that he has the moral right to dictate to Israel how to behave. Not after how we in Europe behaved so despicably just 60 years ago. So, my friend, we now have our silver bench.

He didn't need to say anything more. And he didn't.

During the trek back, Gunter told me about numerous occasions when anti-Israel activists attempted to bully Swiss shopkeepers in his area to boycott the importing of Israeli goods. "It is similar to Nazi party members standing outside

Jewish shops in the late '30s in Germany, bullying locals to boycott Jewish businesses. Too similar for me," Gunter related. "These activists here say there is no connection to the past . . . well, I've actually heard some of them say, 'You are Swiss, the same people as Germans; this is good. We like Hitler, but he didn't do his job well enough'." He continued on, "You know, the Nazis had their political justification in boycotting Jewish shops; the anti-Israel activists have theirs, too. I can't see it boiling down to much more than just hating Jews, whether Jewish people live in Germany or in Israel. The message I hear is that Jews simply have no right to live. Isn't that the message of the suicide bombers, really?" Gunter is a Swiss man with a big conscience.

Unfortunately, Switzerland is not the only landscape experiencing a modern day rise of Hitlerian anti-Semitism. I also am reminded of a 1990 visit I made to London, during which my Israeli companion insisted that I tuck my Star of David pendant inside of my shirt. He did not have to say why. That incident leads me to think of a 2006 trip to Germany, where a local Christian pastor who loves the Jewish people invited me to speak at his congregation. When I arrived, only a handful of senior citizens were in attendance. "I couldn't advertise this event," he sadly told me, "because my congregants, mostly elderly, are terrified that they would be attacked or verbally assaulted on their way here by Middle Easterners who live in their neighborhoods who hate Israel." This congregation is located in the heart of one of Germany's largest cities. A recent visit to Copenhagen, where similar anti-Semitic sentiment has been expressed, was marred by a terror assault while we were there. The Swedish Jewish community in Malmo, Sweden fears for its very life:

> A member of Malmo's Jewish community, an elderly man, recently stated: "I left Poland to get away from anti-Semitism. But at least there I never experienced any violence. That only happened to me here, in Sweden."
>
> The Jews of Malmö, a community of about 1,500 in a city of 300,000, are living through a new form of anti-Semitism. This kind does not stem from neo-Nazis or right-wing extremists—traditional perpetrators of European Jew-hatred—but has come to the city through immigrants from North Africa and the Middle East.[2]

I need not recount the event of the vicious anti-Semitic attack at the kosher delicatessen in Paris in January 2015. France, Germany, England, Sweden, the Netherlands, Denmark, Switzerland, and the USA all are experiencing a rise in anti-Semitism. The relevant question, then, is what will the role of the Church be in combatting the growth of such anti-Semitism?

In conjunction with addressing this question, this book will examine a troubling Church collaboration with this growing sentiment, as opposed to resistance to it. In light of the continuing phenomenon of Christian clergy and movements that blame Jewish people for various ills around the world, of particular concern is the role that the Church now plays in actually fueling anti-Semitism in the world today. Of course, this is not a new phenomenon. It is a 2,000-year-old trap into which the historic Church far too often has fallen. This work will look at some who, perhaps unwittingly, have fallen into this same trap today.

This also is not a new topic for review and comment. Other authors have written extensively on the historic Church's involvement in anti-Semitism. Catholic authors James Carroll and Father Edward Flannery captured the essence of what lies behind historic Christian persecution, slander and libel of Jewry in their respective works, *Constantine's Sword* and *The Anguish of the Jews*. Methodist clergyman Franklin Littell has done the same in his work, *The Crucifixion of the Jews*.

Anti-Semitic incidents in Western Europe peaked to a level not seen since the close of World War II, according to numbers released by the Jewish Agency.[3] As numerous social and political commentators have noted that today's world is evidencing the same level of anti-Semitism found in Europe just prior to the Holocaust, it appears that it is time for another treatise if we are to stem the tide before it's too late.

The Guardian recently reported:

> "These are the worst times since the Nazi era," Dieter Graumann, president of Germany's Central Council of Jews, told the Guardian. "On the streets, you hear things like 'the Jews should be gassed', 'the Jews should be burned' – we haven't had that in Germany for decades. Anyone saying those slogans isn't criticizing Israeli politics; it's just pure hatred against Jews: nothing else. And it's not just a German phenomenon. It's an outbreak of hatred against Jews so intense that it's very clear indeed." [4]

In 2004 America's ambassador to the European Union, Rockwell Schnabel, warned the world that anti-Semitism in Europe was reaching its 1930s levels. A recent survey by Professor Gustavo Frandyck notes that 150 million Europeans believe that Israel practices apartheid, and carries out actions similar to the Nazis. Renowned author Daniel Goldhagen recently wrote that 200 million Europeans equate Israel with Nazi practices.[5] Although not a historical analysis of current anti-Semitism, this treatise *examines* a number of troublesome events and trends occurring in a Christian context, which appear to be contributing to the rise of anti-Semitism. As a Jew with many Christian friends, and due to these recent occurrences, I am constrained by my conscience before Almighty God to write this book now.

D. Friedman
Jerusalem, Israel
September 2016

Chapter 1

Disconnects Between New Testament Faith & the Jewish Messiah

In his letter to Rome, Paul makes a vital point for each and every follower of Yeshua to know:

> But if some of the branches were broken off, and you–a wild olive–were grafted in among them and have become equal sharers in the rich root of the olive tree, then don't boast as if you were better than the branches! However, if you do boast, remember that you are not supporting the root, the root is supporting you. (Rom. 11:17-18, NASB)

Gentile believers have joined Israel through faith in Israel's Messiah. Israel's Messiah brought non-Jews into the world of Israel's God–the One True God–the Creator of all. That is fact. Paul leaves no other option: you are "grafted in among them." Gentile believers have joined something very special. The root of an olive tree supports a branch by feeding it sap. That liquid brings nourishment–that is, *life itself*–to the branch. The root enables each branch to live and grow. What happens if the branch decides that it doesn't want to be connected to the root, and pulls away from it? Death!

For some of the new Gentile believers in Rome, the biblical message was novel. The concepts in the Bible and its lifestyle instructions were not familiar to them. It was not the practice of the Roman Empire (especially in the city of Rome) to live as the Jewish people did. Only in the scriptures, history, and lifestyle of the Jewish world (through Messianic Jews) could the new Roman believers gain familiarity with how to live righteously. In this context, Paul wrote Romans 11:17-20, encouraging the new Gentile followers of Yeshua to understand how intimately connected to Israel they were. He used the image of the olive tree, understood to be a symbol of Israel. Jeremiah (11:16), referring to Judah, states, "God called you an olive tree, beautiful, full of leaves and good fruit. . . . "

If it were so important for the Gentile followers of Yeshua of Paul's day and age to understand their inherent connection to Israel and the Jewish people, can it be any less important today? How is it, then, that some Christians have, as a matter of routine, rationalized their efforts to divorce God from Israel, performing theological acrobatics to distort the simple meaning of the Biblical text?

A worldwide Church that is blind to its connection to the root of the olive tree will be blind to many Biblical truths. Pulling away from the connection to Israel's legacy can only weaken the destiny of the Church. Under such conditions, the branch begins to wither. It becomes something other than what was intended–a dried up, wilted branch, in the process of dying.

In Church history, the Church became in large part anti-Semitic as a result of its "divorce" from its Jewish roots—

that is, its great distancing from the root of the olive tree of Israel. Instead of embracing the Jewish people, after about the 2nd century, the early Church by-and-large pulled away from Israel and created an entity that was far removed from its root. Following teaching rooted in both dislike of Jews and theological supercessionism, too many early Church authorities minimized the connection of Christians to the Jewish people. Thus, the distance between the Jewish world in which Yeshua arose and the early Gentile Church quickly grew, and a wide disparity between the Jewish people and the emerging Christian church became apparent. This historical fact is one of the saddest in human history, because its consequences were devastating.

As one German Christian leader phrased it: "Jesus was welcomed as the Son of God but not as King of the Jews. Thus Christianity was led astray, and instead of being their strongest protector, the Church became the Jews' most avid persecutor."[1]

Unfortunately, the early Church is not the only period in history to fail to recognize the interdependence of the olive tree and its grafted in branches. In Nazi Germany, too many theologians formed their biblical teachings based on the following perspective:

> Jesus was to be stripped of his Jewishness and turned into an Aryan, while Jews themselves were subjected to public contempt, derision and ridicule, and left at the mercy of their killers. . . .Theologians set about "cleansing the New Testament of Jewish influences", with unprecedented blindness. [2]

How can Christians today think that they can avoid erring from Biblical truth if there is severance from the root and branches of the olive tree? Paul's words are reality, and even if someone does not like his imagery or the truths he is teaching, this does not lessen their importance. Whether one believes that the root of the olive tree is Messiah Yeshua, or that the root is Biblical history, the point remains the same: separation from the olive tree (Israel) results in death to the grafted-in branches (Gentile believers). It is imperative that Christians comprehend the grave consequences of renouncing their relationship with Israel and the Jewish people, whether through political maneuvering or rejectionist or replacement theology.

We may hear many politically expedient reasons to interpret the Bible certain ways, or seemingly "just" reasons to hate Israel and work towards dismantling the Jewish state. Reasons to avoid identifying with and loving the Jewish people are being given within many sectors of the worldwide Church. Lurking behind all of this is an ideology that is trying to pry Gentile believers away from their relationship with Israel. Its effect is to uproot Christians from the olive tree. The relationship between the olive tree and its root and the branches, is something that Yeshua paid for *with his life*. He brought Gentiles close to Israel's God and God's people, heritage and legacy—*a Jew* brought Gentiles close to God. No amount of supercessionist theology or political expediency will ever change that fact. To quote a Middle Eastern teacher, whom I heard speak at a conference in the summer of 2015: "The Jewish people brought us the Messiah and the scriptures.

For this reason alone, we should respect them."[3]

Paul speaks similarly to the Gentile followers of Yeshua in Ephesus.

> You were estranged from the national life of Isra'el. You were foreigners to the covenants embodying God's promise. You were in this world without hope and without God. But now, you who were once far off have been brought near through the shedding of the Messiah's blood. (Eph. 2:12b-13)

They had been far away from Israel, that is, from Israel's national life, which would include the Bible and the Messiah. This great distance created no hope for redemption and no hope to draw near to God. Messiah's actions brought these persons *near*. Near to what? Near to God. Near to the scriptures. Near to the hope of redemption. And near *to Israel*, because all of these things have their place and foundation among the people of Israel. Certainly, then, hating Israel is a fundamental contradiction to what God teaches and is a blatant disregard of the blessing from being grafted in and, in a very real way, a rejection of God, himself. This misguided attitude is prevalent in the writing and teaching of many Palestinian Christians, who have exalted politics over the authority of God's Word– the very bible in which they say their faith is rooted.

One weakness of the rejectionist Palestinian Christian wing is that they do not understand the crucial point made in Romans 11:17-20, that Gentiles are "grafted in" with the natural branches (Israel) and "have become equal sharers of the rich root of the olive tree. "They refuse to identify with this imagery or they redefine "Israel" to fit their political goals of rejectionist and supercessionist theologies. Thus they do not follow the *peshat*–plain meaning–of the text. They complicate it to make the olive tree refer to something other than the Jewish people. It is not rare for them to let their political leanings inform the text, instead of the other way around.

I suspect that in lieu of a first identity as Christians connected to the root of the olive tree, their first identity is as Palestinians, and as believers, secondarily. One Palestinian Christian scholar told me, "I am a Palestinian. But I am a follower of Jesus first and foremost. The Bible connects me through him to Israel, and so my Palestinian identity is not as influential to me as the new one which God gave me." He then mentioned to me that another person, present in the room at that time, a Palestinian Christian cleric, did not share his belief, but held *his Palestinian identity* to be *the* key by which he interpreted the scriptures.

The first scholar referred to is able to understand the point made by Paul in Romans 11:17-20, and is able to identify with being connected to Israel's history, scriptures, calling, and Messiah. Yet he certainly does not have to deny his Palestinian identity, nor does he. It all goes hand in hand, if we understand the point that Paul is making here.

The second person mentioned denied that Yeshua was Jewish and that Israel is the Jewish people and not some other ethnic entity. And that is just the starting point for his biblical interpretation. He then interprets the Bible in light of these very denials. For him, his politics informs the biblical text and dictates how to understand biblical history.

Paul considered the connection to the root of the olive tree to be important for the believers in Rome. As a subject of the Roman Empire, the State required absolute obedience within its borders. Messianic Jews of the first century in Rome, and the Gentile believers who were with them, had to have another identity as prime. Their loyalty was not first to the Emperor. For Jews, such a concept was not too hard to understand. The Bible makes it clear, and had done so for 1800 years of Jewish history up to that point, that God is to receive our primary loyalty.

It is my observation that Palestinian rejectionist clerics' perspectives are very reminiscent of those espoused by the German theologians who condoned and supported Hitler's campaign to annihilate Europe's Jewish community. They have attempted to take Yeshua's Jewish identity away from him, trying to substitute it with a "Palestinian identity," whatever that means. Yet, Yeshua is identified–well after his resurrection–by his student John as "the Lion of the tribe of Judah" (cf. Rev. 5.5).

Palestinian Christians, like all Christians, are formed to function in connection to the Jewish people, as explained in Romans 11:17-20. However, the rejectionist wing denies God's promises to restore the Jewish people to the Land of Israel, and then advocates political positions that cause more suffering for Jews. Such attitudes support the positions of Hamas and the Palestinian Authority (PA) vis-à-vis Israel's right to exist. Furthermore, they attempt to draw the Church away from its connection to the root of the olive tree. In doing all of this, I believe that their perspective harms the Church, harms the Jewish people and, ultimately, harms their own people.

Such an assessment would be consistent with what I have heard from a number American Christians, in particular, who have told me that after spending time listening to rejectionist Palestinian Christian speakers, they emerged with great dislike towards Israel (i.e., Jews, since Israel is made up of nearly 80% Jews and is the Jewish state). Yet, God clearly states in Isaiah 49.14-16, what his attitude is towards Zion, meaning Israel:

Zion said: "I am abandoned by God; and Adonai has forgotten me."

> Can a woman forget the infant who came from her womb, from her abdomen? Even if these could be forgotten, I will certainly not forget you.
>
> Look, on My palms I have carved out your (name); your city walls are always before Me. (Isa. 49: 14-16, my translation)

If this is God's attitude, it ought always to be a Christian's attitude, as well. Anything else is simply wrong. This particular text explains that God feels about Zion like a mother feels about her newborn. I have often asked audiences if any mothers among them could ever forget that they gave birth to a baby. No mother has ever responded affirmatively to this question. God takes this example out of the human experience to allow us insight into his thoughts about Israel. Moreover, "Zion" is a cognate term to Jerusalem, and is often used to indicate the Jewish people. In the Bible, tattooing oneself is not acceptable, if the tattoo–as in Canaanite religious practice–involves idolatry. Yet, Isaiah uses this image to show how permanently the love for Israel is carved into God's palms. God does not have a corporeal body, and so the image is meant to inform us of the immutability of his love for the descendants of Abraham, Isaac and Jacob. Jerusalem always drew God's attention. Similarly, Deuteronomy 11:12 states, "(Israel) is a Land that Adonai your God desires; his eyes are always fixated on it, from the beginning of the year till the end of the year" (my translation).

It is not just the physical landscape that would attract God to Israel; most people with whom I speak are more attracted to Switzerland or the Greek Isles. But Israel's attraction is more connected to her spiritual destiny–her calling–which is only fulfilled when the descendants of Jacob with the Word of God live in the Land, and take up our calling as his priests for mankind. If I understand the wishes of many rejectionist Palestinian Christians, the Jewish state would be dismantled by political force or violent means. Jews would need to leave. The PA President, Mahmoud Abbas, has already announced that not one single Jew can ever live in the PA areas in any "final" settlement:

> Abbas said that no Israeli settlers or border forces could remain in a future Palestinian state and that Palestinians deem illegal all Jewish settlement building within the land occupied in the 1967 Six Days War. The forceful statements appeared to challenge mediator US Secretary of State John Kerry's hopes that the terms of the talks, scheduled to begin Monday night over dinner, be kept secret. "In a final resolution, we would not see the presence of a single Israeli – civilian or soldier – on our lands," Abbas said in a briefing to mostly Egyptian journalists. [4]

Thus, any promises of a future for a single Jew in a PA ruled entity cannot be made.

I appreciate the words of a brave Anglican cleric who has lived his life serving his community in Iraq. He recently wrote:

> Much of Christianity has attempted to thrive without its root. . . . I find it incredibly sad that the radical anti-Judaic polemic has found a new foundation in the past few decades. . . . While these people will deny that they are in any way anti-Semitic, their continual bombardment of Israel can be seen as being blatantly anti-Judaic. [5]

The book of Hosea loses its *entire* meaning with such flaky theologies of a God who sometimes is faithful to his people, and sometimes is not; a God who says he made an everlasting covenant with a people, then who decided to revoke it; a God who gives a gift, then takes it right back. When human behavior is given the power to cancel the promises of God, something is wrong with *our perception* of who God is. Hosea's overall message is that Israel, depicted through Hosea's wife, will and does fail in our covenant faithfulness to God. However, the marriage remains intact and Hosea (depicting God in this relationship) redeems his wife and continues to love her. Rejectionist Palestinian Christians and their secessionist theologians render the main message of the book of Hosea as expendable. If Israel–the Jewish people–has no valid covenant relationship with God today, then Hosea has rejected his wife once and for all.

Such thinking represents one clear fact: these individuals do not understand what Paul was trying to emphasize to the Romans. When this happens, the results can lead both to anti-Semitism and to an inability to comprehend the writings of Paul.[6]

Furthermore, attempts are made to divorce the history of the Jewish people from the Land of Israel. This also qualifies as a type of anti-Semitism by outcome, since it works against the welfare of the Jewish people, while also upholding a prejudicial and inaccurate position regarding the history of the physical Land of Israel. One such way this perspective emerges is to try and weaken the ability of Jewish people to worship at Judaism's holiest site–the Temple Mount. Italian Giulio Meotti, a reporter for the daily *Il Foglio*, has seen the Vatican's attempt to finagle this area away from the control of Israel, and set up joint Christian-Muslim control of this area. He wrote:

> The Catholic de-legitimization of Israel passes through the war on Jerusalem and the war on Jerusalem passes through the Temple Mount. The site where the Jewish people worshipped for hundreds of years and the focal point of every practicing Jew's prayers is under assault from the Vatican. The Vatican-PLO agreements have been signed to enable the eviction of the Jews from Jerusalem. This follows a memorandum signed by Palestinian and Vatican officials in 2000 which repeated the Vatican call for an international mandate to preserve "the proper identity and sacred character" of Jerusalem. It means a return to a time when half of Israel's capital was under Islamic control, the Old City was closed to Jews, the synagogues were desecrated, and walls, barbed wire, and snipers divided the city by force. The Vatican is consistent.[7]

The reader should be aware of this persistent and unfortunate influence of the Vatican. On the other hand, it is heartening to know that throughout the years, *many* Catholic clergy and laypersons have expressed their support of a strong Israel behind firm and secure borders to me. I have met, and still meet, many such persons from Poland, Ireland, the United States, and Mexico. Popular Catholic authors Father Edward Flannery and James Carroll have written extensively on Jewish subjects, upholding the right of Israel to exist as the Jewish state. Catholic author Thomas Cahill has nicely summarized the Jewish contribution to the world–and, in particular, to Christian civilization–in his work *The Gifts of the Jews*. I recommend all three authors.

Romans 11:29 loses it meaning entirely if theological systems are conjured up that revoke what is written in the Bible, ". . . for God's free gifts and his calling are irrevocable (11:29). Clearly, in its context, 11:29 was written about the Jewish people.

Yeshua's clear teachings in Matthew 5:17-20 and John 10:35 lose their meanings entirely if we do not take seriously his teaching that the entire Bible with all of its promises are valid throughout human history–that no valid theological system can take things out of scripture, cancel them, or otherwise "hack them up" according to human whims. The Church would do best to remember the ancient Jewish teaching, that "no verse of Scripture ever escapes its simple, literal meaning." This is true especially in our discussion with portions of the Bible texts that address the restoration of the Jewish people to the Land of Israel, as well as the immutability of God's covenants with Israel.

> Don't think that I have come to abolish the *Torah* or the Prophets. I have come not to abolish but to complete. Yes indeed! I tell you that until heaven and earth pass away, not so much as a *yud* or a stroke will pass from the *Torah*—not until everything that must happen has happened. (Mt. 5:17-18)

Palestinian rejectionist Christians must blatantly deny the veracity of this teaching by supposing that any of God's promises to Israel have been revoked, cancelled or abolished. The meaning of this teaching is that nothing in the Torah can be revoked. Yeshua further stated: ". . . the *Tanakh* cannot be broken" (Jn. 10.35b). The word used in this verse for "broken" is *luthenai*, and it means "to be done away with," "broken into pieces," or "eliminated."

None of what I have just stated precludes the pursuit of justice in society, nor would discourage the love of human rights. There is no reason one cannot love Israel and the Jewish people, and still be concerned that civil rights be applied to all persons across the world. There is no reason that the biblical text would eliminate verses that teach about the value or worth of all human life. Reading and understanding the Bible for what it clearly states is paramount in the discussion of the role of Israel and the Jewish people in God's plans of redemption. Recognizing historic Church error towards Jews that were built upon theological airs of superiority and complicated finagling with scriptural texts is a first step toward peace.

If the Church today, as a whole, understood that it should act in a well-connected way to Israel, and share in and encourage Israel's destiny, then the distance between it and between the Jewish people would shrink greatly. Paul presents the Church's close connection to Israel *as a fact*. The legacy of Israel and the Jewish people would be considered part of the heritage of the Church, as well. I recently met an Anglican vicar in the UK who told me, "Although I'd never interfere in the life of the Jewish community (in his city), I am obliged to be the protector of the Jewish community. I keep my eyes open as to how I can oppose anti-Semitism that may threaten them." This vicar understood that he (and his Church's) inherent connection to the Jewish world made this their duty, which he gladly took upon himself. In fact, this vicar has a weekly Hebrew class given by a Jewish community member, in the effort to teach his congregation about the Bible as well as to promote good relations with his local Jewish community.

It is distressing to see that there is still ignorance today in the Christian world about how the Scripture came to the Church via Israel. And this would include both the Older and Newer Testament writings. Many Church members are ignorant of the fact that all the books of the Newer Testament writings were penned by Jewish authors. The books of Luke and Acts are often brought out as exceptions to this, however, many scholars (including me) believe Luke to have been either a convert to Judaism or in the category of a "God fearer."[8] Therefore, it is illogical to reject the very people through whom the portal to God was opened. If the connection of the Church to the olive tree were embraced and understood in its wider background as a fulfillment of Biblical prophecy, the Bible would inform political affairs—not vice-versa.

Sadly, missing the connection to the root of the olive tree is an ignorance which pervades the thoughts and expressions of many church leaders worldwide, including Naim Ateek, the leader of Sabeel—a Christian organization which expresses itself in erroneous and misguided metaphors, thereby rousing anti-Semitic sentiment among its members: "Here in Palestine, Jesus is again walking the Via Dolorosa. Jesus is the powerless Palestinian humiliated at a checkpoint . . . Jesus is on the cross again with thousands of crucified Palestinians around him. . . . The Israeli system of crucifixion is operating daily."[9]

Not one Palestinian has ever been crucified by the Israeli government. Ateek offers no proof of such, either . . . because it did not happen. If Ateek means to tell us that he feels that his colleagues are politically persecuted, he could have said so without invoking language that leads to hatred. Ateek expresses strong dislike for the Jewish state. Understanding and believing Paul's points in Romans 11 should prevent the development of such an attitude. If Ateek disagrees with Israeli policies, fine. If he works to improve or change such policies, fine. Yet, Ateek's images and language do not simply express disagreement with Israeli political policy. They stigmatize the Jewish people in stereotypically anti-Semitic ways.

Zechariah 8:23 depicts a future time period. The events of Zechariah chapters 8, 12, 13 and 14 have not been fully lived out in history; so, many of the depicted events have yet to occur. Zechariah 8:23 notes:

> So states the God of the Heavenly Armies: "In these days, ten people from all the language groups of the nations will take hold, take hold of the corner of a Jewish man's (cloak), saying: 'We will go with you (plural), because we heard that God is with you!'" (Zech. *my translation*)

In future days, following the lead of the Jewish people, the world's ethnic groups are pictured as coming to Israel (also cf. Zech. 14:16ff). Why? To be in God's presence because God is with you the people of Israel. This is a beautiful depiction of what it means to be connected to the root of the olive tree (cf. Rom. 11:17-20). This image relays either great desperation on behalf of the nations to experience God, or great enthusiasm to do so–or both. Ten people will attach themselves to one Jewish man to find God! This is an international reconciliation project between God and man that is staffed by Jewish people.

In view of this, it seems hardly beneficial for Christians today to foment, encourage, and display hatred towards Israel. Such anti-Semitism does not bode well with God's actions in the future, which is to cause peoples–to some small degree–to rely on Jewish people to bring them before God, to Israel. The old English proverb that states "don't bite the hand that feeds you" is relevant here.

God has not rejected Israel or the Jewish people. The prophet Jeremiah addresses any disobedience that Israel has committed, which should *not* be judged by humans, but only by God.[10]

> This is what Adonai says, who gives the sun as light for the day, who ordained the laws for the moon and stars to provide light for the night, who stirs up the sea until its waves roar—Adonai-Tzva'ot is his name: "If these laws leave my presence," says Adonai, "then the offspring of Isra'el will stop being a nation in my presence forever." This is what Adonai says: "If the sky above can be measured and the foundations of the earth be fathomed, then I will reject all the offspring of Isra'el, for all that they have done," says Adonai. (Jer. 31:34-36)

Unless a spokesman or theologian has the power to cancel sunlight and moonlight, it is not wise to declare that Israel is rejected due to any acts of disobedience towards God. The text above is written in fairly clear language. Jeremiah lived in a day of unprecedented poor political and spiritual decisions made by the government in Judah. Yet, in spite of this, God's call and love towards Israel never ended–a 70-year dispersion notwithstanding.

I do not deny that my people have had behavior issues with God in history. But, every nation has been disobedient, *as has the Church*! (e.g., the Church's role in the Crusades, the Inquisitions, and in compliance during the Holocaust, etc.). The fact that the Church continues on today is nothing but a sign of God's mercy; the same is true in the case of the Jewish people. Had he ever rejected the offspring of Israel, he would have grounds by which to reject the Church, as well. But this has not happened in either case.

Jeremiah also penned these words:

> Here is what Adonai says: "If I have not established my covenant with day and night and fixed the laws for sky and earth, then I will also reject the descendants of Ya'akov and of my servant David, not choosing from his descendants' people to rule over the descendants of Avraham, Yis'chak and Ya'akov. For I will cause their captives to come back, and I will show them compassion." (Jer. 3:25-26)

God described his attitude towards Israel as "compassion," which in the original Hebrew means the care and emotions that a mother has for a child in her womb.

Paul wrote:

> The people of Isra'el! They were made God's children, the Sh'khinah has been with them, the covenants are theirs, likewise the giving of the Torah, the Temple service and the promises; the Patriarchs are theirs; and from them, as far as his physical descent is concerned, came the Messiah, who is over all. Praised be Adonai forever! Amen. (Rom. 9:4-5)

In Romans 9, if Paul had wanted to indicate that Israel's covenants with God were no longer valid, he would have put his verbs in the past tense in Greek; they are in the present tense: "the people of Israel–that have the status as sons, the Presence of God [in Temple], the covenants, the gift of the Torah, the Temple worship, and the promises (in the scriptures re: the future)." None of this indicates that these gifts have been revoked. In fact, Paul's summary statement in Romans 11 refers to the Jewish people: *"The gifts and callings of God are not taken back/cancelled"* (vv. 28-29, my translation).

Additionally Paul wrote:

> In that case, I say, isn't it that God has repudiated his people? Heaven forbid! For I myself am a son of Isra'el, from the seed of Avraham, of the tribe of Binyamin. God has not repudiated his people, whom he chose in advance. (Rom. 11:1-2)

Romans 11:1-2 and 11:28-29 directly tell us that Israel had not lost its place or function in God's overall plan. Furthermore, whatever "rejection" is being talked about here, it is a temporary one.

Much of Church history has interpreted Paul as having said that God once and for all rejected Israel's calling and gifting;

rejectionist Palestinian Christian thought supports this misguided notion. If that were Paul's intent, he not only would be contradicting the aforementioned verses in Romans, but how he lived his own personal life as well (cf. Acts 28:17)–to the very end, he was a Torah-loving, covenant faithful Jew. In fact, my book *They Loved the Torah* chronicles how Paul lived his entire life as a Torah-fearing and observant Jew, just like his messiah! *If God had cancelled the covenants, Paul would not have lived this way, or he would have been hypocritical.*

So, if many throughout the history of the Church have not understood the proper role of Israel, and if rejectionist Palestinian Christians and their theological supporters in the West do not see that the "root supports them," then *how should we understand the role of Israel, and the relationship of God to Israel and the Jewish people?* Let the very words of the Bible speak for themselves.

> I will not reject them when they are in the lands of their enemies, nor will I loathe them to the point of utterly destroying them and thus break my covenant with them, because I am Adonai their God. Rather, for their sakes, I will remember the covenant of their ancestors whom I brought out of the land of Egypt—with the nations watching—so that I might be their God; I am Adonai.'" (Lev. 26:44-45)

I am not suggesting that everyone within the Church today, or even specifically among Palestinian Christians, is politicizing the Biblical narrative, taking it out of its context, and seeking to use it as an anti-Semitic weapon against the Jewish people. I am intimately familiar with a number of Palestinian Christians who are grateful to live in the state of Israel, and who support the right of the Jewish state to exist. I have met with such persons on numerous occasions for networking, friendship building, and for our families to befriend each other. But the evidence that opposition to Israel and resurging disdain for the Jewish people is on the rise within a broad spectrum of Christendom is alarming and irrefutable.

Many in the rejectionist Christian camps claim that God has rejected the Jewish people and that, after the last dispersion–70 C.E.–God no longer has valid covenants with the Jewish people.

Our text clearly indicates that God foresaw the Jewish people would have trouble staying faithful to their covenant with him. But what is God's response? No rejection–no termination of obligation on his part, but remembering that he has a valid covenant with the Jewish people. That is the clear message of Leviticus 26:44-45, as quoted above. Nothing in the text indicates that God's faithfulness to his covenant with Israel is in any way temporary.

And so I ask, in all sincerity, since the scriptures indicate that God has not rejected Israel despite any transgressions, which Christian wants to stand up today and declare something contrary to what is written in the scriptures? Any declaration that God has rejected Israel's calling is untrue, according to words of the very Bible on which the Christian faith is based.

Rejectionist Christians, at times, refer to Israel's birth in the modern era as the "al-nakba" (Arabic for "the disaster"). However, if the following verses describe what the return of the Jewish people meant to God's plans, then Christians should refrain from ascribing any negative context to the birth of Israel:

> Don't be afraid, for I am with you.
> I will bring your descendants from the east,
> and I will gather you from the west;
> I will say to the north, 'Give them up!'
> and to the south, 'Don't hold them back!
> Bring my sons from far away,
> and my daughters from the ends of the earth. (Isa. 43:5-6).

Prior to the modern time period, never had there been a time in Jewish history when our people have returned from a diaspora from all four geographical directions. The Egyptian dispersion was a return from the west or south; the return from Babylon came from the east and north. The "ends of the earth" would well describe the Americas, Africa and Asia, from where Jewish persons have returned to Israel in more recent times. Moscow is due north of Jerusalem. Ethiopia is due south of Israel. Only within the last two decades have returns from those two geographic diasporas occurred in any large numbers.

The language of scripture is clear concerning God's everlasting love for the Jewish people. Yeshua, himself a Jew, taught in John 10:35 that it is unrighteous to twist, attempt to cancel, eliminate or hack apart the scriptures. This is exactly the type of finagling that has to happen to contradict the clear meaning of the text, in particular with respect to Yeshua's straightforward message affirming the principle that whatever is written in the first five books of Moses, the Prophets and the Writings is eternally valid. These writings include God's call to Israel as enumerated in Exodus 19:5-6 and in Deuteronomy 4:5-9.

Further scriptural evidence that God has not revoked his promises to Israel is found in Malachi 3:6: "But because I, ADONAI, do not change, you sons of Ya'akov will not be destroyed" (CJB). By the way, if God did destroy the Jewish people, then Gentile believers in Yeshua would be grafted into nothing. Since it is the root of the olive tree of Israel into which non-Jews are grafted, if Israel doesn't exist, no grafting can take place.

As mentioned earlier and recorded in Zechariah 8, there is a future role yet unfulfilled by Jewish people in the Land of Israel by which we will serve the nations. Contrary to the view presented by many rejectionist Christians that we Jews believe we are better and are more privileged than other peoples due to our calling, I was taught by all of my Jewish teachers, my grandparents, and my rabbis that we are *not* better than any peoples–and this is *commonplace* within Jewish culture. We do not have privilege, but responsibility.

Almost every Jewish family all around the world, including in Israel, is imbued with the concept of *tikkun 'olam* (repairing the world). This means, practically, that it is the responsibility of each Jewish individual to contribute to doing positive things during his or her life to help mankind and benefit those in need. *Our national calling is one of service.*

If rejectionist Christians would team up *with us* to try and find ways that we can best carry out our national calling (found in Ex. 19:5-6 and Deut. 4:4-8), rather than blaming Jews for allegedly thinking we are superior, things would be a lot different!

A time of rabid opposition to Israel's presence, with some type of division of the Land as a consequence, is a part of prophecy concerning Israel that has yet to be fulfilled:

> For then, at that time, when I restore
> the fortunes of Y'hudah and Yerushalayim,
> I will gather all nations and bring them down
> to the Valley of Y'hoshafat [*ADONAI* judges]
> I will enter into judgment there
> for my people, my heritage Isra'el,
> whom they scattered among the nations;
> then they divided my land. . . .
> Let the nations be roused and come up
> to the Valley of Y'hoshafat [*ADONAI* judges].
> For there I will sit to judge
> all the surrounding nations (Joel 4:1-2, 12).

It appears that, in the future, peoples will be brought to the Wadi Joz area (identified as the Valley of Y'hoshafat today) to stand judgment for being in conflict with Israel. Psalm 83 specifically notes an international coalition that gives political opposition to Israel. The coalition's goal is: "*Consulting together against those you treasure. . . . They say, 'Come, let's wipe them out as a nation; let the name of Israel be remembered no more!' With one mind they plot their schemes. . . .* " (v.4). This coalition consists of the peoples of Edom, Ishmaelites, Moab, Amon, Amalek, Tsur, Assyria and Lot. Lands encompassed by this description include a large section of today's Middle East. Ancient "Ashur" (Assyria) alone consisted of today's Lebanon, Syria, Iraq, Turkey, Azerbaijan, Armenia, parts of Iran, and possibly Jordan. Since the Psalm also foretells the end of this coalition's efforts is doom, Christians would be advised to steer clear of supporting any plot to destroy Israel's existence.

The prophet Zechariah also addresses a coalition that comes to militarily attack Israel, which also will end up being thwarted:

> . . . in the siege against Jerusalem . . . I will strike all the horses with panic, and their riders with madness, I will keep watch over Judah, but I will strike blind all the horses of the peoples. . . . When that day comes, I will make the leaders of Judah like a blazing fire pan in a pile of wood . . . they will devour all the surrounding peoples, on the right and on the left. . . . ADONAI will save the tents of Judah first. . . . When that day comes, I will seek to destroy all nations attacking Jerusalem (Zech. 12:2b,4,6,7a, 9).

A Polish Christian woman, who was a strong Baptist and who helped save Polish Jews during the Holocaust, told me many years ago: "I see it as my job to make sure that not one Polish soldier is there when this attack in Zechariah 12 happens against Israel." Only failure and the opposition of God await any Christians who elect to participate in such activity against Israel.

Then Zechariah ch. 13 describes a wonderful event, involving the spiritual awakening of the people of Israel, culminating in the nation's ability to once again serve God in an effective manner for the benefit of the entire world. The Church, in the spirit of Psalm 122:6, ought to be praying for, and supporting Israel to reach that day.

Some Christians will attempt to convince you that Jews do not deserve God's calling because we somehow have failed God. Such persons often will teach that because Jews do not believe in Yeshua, God has dropped them as his covenant partners. Let us however, set the facts straight:

1. All the first believers in Yeshua were faithful, Torah-loving Jews.
2. Those who spread the good news to the pagan nations around Israel–including the twelve Apostles, Paul, and Barnabas–were all Jews. The Christian world should forever be grateful towards the Jewish people for this!
3. According to Acts 21:20ff, there were a large number of Jews who believed in Yeshua in Jerusalem by the year 60 C.E., The word used to describe this number is *myriades* in Greek, which literally means 20,000 men. If any percentage of these men were married with children, the number rises! Acts 6:7 also informs us, some years earlier, that a significant number of priests (cohens) had become believers in Yeshua. Luke emphasizes this point to Theophilus, who would have been a Sadduceean priest, in order to emphasize his point that belief in Yeshua is acceptable practice for priests.

This evidence dispels the idea that the Jewish people wholesale rejected Yeshua. Church history–from the 2nd century onward–divorced itself from its Judaic roots, further pushing the Jewish people away due to anti-Semitism among other things. The two wars against Rome also alienated the Messianic Jewish population of Israel from the larger Jewish population. Coupled with the outright rejection of the Jewish people by the Gentile church, the Messianic Jewish community for the most part died off by the 5th century.

Interestingly enough, it was Jewish men and women who spread the good news into Africa, Asia, and Europe. Jewish believers in Yeshua were instrumental in the nations of the world being able to believe in One God and in the Jewish messiah. Without them, Europe may not have gotten the good news till much later. These Jewish believers opened the door for all people to believe in the Messiah by the Acts 15 decisions–made by an all-Jewish court–which paved the way for non-Jews to approach the One True God without needing to formally convert to Judaism. This knowledge should engender gratefulness to God for the Jewish people who were indeed faithful to Him! Yet some Christians today want to expunge this history out of their narrative concerning the Jewish people.

As odd as the grafting in of the Gentiles seemed to the Jewish believers, it was all a part of God's plan. To paraphrase Paul in Romans 11, vv. 11-15:

> A mysterious, tough situation has occurred. Many in Israel do not believe in Yeshua as Messiah. But God will work this for the good . . . Gentile (and Jewish) students of Messiah can love and serve Jewish people so much, that it will make us ask, 'Why are you doing this, and so make us jealous of so wonderfully living out the calling with God?' In the end, things will come full circle, and all Israel will experience life from the dead.

So there has been a partial rejection, as v. 15 notes. But it is not permanent. And the rejection is not God rejecting Israel—it is Israel not believing as a nation in Yeshua. But that too is temporary. The "casting aside of Yeshua" turns into "their accepting him" (v. 15).

If the Church throughout its history had made showing love to the Jewish people an aim, then the Church today would likely be viewed by the Jewish world with far less skepticism and distrust. Instead, an unfortunate turn of events began early on in Church history. Teachers like Marcion and Chrysostom came and spouted anti-Jewish rhetoric. Marcion taught that there were two gods–one in the first 39 books, and another in the last 27. Chrysostom taught that God rejected the Jewish people because they were unfaithful to him. These teachers were wildly popular and set the foundation for the Church's view of the Jewish world for almost two thousand years. Martin Luther–at the end of his career–tore into the Jewish people with vicious and violent language. For example, he wrote that:

> We (must) eject them forever from this country. For as we have heard, God's anger with them is so intense that gentle mercy will only tend to make them worse and worse, while sharp mercy will reform them but little. Therefore, in any case, away with them.[11]

And again, he wrote:

> . . . set fire to their synagogues and schools . . . so that no man will ever again see a stone or cinder of them. This is to be done in honor of our Lord and of Christendom, so that God might see that we are Christians . . . (if) we were to protect and shield such a house for the Jews . . . in which they lie about, blaspheme, curse and vilify and defame Christ and us, it would be the same if we were doing all this. . . . Second, I advise that their houses also be razed and destroyed. . . . This will bring home to them that they are not masters in our country. . . . Third, I advise that all their prayer books and Talmudic writings . . . be taken from them. Fourth, I advise that their rabbis be forbidden to teach henceforth on pain of loss of life and limb.[12]

He never repudiated his statements. *The Church has been a vehicle of rejection, hatred and hostility towards Jewish people for most of Church history*. These are undeniable and sad facts. If under the auspices of the BDS movement, replacement theology, false apartheid accusation, rejectionist Palestinian theology, or any other waves of contemporary misguided anti-Semitism these same attitudes are promoted by the Church today, I can only say that it advances this most disturbing trend of history.[13]

Church members who hate Israel today can claim, "I am not Chrysostom, and I'm not a Crusader, nor do I take part in any forced Inquisition of the Jewish people. That's not me." And they would be right. Yet adopting pro-Palestinian and anti-Israel stances in the name of Yeshua simply perpetuates the perception that "there go those anti-Semitic Christians once again, doing what they have always done–hating us." It's important that Gentile believers are aware that Church history and a resurgence of these attitudes have influenced many Jewish people to reject Yeshua in more recent times. For how can the Jewish Messiah, if he were the real one, *hate the Jewish people?* It is not logical. From there, the argument flows, if *his followers* hate us, it is a reflection of him–thus, he can't be the Messiah!

The Church's task vis-à-vis the Jewish people was to love. In Romans 11, v.19 Paul writes: "Remember that you (Roman Gentile believers) do not support the root, the root supports you." There was supposed to be a loving and supportive relationship between Gentile believers in Yeshua and the Jewish people. Such a loving relationship would have drawn the attention of Israel. After all, nothing draws people to God like human love expressing the Divine love.

Not being aware of the truth of Gentile believers' strong connection to Israel can render Christians unaware of their need to love Jewish people. One example of how this ignorance can lead to anti-Semitic actions is from Holocaust history. A Franciscan Catholic priest named Andreas Kun, who helped the Nazis murder Jews in wartime Budapest, would do the following:

> . . . (He) wore a black cassock and carried a giant crucifix and snub-nosed revolver. By his own admission, Kun personally killed more than five hundred Jews . . . He would . . . order his mostly teenaged followers to line up Jews on the banks of the Danube, and then, as they took aim, he would cry out, "In the holy name of Jesus, fire!" [14]

"In the holy name of Jesus, fire!" What a tragic line. Christian religious motivation is conjured up as a motto for "Jew-killing." The Crusaders engaged in similar persecution of Jewish communities. Religious motivation was used to fan the flames of anti-Semitism, then as a platform for murdering Jews. I sincerely hope that each reader of this work decides never to allow himself/herself to take part in anything that will enable "Christians", once again, to help destroy the Jewish people–whether in Europe, America, Africa, or the Middle East. How many more Christian clergy will contribute towards the death of Jews in their naïve contributions to Israel-hating movements?

Mark Dankof is a Lutheran cleric and broadcaster whom I apparently had as a classmate at Valparaiso University in the mid-1970s. I am distressed to see that the tolerance, friendliness, and support which was exhibited towards the Jewish world by Valparaiso clergy and faculty members–in particular, Prof. T. Jungkuntz, Prof. W. Keller, Prof. W. Rast, and Prof. D. Nagle in those years–failed to take root in Dankof. Today Dankof's accusations have included blaming the Mossad for carrying out the Twin Towers attacks, as well as murdering John F. Kennedy, blaming the Jewish people for destroying Christian values, and claiming that Israel provides the financial backing for all war making in the Middle East–". . . the perpetrators of this never-ending tragedy are all policy makers with provable political and money trails that lead back to Tel Aviv." [15]

All Christian clergy have a moral obligation to discourage any future incident of a colleague's taking part in anti-Semitic propaganda of which they are aware. If thwarting such behavior does not occur, then "*In the holy name of Jesus, fire!*" will inevitably happen again. At this prospect, the Jewish Messiah would weep in deepest sorrow and mourning. It was not the Jews who failed him in the above-described event in wartime Budapest. To quote Israeli journalist Avraham Avi-Hai:

> Come, come, gentlemen in the (Christian) clergy: without Israeli power, the Middle East would be as Christianrein (without Christians) as is Saudi Arabia. Why not speak the truth? It's time to end the double standard. Speaking the truth is a Judeo-Christian virtue, is it not? As the prophet Zechariah said: Truth and peace shall ye love. [16]

Yeshua's name never again should be used as a rallying cry against Jewish people, as it was during the Crusades, pogroms, World War II, and in today's BDS movement. His name should not be used to affirm anti-Jewish, rejectionist Christian theologies, as well as any Christian version of the apartheid slander. My Christian friends, please do not repeat the mistakes of the past in today's world by promoting lies and aiding and abetting further conflict. Instead, it is time to grasp the biblical message of loving Jewish people, and to help ensure that Israel reaches her God-given destiny.

Chapter 2

Dangerous Influences of the Checkpoint Conference

The late Robert Wistrich, Hebrew University professor, historian and author of works on the Holocaust, noted that anti-Semitism in its modern context can be defined as: "depicting the Jewish state as a criminal entity that has no right to exist."[1]

Fiamma Nirenstein, a former Italian Parliament Member, recently stated: "You will not find a politician that will call himself an anti-Semite but if you talk about the issue of Israel, [you will find an] unashamed attitude of lies about the Jewish people," she said.[2] May I add this holds true for increasing numbers of Christian religious leaders, as well, and not just politicians.

One of the forums of the Christian world in which anti-Semitic posturing has been regularly expressed is the "Christ at the Checkpoint" conferences. Started in 2010, this conference is under the direction of a small group of persons with strong connections to the Bethlehem Bible College. The conference sponsors have stated that they are directing a reconciliation effort and a Bible conference between Arab and Jewish believers.

I hope to mitigate further adoption of theologically based anti-Semitism by the Christian world. I have live-streamed three Checkpoint conferences and read every essay posted on line at their website. Additionally, I have debated two of the Conference sponsors in international forums. I have dialogued with three of the sponsors over many years on a more personal level on the issues I raise in this chapter. Finally, I have talked to many Checkpoint participants to gauge the affect that this Conference has had on their thoughts about Israel and the Jewish people. My conclusions are drawn from these interactions.

My criticisms of the Checkpoint conferences are based, as well, on their abject failure to accomplish what their own" Manifesto" declares. Instead of being a forum for reconciliation between Israelis and Palestinians, it has been a place of severe judgment towards Israelis, lacking "Christian love"; it has been patently anti-Israeli from its inception. The conferences have furthered negative stereotypes of Jewish people, while blaming only Israel for the major problems that Palestinians experience.

There has been zero balance in presentations, with the focus on perceived Israeli wrongs far outweighing any discussion of how the PA, the Palestinians or the wider Arab world may possibly have wronged Israel or the Jewish people. That "side" of matters has been widely ignored in the discussions that have taken place over four conferences. In particular, Conference Manifesto points 1, 6, 7, 10 and 11 have been sorely forgotten in the content and thrust of the four Checkpoint conferences.

Individual names of persons involved in the Christ at the Checkpoint Conference will be used as little as possible. It is not my desire to attack any conference sponsor or participant on any personal level. There are perspectives espoused by the sponsors, however, which I deem to be harmful to the health, function and direction of the Christian world vis-à-vis the Jewish world, as well as in violation of the clear teachings of the Bible on which their faith is based.

Conference Manifesto Point 11 declares that a "respectful discussion: must occur between Israelis and Palestinians at the conference." This is hardly what has been happening by slinging emotionally-charged accusations at Israel. Englishman Ben White, a Christ at the Checkpoint participant, for example, wrote an entire book claiming that Israel is an *apartheid* state. The Anti-Defamation League watchdogs on anti-Jewish behavior worldwide consider White's book to be anti-Semitic in nature. It is one thing to say, "I think your nation needs to improve in this area and in that area to insure civil rights across the board for all its people." That is a legitimate item of discussion. But it is quite another thing to sling accusations of being an *apartheid state*. White's input did not promote reconciliation and does not carry out a respectful discussion with the "other", thus it greatly failed the Manifesto's directives. Wistrich and Nirenstein's definitions of anti-Semitism have matched much of the language that is being used today in the international community regarding

Israel. Calm discussions centering on the actual facts of the Israeli-Palestinian situation are less common today, in my opinion, having given way to language full of hatred, extremism and of *blaming the Jews*.

Agreement with White's apartheid charge may be logically inferred if the Checkpoint sponsors do not publicly renounce White's ideas on this matter. I, for one, have not heard any such opposition to White's thesis by any Checkpoint sponsors. Perhaps one of the Checkpoint sponsors has indeed rebutted White's ideas. If so, I would like to hear about it.

As a Jew born in the land that produced the most lethal anti-Semitism of the 20th century Germany at an early age I became very sensitive to the presence of anti-Semitism. My father was one of the evidence gatherers for the prosecution of Nazi war criminals in Germany after World War Two. I recently turned in files of his work to the Yad VaShem Holocaust Museum in Jerusalem, for public recording of what he had found. I listened to the screams of pain from Holocaust survivors in my home as one of my first memories of life. Their grief was engraved in my mind from my childhood. So my ears became perked as a youngster when Jewish people, and when the country of Israel, were being talked about.

I am fairly experienced at filtering out idealistic, political talk that harms no one, from verbalized aims and ends that express an existential threat to my people.

The late Professor Frank Littell, a Methodist cleric and my father's roommate during the American occupation of West Germany in the late 1940s, penned these words: "The (political and theological) double-standard, bolstered by the endemic anti-Semitism of Christendom, finds fault with the Jews whatever they think or do."[3] I believe some of the Checkpoint conclusions–as well as the historic Church minimization of our Jewish people which has been repeated in the rhetoric of the Checkpoint proceedings–continue on the very path that Rev. Littell described. In reply to White's apartheid accusation, I repeat author Steven Apfel's questions to the Checkpoint sponsors: "When last did a Jew kill a person for being a Christian? When last in the Holy Land did Jews burn down a church? When last was a Christian converted to Judaism under pain of death? Yet where do churchmen aim their diatribes?"[4]

I believe in free speech–a right, which according to the 2013 Freedom House report, Israel excels in offering all of her citizens.[5] Criticism is not necessarily a negative thing, at least self-criticism is not always such. One of the Checkpoint's Manifesto points extols the virtue of self-criticism. But when criticism is focused on "the other", and grows in intensity, then purports untruths and/or taking action to harm "the other"–especially over a long period of time–then a reasonable person should find cause for concern. Three Checkpoint conferences and the writings of its sponsorship have harped on the same anti-Israel political agenda repeatedly. The words have become less abrasive, the speakers less agitating, but the points remain basically the same–blame the Jews for all the ills of Palestinian society. If over a period of years, the very same people say the very same things over and over during such a process, I cannot escape the conclusion that this constitutes anti-Semitism by *outcome.*

The Nazis made claims that the Jews were responsible for Germany's ills–that Jews were *occupying physical German space* and had no legitimate place in the land of Germany:

> The Jews must be removed from the German community, for they endanger our national unity. . . . The fact that the Jew still lives among us is no proof that he belongs among us. . . . They want to destroy the German Reich and our people.—Joseph Goebbels[6]

The Nazi claim further emphasized that Jews were not the original inhabitants of Germany. As a result, expulsion–then death–was their due. Similarly, Checkpoint participants have affirmed that Jews again are taking up residence in a foreign place ("Palestine"), profiting at someone else's expense, and are not the original inhabitants of Israel. The same tune is being played seven decades after the Nazis strummed it. Today, at Checkpoint Conferences, the name of the land is different (Israel or Palestine as opposed to Germany), the name of the claimants differs, the decade is different, but the contents of such thought are no less frightening. This is due to the similarity with the same exact ruminations that Adolf Hitler and Joseph Goebbels made only seventy two years ago. This eerie likeness between these sets of political claims is disturbing, particularly since there are Christians who buy this line of reasoning. If Checkpoint sponsors claim that they do not share the above stated Nazi beliefs, they have yet to repudiate such in public, while giving space to speakers in conferences who affirm the above-stated points.

Checkpoint speakers refer routinely to the inception of the State of Israel in rejectionist terms, using the two words *al-nakba* (Arabic for *the* great disaster", emphasis mine. The use of this term is derogatory towards the State and people of Israel. Thus it violates the Manifesto of the conferences that had declared that "respectful dialogue between Palestinian and Messianic believers must continue." The unwillingness to recognize the world's only Jewish state by referring to its inception as "*the* great disaster" does not fit the atmosphere for conducting a respectful discussion. Yet, this phrase is used commonly in the speech and writings of Checkpoint contributors, including one Checkpoint participant who wrote the following: "I am the product of the al-Nakba, the 1948 war that we call "The Great Catastrophe."[7] He continued, noting that "Zionism is militarizing the Church."[8] Charges like these create an atmosphere where discussion is nearly impossible. They violate Checkpoint Manifesto Point 10: "Criticism of Israel . . . cannot be confused with anti-Semitism and the delegitimization of the State of Israel." This point recognizes that if one does try to delegitimize the Jewish state, that such action would be wrong.

In fact, this criticism *does* indeed challenge the legitimacy of the State of Israel. The meaning of his charge–"militarizing the Church"–is ill-defined. Yet it is overtly negative and suggests that somehow the existence of the Jewish state harms Christians. The logical conclusion drawn based on his words is that the birth of the Jewish State is a "disaster" and a threat to Christians. How is this not a contradiction to Manifesto Point 10?

In fact, the use of this politically charged term "al-Nakba" violates the spirit of Checkpoint Manifesto points 1, 10 *and* 11. If "bringing reconciliation" as espoused in Manifesto point 1 is a sincere aim of the conferences, I doubt this can be attained when derogatory terms such as "*the* great disaster" are used by Conference sponsors and participants in relation to Israel's birth. The starting point for reconciliation is accepting the "other one's" very being. If I am to accept Palestinians as a people with political aspirations, why should I not be accepted as an Israeli who already lives in the UN approved Jewish state? Reconciliation can only occur if the Jewish state is accepted by all conference participants as a valid entity. Anything less than this is hypocrisy for a purported "reconciliation" conference. Perhaps doubts on this issue contribute to the extremely low turnout of Jewish participants to the conferences. This factor contributes to making the conferences appear to be a radical, leftist Christian and Palestinian rejectionist summit against Israel.

Additionally, Checkpoint speakers have supported the use of violence against Israelis as a political strategy, thereby violating Manifesto Point 5: "All forms of violence must be refuted unequivocally." Ben White has been a featured Christ at the Checkpoint speaker, and he stated: "Popular struggle, like violent resistance, is not an end in and of itself; it is a method, a strategy."[9]

Another Checkpoint speaker and sponsor stated the following:

> Our goal is to involve all people in the popular resistance. I call for every person to ask themselves each day when they wake up what they can do that day to resist the occupation.... What does matter, what is crucially important, is that all people are engaging in this popular struggle. This is not a substitute for the armed struggle. This not a method for normalization with the occupation. Our goal is to revive the popular resistance until every person is involved in dismantling the occupation.[10]

Yet another Checkpoint sponsor and speaker stated these words:

> When we fight for a piece of land, we use religion to rally people, to excite people, to build zeal among the people so they will help to accomplish a goal. Religion is used in the conflict, but it's about land. The Muslim is fighting the Jew because of what the Jew took by force.[11]

These words, in my reading, constitute verbal support for violence. One Conference speaker accepts violence as a "method, a strategy", while another infers that violence has no substitute for its role. The willingness for this Christian speaker to incite people to use violence, or to laud that practice, is certainly hypocritical if not worse, in the context of sponsoring a "reconciliation" conference that has no room for violence (according to its Manifesto Point 5).

How can such expressions emerge from a conference that purports to be a Bible and reconciliation conference? These statements that emerge from its sponsors are hardly helpful in creating an atmosphere of reconciliation. They bring the sincerity of the stated aims of the conference into doubt. The last quote, in particular, used jihad-like language to justify opposing the physical presence of Israel. Is a jihad-like war in the name of Jesus to be carried out by believers to destroy the Jewish State of Israel?

Clearly, such language fails to promote reconciliation. The quoted sponsor accuses "Jews" of "taking land by force." Some of the ideas that were expressed by the Nazi hierarchy are expressed by the PA's hierarchy one generation later. These include that Jews have no right to have a physical presence in "*foreign* land." The repeated claim is that Jews stole their land and ensuing wealth, and must be both expelled and destroyed to rectify the situation. This is an ideological background that Hitler and rejectionist Palestinians Christians share. It was disheartening to hear this same attitude reflected in a statement by a Checkpoint sponsor–"the Muslim fights the Jew because of what the Jew took by force." Why is this accusation framed in religious terms–Muslims fighting Jews? If he breaks down the Israeli-Palestinian conflict into being a religious war, then he has exposed an entirely new side to the conflict, one that should be seriously considered.

The Conference's spokespersons framed their situation in a similar way to commentary found in the PA's official newspaper–a government mouthpiece:

> "They (the Jews) plundered the Palestinian land and national interests, established their state on the ruins of the Palestinian Arab people . . . [12]

The three quotes given above do not refute the use of violence. In fact, these words can easily be taken as promoting violence.

Suffice it to say that no one can talk their way around this glaring contradiction. It is there for all to read.

Perhaps this does not include the thought that all forms of violence are equal, because we hardly hear of any violence refutation at Checkpoint conferences other than alleged Israel-on-Palestinian acts. To a Western audience, this manifesto point sounds great. But the evidence belies their adherence to their own code. Consider the following newsworthy situations.

The Jerusalem Center for Public Affairs, in its report "Palestinian Crimes v. Christian Arabs and their Manipulation against Israel," cites "the routine extortion of Christian businessmen by PA officials and police," as well as by "street thugs." I can venture a guess that if they began to tell the whole truth of what was happening, no doubt that the PA and those who support jihad would "be on their case" quickly. The Jerusalem Center for Public Affairs concluded, after studying the situation in the PA areas for a 10-year period, that "they (Arab Christians) fear for their own lives"–not from Israel, but from the Muslim majority. If this is true, why do the Checkpoint personnel not give energy to attempt to bring this wrong to public exposure *with the same intensity* with which they blame Israel for their social ills?

Here are other conclusions that the Center reached in its landmark study:

> Harassment of Christian Arabs is widespread under the Palestinian regime . . . they have had their land taken over by criminal gangs in cooperation with the PA Land Registration Office, and Christian women have resorted to wearing conservative Muslim garb so as to not be harassed.[13]

If the rights of Christian minorities in the Middle Eastern are a priority, here is something to be alarmed and active about:

> More than 125,000 Christians have been forced from their homes over the past 12 months. They now live as refugees, most of them in the semi-autonomous state of Kurdistan. ISIS has previously vowed to destroy all Christian historical sites in the areas that fall under its control. In March, it destroyed the ancient Christian Mar Behnam Monastery in the predominantly Christian town of Qaraqosh in northern Iraq. The jihadists have desecrated Christian cemeteries, seized Christian girls for sex slaves and killed other children in front of their parents' eyes. ISIS destroyed Jonah's tomb in Mosul in July and destroyed countless Assyrian artifacts in Nimrod in March. The jihadist organization believes Christian relics represent a religion of polytheistic infidels and are an affront to Islam. . . . Mosul has been completely emptied of its 10,000 Christians. . . . Nicodemus Sharaf, the archbishop, now lives as a refugee in the Kurdish capital of Erbil along with 60,000 other Christian refugees. . . . Christian relics dating to the first century B.C.E. fell into the hands of ISIS. ISIS uses the Arabic letter "N" for Nazarene to mark the homes of Christians. When they use red paint to put the "N" on a home, the occupants can expect a visit soon by ISIS fighters. They are given a choice: Convert, pay the Islamic head tax, or die.[14]

Forced expulsions of Christians. Destruction of holy sites. Forced sexual slavery. Murder. The singling out of only Christian homes for "observation" and "visits" by soldiers. Is this happening in Israel? No. It is *in Syria and Iraq*.

The *Israel Hayyom* daily of June 24, 2015 noted in a feature article that ISIS crucified a number of children who did not keep the Ramadan fast. Does this not deserve the strongest of public rebukes? The same article stated that five Iraqis were locked in a cage and drowned in a swimming pool by the hand of ISIS during this same time. ISIS apparently also locked some Arab citizens in a car then blew it up with an RPG hit. With this savagery being rampant in Syria and Iraq, why has there been no strong reaction or focus from the Checkpoint sponsors? Israel continues to be the Conference's sole "bad boy" focus.

The Syrian Observatory for Human Rights has communicated that 3,000 people have been summarily executed by ISIS over the past calendar year–1,800 were civilians, and this statistic does not include battle fatalities.[15] As the MEMRI organization has stated the situation:

> ISIS, has cut a wide and bloody swath through the Middle East, especially in Syria and Iraq. Many of its most notorious, high-profile actions involve ethnic and religious groups that ISIS has declared fair game: numerous massacres of every type against Iraq's Shi'a population, culminating in the 2014 Camp Speicher massacre; targeting Iraq's Yazidi population for extinction, including the August 2007 Qahtaniya bombings; and multiple attacks against Christians, including the October 2010 attack on the Syrian Catholic Cathedral in Baghdad and the total expulsion of historic Christian communities in Mosul and Nineveh Plains in 2014. . . . ISIS now extracted a terrible vengeance with hundreds of men and boys over the age of 15 shot or beheaded on April 13. Supposedly, this was retribution modeled on the destruction of the Jewish Banu Qurayza tribe at the time of the Prophet Muhammad, with ISIS considering the tribe to be entirely in apostasy. The video of the mass beheadings, taped live with no cutting away of the camera, is among the most terrible ISIS has made. This is no slick production, but raw, immediate savagery.[16]

Online bloggers who are in these nations are posting cries for help:

> The Yezidi refugees in Turkey are facing a tough situation . . . more than 10 months have passed since Yezidi genocide by Islamic state. They are living in a tough situation in the camps in Turkey and calling the world for help many times, but no one cares and listens to them. They had to make decisions to go to Turkey or Bulgaria to go to the lands of peace (European countries), but the Turkish authorities are preventing them to go . . . and now all of them got out of the camps onto the streets and want to leave...please do something for these hopeless people in (the) Middle East.[17]

It is simply shocking to see the tremendous and unwarranted focus on Israel by alleged human rights activists and Palestinian rejectionist Christians, as well as the Checkpoint sponsors, while events in Iran, Iraq, Syria, Nigeria (and recently in France, Tunisia and Kuwait) fly by with little notice. These events all violate the most basic human right: the right to life itself. The Yezidi situation mentioned above is one of these events. The reader can draw his or her own conclusion as to why continued attention is put on Israel while serious crimes are being committed in the same region, and *so little* is heard by the supposed voices of conscience around the world. My conclusion is that anti-Semitism produces an obsession in such persons about exacting a toll on Israel for just existing, while real murder in real time is more or less passed over by them.

What is occurring in Syria and Iraq is a real genocide against Christians. Although this is happening in the same regional neighborhood that rejectionist Palestinian Christians live in, one strains one's ears to hear them address this real genocide. Instead, their focused energy, subject matter and finances are spent trying to vilify Israel. Is something wrong with this picture? For me, the answer is an unqualified "yes." Why is it when Jews are not involved, there is no ongoing, loud protest? Why are no conferences held by Checkpoint persons to find a way to address the above-mentioned situations? One of the other Israeli-Arab reconciliation thrusts with which I am familiar already has done so, because an overriding concern among those people is helping the threatened Christian communities in Syria and Iraq.

By his own admission, a rejectionist Palestinian Christian pastor who is quoted earlier, cosigns Muslim efforts to "build zeal" for the goal of fighting the Jews. He also accuses Jews of theft of the land. This meets the definition of an anti-Semitic comment. Had the author been using "we" in a general way to speak about the political sentiment in the Muslim Middle East, he should have stated such and distanced himself from the attitude that he described. But he does not do this. So what conclusion are we to draw?

Even though some of the sponsors deny any political goals were ever on the Conference agenda, listening to the content of the past three conferences has led me to the exact opposite conclusion. We, therefore, should examine the political goals being advocated by this Conference and their affects upon Israel. Compared to the other two Arab-Israeli reconciliation conferences with which I am familiar, this one is the most highly political, *by far*. To quote an author who was present at the third Checkpoint Conference: "It relies on the bible to make the political views and world vision of the authors sacred. The approach is to convert Christianity into a very human ideology."[18]

I see the situation similarly. It is clear that the execution of a political agenda was part and parcel of this Conference, as evidenced by this statement from the opening sessions of the third Checkpoint Conference: "As evangelicals we pledge our allegiance to Palestinian President Abbas and the Prime Minister."[19] What other than the term *political* could be used to accurately describe such a commitment?

To deny the political agendas of the conferences is to be grossly disingenuous. To pledge alliance to the leader of the PA–who has declared there will be a Judenrein Palestinian state–is a highly questionable act for a "Biblical reconciliation conference." Such a declaration is a divisive act, not a reconciliatory one. I know of no other Arab-Jewish reconciliation conference that has included a political pledge of allegiance as part of its program. I know of no other Arab-Jewish reconciliation conference whose sponsor has stated: "I call for every person to ask themselves each day when they wake up what they can do that day to resist the occupation."[20]

A leading Iraqi-based cleric, having observed Palestinian rejectionist theology, noted: "The leaders of so many of the churches in the Holy Land have, in essence, become more political than theological leaders. . . ."[21]

To share the assessment of another observer:

> "Most of them (Checkpoint sponsors) claim to be pro-Israel, pro-Palestinian and pro-peace," Brog told *JNS.org*. "But

> almost every speaker will focus on Palestinian suffering and ignore Jewish suffering. And almost every speaker will blame Palestinian suffering on Israel and Israel alone. . . . In the guise of love, they continue a dangerously one-sided propaganda campaign against Israel," Brog added.[22]

No one–with the exception of one Jewish presenter at one conference for five minutes–ever spoke about what Israelis went through in 1948, when after a seven month starvation siege against the Jewish civilians of Jerusalem, five Arab nations rejected a two-state solution and attacked the infant Jewish state a day after Israeli independence. In my opinion, *that* was the "nakba"–Arabic for "the disaster"–*that the Arab political leaders of the Middle East could never accept a Jewish state in their midst*, and make room for people who had just undergone a six million person slaughter, when there was enough room in the area to do so. The UN partitioned Jewish state would hardly have made a ripple in the water in terms of its physical size among the nations of the Middle East.

The lack of allowing a strongly Zionist perspective at the conferences is in violation of Manifesto points 7, 10 and 11. There cannot be a sincere reckoning of problems without hearing the Israeli "side of the story", which Checkpoint conferences have to date sorely been lacking. There has been a heavy emphasis on hearing the rejectionist Palestinian side. Palestinians, both Christian and Muslim who, for example, love Israel and are happy to live there peacefully, are also not invited to share their perspectives. I would personally be happy to suggest such speakers to the conference sponsors. There is no fair and unbiased hearing of issues and perspectives at this conference. A look the four conferences' agendas, including the featured speakers and given topics from 2010 to 2016, will confirm my point.

I fear that the perspectives espoused at the Checkpoint Conference will further enable fascists, jihadists and anti-Semites to attain their one solitary, overriding goal: destroying–by whatever means–the world's only Jewish state. Simply by publicly blaming Israel for most Palestinian ills, the current thrust by the anti-Israel world is being bolstered by the Checkpoint Conference. Through this Conference, Christians are agreeing with Islamists as to the necessity to harm or dismantle the Jewish state. I cannot reach any other conclusion.

Another Checkpoint sponsor, in what I believe is an accusatory tone, portrayed almost any Israeli as being arrogant, unjustly proud, ultra-nationalists, racists, and unconcerned with world affairs:

> . . . the idea that we are members of the chosen people is planted far deeper. . . . If you scratch beneath the skin of almost any Israeli, you'll discover that he really is convinced of that: We're the best; the 'Jewish' is the most successful; the Israel Defense Forces is the most moral. Nobody will tell them different, we're simply the best in the world. This is not only unnecessary and groundless arrogance, it's also an idea that enables Israel to behave as it does, with blatant disregard of the world's feelings. Nor does it lack benighted ultra-nationalist and racist foundations.[23]

This tone is hardly compatible with working toward reconciliation with Israelis. It is violating Manifesto points 8 and 10 by its very tone and content. Do these words sound like the basis for relating with respect to the Jewish people, to you? Romans 11:20 instructs Gentile believers to" not be arrogant" towards the Jewish people. The accusations being made here appear misguided and contrary to the clear meaning of Paul's teaching, in addition to contradicting their own stated mission.

The spread of misinformation that has occurred at the Checkpoint conferences also has disturbed me. An American acquaintance of mine attended the 2010 Checkpoint Conference as a participant for the entire time. This person later spoke at a gathering in the USA which I happened to attend. He shared an alarming statement which had been espoused at that 2010 Conference–that "Israel has the 4th largest army in the world." He repeated that fact, then asked his audience, "Why do you think t*hat* is?" This speaker was publicly criticizing Israel's right to exist *with* an army. This alleged "fact" about the size of Israel's army was told to him by one of the Checkpoint speakers, whom he refused to identify for me. Yet he admitted where it was that he "learned this *fact*." This American lecturer was affected in a negative way towards Israel because of that piece of misinformation.

I believe that Israel has the 18th largest army in the world, with those of its neighbors Egypt, Turkey and Iran being a good deal larger than Israel's. After he spoke, I approached this lecturer in private and corrected that piece of misinformation. He then looked at me, quite surprised, and genuinely asked me, "Really? If what you say is true, then why was I told what I was told at the Checkpoint Conference?" That is a very good question. Having reviewed various assessments of the size of the world's armies myself, the consensus is that the People's Republic of China, the United States, India, North Korea, Russia, South Korea, Turkey, Pakistan, Iran, and Egypt comprise the top ten. One single source ranks Israel's military as the 11th largest in the world, but I could not find a source with a higher ranking!

Why would this "military affairs" informant at the Checkpoint conference not complain about the size of China's army? Or North Korea's? Or any other army on the face of the earth? Why single out Israel's army with the insinuation that was given? Why does China have such a large army?

The effect of misinformation is to negatively influence the general attitude towards a people–in this case, that people happened to be the Jews. This piece of misinformation occurred at the Conference and affected at least one person's judgment towards Israel quite negatively. I do not know if this misinformation was shared publicly or privately, but the effect and the source of this misinformation remains the same. A whole audience in the USA heard this fabrication, and who knows if any others were affected by this untrue statement and its anti-Israel insinuation. "Well, that's just one person and just one event," one could retort. "No big deal." I want to say it *is* a big deal. It is a piece of misinformation that leads to stereotyping Israel and smirks of anti-Semitism.

It is both counterproductive and highly questionable to the aim of peacemaking to have misinformation disseminated at a supposed reconciliation conference. I do not know how this particular insinuation is relevant to a Bible conference. Listeners who know little of the facts on the ground will hear this false "fact" and be led to draw untrue conclusions, as indeed happened in the incident that I describe above. This constitutes manipulation of the audience, and is not appropriate for sincerity, honesty or reconciling anyone to anyone else.

Yes, the American lecturer should have checked his facts before talking about Israel. Yet he never should have been told what he was told in a conference purporting to tell facts, and supposedly reconciling the Israeli-Arab situation. Reconciliation was not an affect upon this person. To the contrary, the hearer was influenced to dislike the Jewish State by the insinuation that Israel is nothing but a gigantic military machine.

Point 10 of the Manifesto advocates the challenging of "injustices in love". Such was not carried out here. I can only surmise that an attempt to delegitimize Israel was made here by the portrayal of the state as a war-mongering throng. For, such delegitimization was the outcome in at least one person's mind. Additionally, in my mind "love" includes speaking truth, not exaggerated numbers in service of a particular political agenda.

Anti-Semitism is not always visible, or even present, as a motivation. *It can be a function of* ***outcome***. In other words, one can say and genuinely intend," I am not anti-Semitic." Claims to the contrary aside, if the end result of one's work is to *lower the value of the Jewish people in the eyes of others, or lower the value of Jewish civilization, or lower the validity of Jewish statehood,* then anti-Semitism has been invoked. Both the perpetrator and the supporter have, indeed, involved themselves in anti-Semitic activity–their participation has de facto contributed to harming the Jewish people.

Outcomes are outcomes. I have never heard anyone tell me that after attending or live streaming a Checkpoint Conference, that they felt a need to love Israel, or pray for the destiny of Israel.

> (This Conference) includes a heavy emphasis on replacement theology, which teaches that the Christian church has replaced Israel or the Jewish people regarding the plan, purpose, and promises of God. Adherents of the theology believe that the Jewish (people) are no longer God's "chosen people." While once a popular belief among Christians, replacement theology has been thoroughly discredited within the modern Evangelical movement . . . The speakers at CATC "represent a who's who of the new, anti-Israel Christian narrative," said David Brog, executive director of CUFI. "Most of them claim to be pro-Israel, pro-Palestinian and pro peace," Brog told *JNS.org*. "But almost every speaker will focus on Palestinian suffering and ignore Jewish suffering. And almost every speaker will blame Palestinian suffering on Israel and Israel alone. In the guise of love, they continue a dangerously one-sided propaganda campaign against Israel," Brog added. "You can't honestly criticize Israel's security barrier without discussing the suicide bombings that it stopped. You can't honestly criticize Israel's presence in the West Bank without nothing that it would have ended long ago had the Palestinian leadership said 'yes' to generous peace offers in 2000 and 2008. But at this particular checkpoint, context and nuance are confiscated at the front door."[24]

How can followers of the Jewish Messiah spout anti-Semitic ideas? The Jewish world is discouraged from looking at who Yeshua is by listening to the words of his followers throughout history. Professor Littell, a Methodist clergyman from Temple University who understands Jewish history and sentiments very well, expressed a perspective often shared by skeptical Jewish non-believers,

> The Christian establishment cannot be counted on for humanitarian, let alone fraternal, intervention to prevent or even impede the mass murder of Jews. The lesson was taught by the heads of the Roman Catholic, Protestant and Orthodox churches during the Holocaust and during subsequent threats such as the Yom Kippur War.[25]

Today, rejectionist Palestinian Christians, in particular, influence the Jewish world in similar fashion. Rejectionist Christians continue to drive a wedge between Yeshua and his own people, then add to that insult by denying that Jewish people are his own people.

B'nai B'rith, a mainline Jewish organization, sees the Checkpoint Conference as a negative presence in relation to world Jewry, and as an expression of anti-Semitism from within the church world. We can see B'nai B'rith's assessment of Christ at the Checkpoint in this statement:

> The B'nai B'rith World Center in Jerusalem calls on the Van Leer Institute in Jerusalem to withdraw all connection and support for "Christ at the Checkpoint," a conference that will take place in Bethlehem March 5-9, because of the clear anti-Israel and anti-Jewish posture of the event.[26]

Let us consider what Israelis are likely to infer about Christianity from the anti-Israel messages of the Checkpoint Conference. The historical figure of Yeshua is perceived as having followers today who continue in a *legacy* of historic Christian sin against the Jewish world. This consists of minimizing the Jewish people, attempting to humanly repudiate our holy covenants with God, slandering us, and blaming us for all manner of ills, as well as casting us in the image of the *wandering Jew* by emphasizing that we do not merit our homeland. Israelis internalize from such messages that Christians today, as throughout Church history, hate Jews. Many Israelis perceive the religious Christian world in such a light. *The Conference only exacerbates and perpetuates that very perception. This repeats a historic wrong vis-a-vis Jewish civilization, and it is Jewish civilization which happens to be the bedrock and birthplace of the Checkpoint sponsors' own faith!*

Political activities as a thrust of an Israeli-Arab reconciliation conference that supposedly is centered on the Bible is misguided, at best. Does this Conference promote Psalm 122:6? Does it promote Leviticus 19:18? Rather political action in opposition to the Jewish state of Israel is promoted. Such posturing has been carried out at the Checkpoint Conference through various activities, including a demonstration march to the *Bethlehem security barrier* and screenings of provocative and politically anti-Israeli movies.

This Conference bills itself as a Bible-based reconciliation meeting. As a Jew and an Israeli, I do not find this reconciliatory. Point 1 of the Conference Manifesto states: "The Kingdom of God has come. Evangelicals must reclaim the prophetic role in bringing peace, justice and reconciliation in Palestine and Israel." But by promoting one-sided presentations, clearly no peace has been brought, no justice or reconciliation can occur, nor has it. I find nothing "prophetic" in it. Thus, the failure in attaining this point is prominent.

So many people, in fact, have charged that it is a political conference, that this response was evoked from the Conference sponsors: "This is a Biblical conference, to study what the bible says about the land (of Israel). Nothing at all has been mentioned about Replacement Theology or the destruction of Israel. These are unfounded claims."[27] That retort is, at the very least, inconsistent with their recorded pledge of allegiance to Palestinian leadership.[28]

Such can *only* be construed as a political act. Again, this constitutes a major failure in realizing points 1 and 2 of the Conference Manifesto, which cannot be attained in such an atmosphere of insincerity. As I previously noted, 95% or more of Messianic Jewish leadership in Israel does not attend the conference due to the presence of these factors.

Revisionism was part and parcel at another Checkpoint speaker's seminar. He misguided the audience with such tidbits as: "The Palestinian Church was started on Pentecost 2000 years ago" and "The gospel was proclaimed in Palestine on Pentecost," as well as, "The gospel is a product of Palestine."

According to the book of Acts, ch. 2, *Jewish* pilgrims who came to Jerusalem spoke many languages. It is important to realize that these were *Jewish* pilgrims, a small number who possibly lived in Nabatean areas, or Yemen of today, or possibly in today's Saudi Arabia–"Jews by birth and proselytes; Jews from Crete and from Arabia! How is it that we hear them speaking in our own languages about the great things God has done?" (Acts 2:11).

Historian Michael Grant informs us that the Jewish population of the world at that time was about eight million people. Two million lived in Israel, two million in ancient Babylon (Iraq and Iran of today), one million in Egypt, and one million in Turkey, Syria and Lebanon of today, with the remainder in Europe and Africa. Those mentioned in Acts ch. 2 were all *ethnic Jews*, or they would not have been at the Shavuot gathering in Jerusalem. The language being referred to in Acts 2:11 probably refers to the local dialect of the area where these pilgrims resided (referred to as "Arabia" in Greek).

In a recent private conversation, a linguistics professor in Jerusalem assured me that it is unlikely that Arabic was the language referred to in Acts 2:11; rather, again, Aramaic or a dialect or offshoot of Aramaic, would have been the likely language referred to in the reference to the "Jews from Arabia." "The word 'Arab' has had a wide variety of uses over the centuries . . . the majority of ancient historians who wrote . . . considered the Nabateans to be Arabs and the Arabs to be Nabateans."[29] It is *not* true that all non-Jews, or any significant number of them, spoke anything that we would identify as modern Arabic in that time period in that given location. Those Jewish believers identified in Acts 2:11 were likely speaking the Nabatean dialect of Aramaic. Where Aramaic was not spoken or popular in the ancient Middle Eastern world, often Greek was—not Arabic. Only *from the fourth century* did Arabic become the spoken language of the ancient Nabataean areas. From 66 B.C.E.-93 C.E., in Judaea, Galilee, Perea, Gaulanitis, and the later provinces of Syria, Nabataea, Mishnaic Hebrew, Greek, Aramaic, Samaritan and a touch of Latin would have been spoken. There is no area in these regions, to my knowledge, where Arabic–as the language is known today–would have been spoken or written. My point here is that whatever language these people from "Arabes" spoke, they were *Jews*.

His further statement, that "It (the good news) is a product of Palestine" is a misleading statement to make, as well. There was no ethnic identity as "Palestinian" in the first century. Only the Romans, for governmental/administrative purposes, termed parts of the then Jewish inhabited land of Judah as "Palestina." And they meant the "Jewish province." There were other ethnic peoples, such as Samaritans, and Nabateans, but there were no identified Arab "Palestinians" who existed. Historically speaking, it is more correctly stated that *the gospel is a product of ancient Israel, and a legacy of the Jewish people.* Paul makes this clear when he writes, "from them (the Jewish people), as far as his physical descent is concerned, came the Messiah . . ." (Rom. 9:5). Any true believer would trust Paul's summation here above the historically baseless assertion made by this particular Checkpoint sponsor.

As this particular group of Jewish pilgrims became empowered to take the good news back to their lands of origin, their identity certainly would not have been "Palestinian." Their identity would have been as Jews, descendants of Abraham, Isaac and Jacob, who happened to believe in Yeshua from the tribe of Judah as their Messiah. This underscores the fact that the good news was brought to the world by the Jewish people. That is a basic historic fact that all modern-day Christians should support. Only anti-Semitism or a self-serving political agenda would prevent such an affirmation.

An identified problem: the outcome

My major problem with the Conference is that I believe it furthers what I have defined as *anti-Semitism by outcome*. The first Conference included at least two featured speakers who are considered by major Jewish organizations to be anti-Semitic. When we look at what *anti-Semitism by outcome* is, it is a slippery animal to capture. But it truly exists. This type of anti-Semitism communicates things that lower opinions about the value of, and the rights of, the Jewish people. Joseph Goebbels's type of oratory skills are not needed to participate in "anti-Semitism by outcome." Screaming, yelling, nor being loud and vicious is required to communicate negative and stereotypic messages about the Jewish people. When sandwiched in religious language–especially by calm, gentle clergymen–this type of anti-Semitism is harder to recognize. When communicated around "Biblical" messages that minimize the connection of the Jewish people to God and that deny our history to the land of Israel, anti-Semitism by outcome becomes flammable and insidious.

There are standards of anti-Semitism that have been defined *by the victims of anti-Semitism*, and it is the Jewish world that will define what anti-Semitism is, *not* the Checkpoint sponsors. Criticism of Israel–as it has been carried out by the Checkpoint Conference in the past–has produced *anti-Semitism by outcome.*

I am not sure that the Conference sponsors are aware of how they have spread *anti-Semitism by outcome*, but they should become aware of how their seminars impact both the Jewish and Christian worlds. For example, one featured Checkpoint speaker and participant recently has been censured by his local supervisors in Europe due to the flammability of his anti-Israel statements. His local Jewish community was up in arms about his ongoing Israel-related statements, which they assessed to be anti-Semitic. Although the Checkpoint sponsors were aware of this situation, they never did anything public to denounce this spokesman's statements. Granted he is no longer a speaker at the Checkpoint Conference, but no formal statement of repudiation of this person's approach to the Jewish world was ever issued by the Conference. At least one Israeli leader attempted to convince a lead sponsor of the Conference to issue such a statement. This would have gone a long way in displaying recognition of having committed *anti-Semitism by outcome*. It would have demonstrated a desire to promote healing and reconciliation. It would have been a positive step towards the Jewish world by the conference sponsors. But it never happened.

Why is the only concentration at the Conference on Israel as the political wrongdoer? Why not give *equal time* addressing the myriads of political harms routinely carried out by Hamas, Hezbollah, Iran and the PA? What about sponsoring a demonstration *against* Hamas, or against Hezbollah, the Ayatollahs and Mr. Khamenei at the next

Conference? Or do these governing authorities not oppress Iranian Christians? Or how about demonstrating against the Ministry of Education of the PA, whose personnel continue to promote suicide bombings to its middle school pupils? To me, this fits into the definition of *anti-Semitic by outcome*. Why do the Checkpoint sponsors not spend the same energy and effort publicizing these situations as they do in asserting that Jews are responsible for their social and political ills? At the very least, this violates Manifesto Point 12, which notes: "Christians must understand the global context for the rise of extremist Islam. We challenge stereotyping of all faith forms that betray God's commandment to love our neighbors and enemies." In my opinion, the Conference sponsors largely ignore such global context. Little is said that addresses the humanitarian crises in Syria and Iraq, the murderous policies of ISIS, and the gross persecution of Christians in Iran, all of which really *do* threaten the stability of the entire Middle East.

The Jerusalem Center for Public Affairs summed it up:

> Often in cooperation with the Palestinian leadership, they claim that the situation is not bad for the Christian Arabs . . . In private . . . Christians will tell you that they are suffering from the pressures by the Muslims. In public these same people will berate Israel for the security fence. It has become an old game and Israelis understand it. One wonders when foreign journalists and NGOs will finally start to understand it. . . . Rather than identify the true Palestinian perpetrators of crimes vs. their own people, they take the politically correct path by blaming Israel. All unrest and suffering in the region is routinely attributed to actions by Israel without acknowledging or condemning Muslim violence.[30]

Silence in the face of this type of misbehavior in favor of harshly criticizing Israel for Palestinian ills can only be seen as anti-Semitic manipulation that serves a political agenda that is not being openly talked about. I can reach no other conclusion.

Point 8 in the Conference manifesto states: "Any solution must respect the equity and rights of Israeli and Palestinian communities." Again, I must say this sounds fair enough and like a good ideal. However, after listening to three Checkpoint conferences and reading all the online posted essays by Conference sponsors–plus Mr. White's book–the practice of what is written and the words that are written leaves one huge disparity. My personal opinion is that the Checkpoint sponsors and speakers have not agreed on what "respecting" means, what it looks like, and how to actually do this. Some of the presented materials, if followed to their logical political conclusions, would result in the dismantling of the Jewish state of Israel. *How would such a situation respect the "rights of Israeli . . . communities?"* Again, such an outcome violates Manifesto points 7 and 8, where the rights of Israeli community are mentioned, but not defined. The rights of (the) Israeli community must include the right of Israel to exist as the Jewish state, which right is not shared by all Conference sponsors.

These points will continue to be violated if Checkpoint sponsors do not crack down on all political statements that their members issue, for which the logical outcome is Israel's demise.

In fact, if one listens to all of the presenters and their materials, and reads all posted Conference essays, very little is discussed regarding how to insure the rights of Israel. In stating this, I include the most basic right: how to insure that Israel simply exists as the *Jewish* state. Quite a lot *is* discussed concerning how to advocate for Palestinians. I cannot recall one Conference speaker being asked to give a seminar on "How can we insure that Israel enjoys the right to exist as the Jewish state, given the political and religious climate of the Middle East?" Perhaps I am wrong, but I certainly do not recall even a single Israeli speaker on that topic, yet it is presented to the public as a priority, since it is included as a manifesto point. Yet, there is no effort given to relate to this very point: "Evangelicals must reclaim the prophetic role in bringing peace, justice and reconciliation in Palestine and Israel." (Manifesto Point 1) How can this be accomplished if the need and ways to insure the very existence of Israel is never taken up as a Conference topic? "Peace" and "justice" would appear to be one-sided in such a presentation.

At a *reconciliation* conference, I would think equal time would be given to presentation of this need as much as any other need. But that never happens here. After all, are not two disparate sides supposed to be presenting their points of difference *with each other*–and not just in front of Western media and Western sympathizers–to qualify as reconciliation? Yet the great majority of the few Israelis taking part in the Conference are those who are already in the leftist camp of political affairs. There is no representation, and certainly no equal representation, from opposing political views, leave alone theological views. I can recall three speakers who were invited to Checkpoint conferences to present *the other side*–

yet one was neither Israeli nor Jewish, one was already fairly sympathetic to the Checkpoint beliefs, and the final one was a fairly new immigrant who could not be said to represent the sentiments of the bulk of Israelis. All three were from the same city. The foundation for reconciliation and representation were not present here. Additionally, one speaker who requested to speak at the Conference, who *did* represent a disparate theological and political stance, and who was a veteran Israeli, was outright rejected as a speaker after asking to come and present his case.

Point 10 of the Manifesto notes that *criticism of Israel* "must be done in Christian love. Criticism of Israel and the occupation cannot be confused with anti-Semitism and the delegitimization of the State of Israel." This again sounds good to the Western audience. But it is hardly the reality of what occurs at the Conference. First of all, what is "Christian love?" Subjective terms like this have no real meaning in practice in the absence of clear definition. I have a definition. Jewish people on the whole may have a definition of what this means to them. Do the Conference sponsors have a definition? If so, it is not clearly stated. Precise definition is needed.

I have heard a number of Conference speakers and participants during three conferences *harshly criticize* Israel without meeting my definition of practicing "Christian love" towards Israeli Jews.

Checkpoint speakers promoted the delegitimization of the Jewish state which violates Point 10 of their Manifesto: "Criticism of Israel . . . cannot be confused with anti-Semitism and the delegitimization of the State of Israel." Here is an example of a characteristically harsh and delegitimizing statement:

> The State of Israel is built on the principle of discrimination, by Jews against non-Jews . . . There is only one humankind, not different kinds of races, some more privileged and some needing to make space for these in compensation for their suffering.[31]

Such an analysis by a prominent participant in the Checkpoint leaves no room for a Jewish state. There is no Christian compassion expressed there, at least not for Jews. In fact, by lumping all ethnic groups together as "only one humankind", the calling of Israel by God and the existence and history of the Jewish people are strongly minimized. Furthermore, this Checkpoint sponsor seemingly denies the history and relevance of all other ethnic peoples. Additionally, there is no reckoning with the fact that any state founded on nationalist platforms are also "discriminatory"–including a future Palestinian one, whose reigning President has declared that it will be free of Jews. Is this not discriminatory?

Point 10 also has also been violated by the Checkpoint's screening of two movies, "Little Town of Bethlehem" and "With God on Our Side" as part of the Conference curriculum. These movies reflect a blaming and victimization narrative, and are built upon the strategy of playing upon the emotions of the audience. They are both highly propagandized with very questionable recollections of history. Both films serve to delegitimitize the State of Israel, in contradiction to points 1 and 10 of the Conference's Manifesto.

Another prominent Checkpoint sponsor noted that:

> Israel's dream of being a Jewish state "has become more sacred than human life and that human rights are transgressed for the sake of this dream. . . . Jewishness in Israel has become an obsession for Israeli Jews and a nightmare for Palestinians because of its extremist views and determination to create a world filled with masters and slaves. The Jewish dream has become a mantra for the hatred of one's neighbor.[32]

When one equates the forging of a Jewish identity *in the Jewish state* to being obsessed with extremist actions, anti-Semitism lurks at the door. I see no Christian compassion whatsoever in such a harsh assessment of the 'goal' of we Israelis. Additionally, the allusion to 'slaves and masters' is not accurate to the social structure in Israel today, and thus has a deceptive emotional pull at its center.

Point 11 of the Manifesto says: "Respectful dialogue between Palestinian and Messianic believers must continue. Though we may disagree on secondary matters of theology, the gospel of Jesus and his ethical teaching take precedence." Who from the West would not agree with such a religiously sound statement? But again, these words and the reality as practiced by the Checkpoint conferences in the past do not match. First of all, most Messianic Jewish leaders in Israel flat out refuse to attend the Checkpoint Conference. One reason for this is due to the perceived anti-Semitic nature of the content of past conferences. I am included in this set of leaders. Yet many of us participate in other reconciliation conferences.

What are noted above as the "secondary matters of theology" are not "secondary," but are an essential part of the disparity between Israeli Messianic Jews and Checkpoint sponsors. These would include what is termed "replacement theology", or supercessionism.[33] Why is this matter indeed *primary* in focus, and not one of secondary importance?

Because it affects my life, my family's life, and my people's life very directly; this does not just touch on the quality of our lives, but on *our very ability* to live in our nation, and then *simply to live*, period. If, as some of the rejectionist Palestinian Christians claim, that we Jews have no right to live in our Jewish state, and that the covenants of the Bible are no longer valid for Jews, then this is *not secondary* to me, because the implied consequences of my "theological mistake" are rather massive. The results of such belief, besides being contrary to a sound understanding of the Biblical text, affect how the Christian world perceives Jews. Just consider the rather horrid history of relationships between the Church and my people; these "secondary" theological matters have contributed greatly to Christian persecution of Jewish people throughout the past 2,000 years.

And this begs another question: What does "the gospel of Jesus" imply? What is it? What is it that is "primary" to the Checkpoint sponsors? I can venture a pretty good guess, but again, this is ill defined and up to anyone's guess. Does it involve the future, fate, and call of the Jewish people? These are not secondary matters, but in my opinion are strongly connected to the message that Yeshua himself taught in Matthew 5:17-20, and which is corroborated in Romans11:17-20, Zechariah, chs. 12-14, among many other scriptural texts. One cannot hack the Bible apart, saying "this is the gospel only, so only believe this version of it, and throw the rest away." The entire Bible's message is needed by all of us today, and it is founded in the history, culture, language, poetry, thought processes, ideas and Biblical interpretations of the ancient Jewish world. If you divorce yourself from that world, there is little chance of understanding the Bible.

Conference sponsors and participants attempt to differentiate between Zionists and the Jewish people. Some believe that it is possible to love all Jews, but hate Zionists and Zionism. Yet, this is a falsehood, and not a new one endemic to rejectionist Palestinian Christians:

> The new code word for Antisemitism is *Anti-Zionism*, whether the slogan is uttered by Communists, Arab League propagandists, adherents of the "New Left" or liberal Protestants. . . . No one can be an enemy of Zionism and be a friend of the Jewish people today—not the czar, not the Soviets, not the *Deutsche Christen*, not the *United Church Observer.* (my italics) .[34]

Reverend Littell wrote these words in 1975–a generation ago. The operating principles found in his quote have not changed since then. The appeal to be *against Zionism* means opposition to the existence of the world's only Jewish state, Israel. It means attempting to cause the downfall of the state, either by violence (jihadists) or by political maneuverings (BDS, et al.). Reverend Littell was perceptive to categorize all such activity as anti-Semitic activity. I see no huge difference between what

Reverend Littell describes and the logical outcomes of the religious and political content of the past three Checkpoint conferences. Another Conference observer wrote:

> . . . an ominous . . . underlying message of the conference: Evangelical Christians in the United States and Europe must choose between spreading the Gospel in the Muslim Middle East and supporting the Jewish state against its enemies in the region.[35]

Those Christians who support anti-Zionist movements are in full agreement–whether they know it or not–with the sharp beliefs of the PA's spokespersons, such as ". . . an aggressive foreigner occupies our home and steals it."[36] (Official PA reporter Yahya Rabbah)

The presence of one German speaker at the Checkpoint Conference adds to my skepticism about their definition of "the gospel of Jesus." Just at a time when Germany and Israel are enjoying a fruitful relationship after the Holocaust, this particular German Christian speaker participated, and stated, ". . . jumping from God's promise to Abraham to the modern State of Israel is to nullify the cross of Jesus Christ."[37] Additionally, he made a demeaning statement in saying that anyone who believes that the Jewish people have special and still valid covenants with God is "stupid" (he used the German word *dumbkopf* I believe this to be in direct violation of Checkpoint Manifesto point 11, which emphasizes the need for respectful dialogue with the "other".

As a Jew born in Germany, I cannot fathom either the rationale or the timing of such a statement, let alone its theological integrity. Further, these very words can only fan the flames of friction between Jews and Christians. In addition, this speaker obviously has no idea of the ramifications of Jewish history when he noted, "When the focus moves to Jesus, the issue of the land (of Israel) or of Jerusalem becomes secondary or even obsolete. To continue to fight . . . is to disclaim what Christ has done or what he stands for."[38]

The speaker intimates that if the Jewish people continue to fight for our existence, nationally and as a people, that we are opposing the purposes of our own Jewish Messiah. This thought lacks logic as well as compassion. After what happened between Germany and the Jewish people in the recent past, it was hardly fit for this speaker to utter what he said. Furthermore, if the issue of "the land" is not supposedly so important, why would the speaker participate in a conference where the issue of the land in its most political terms *certainly is the focus*? I would have thought he would have refused the invitation to speak at the conference, given his words that the issue of the land of Israel is of no importance to God. Obviously I would have been mistaken.

Perhaps this speaker is a good human being with integrity, but he does not have a logical, compassionate nor fruitful way of relating to Israelis nor to the Jewish world. Additionally, he exhibited little understanding of God's purposes towards the Jewish people. As a Jew, and as a Messianic Jew, I have not "disclaimed" anything that Messiah has done or what he stands for. That is a harsh judgment that he publicly made against many people, including me. And I believe in the need for Israel to exist behind firm and secure borders. Through this rationale, the speaker unfairly infers that I and other Messianic Jews are false believers in Yeshua. This particular speaker's input into the Checkpoint Conference was provocative and hardly would lead to any reconciliation. It was simply out of place in every way possible.

Real reconciliation will require a total change of approach. For example, I wonder what would happen if the Checkpoint sponsors would drop the delegitimizing banner and stand *with* Israel. Perhaps they should post the following on their website: "Israel, you have a right to exist as the Jewish state. Israel, we stand with you in opposing and resisting all forms of Islamic terror and anti-Semitic propaganda. We have room enough in the Middle East for you, and we will stand by you in your fight against terror on your borders and in your struggle against political delegitimizing. We renounce any connection with persons attempting to expel you from your nation, and we oppose the use of secessionist theology to delegitimize your nationhood. We oppose the attempts of the Iranian government, Hezbollah and Hamas to destroy the state of Israel, no political strings attached. We will encourage our children to embrace you and work so that our educational system does nothing but teach tolerance and acceptance of you." Such a statement, followed by changes to confirm the words, would be a catalyst for real peace and reconciliation. I wonder what could happen then between Israel and the Palestinians.

And then, finally, if the sponsors would drop political alliances with persons who promote theologically based anti-Semitism, something incredibly good would occur. Israelis would be able to embrace such sincerity and risk-taking with less shyness. And we would think a tad higher of the Christian world, as well. *But I hardly hear one Checkpoint person ever express concern with how to shine God's love to the Jewish people.* That has not been any priority on the Conference agendas.

Recently, the *Times of Israel* expressed concern over the message being disseminated by the Checkpoint sponsors to youths who are associated with their attendees and supporters. The Times reporter relayed that a recent youth conference intended for young Arab Christians used advertising to recruit attendees via You Tube. Their You Tube video, posted on March 26, 2015, was assessed to be "nothing more than an inflammatory piece of anti-Israel propaganda in which Israel is equated with ISIS through the use of explicit imagery."[39]

I examined this You Tube segment. It was totally unclear whether or not the images of ISIS terrorists and their captive victims included in the video were meant to be connected conceptually to the situation with Israeli traffic jams which occur at various security points. If Israel were *the* major discussion point of this youth conference, and separate discussions of the threats posed by ISIS and allies were not conducted, then indeed the You Tube video should be seen as propaganda, and anti-Semitic at that. If however, the nature, makeup, aims and threats of ISIS and their ilk were major discussion points of this conference, then I can make room for the ISIS portions of the You Tube video not being intended to vilify Israel. However, the lack of explanation once again contributes to Checkpoint-related confusion. No follow up reports of this conference are available in public forums that I could access.

It is clear that the bulk of Israeli Messianic Jews do not have enough faith in the motivations of the Checkpoint Conference to attend it. This certainly lowers the believability of the claim that this Conference is a move in the direction of reconciliation with Israelis. In fact, an American Christian reporter who *did* attend the 3rd Checkpoint Conference wrote the following comments in the *Jerusalem Post*:

> (The conference sessions were) selling its, rhetoric, to a non-Jewish audience of Christian clergy, Christian pastors, Christian students, Christian publishers, Christian authors, Christian Jews, Christian reporters. Lots of Christians. (Yes, me too.) Oh, and an Islamic spokesman for the Palestinian Authority's foreign minister who kicked off the conference right after everyone stood to sing the Palestinian National Anthem. . . . The obvious problem, of course, is that there were no Jewish Jews on the roster. This was puzzling in light of proud and repeated claims by leaders that the conference included all points of view with respect to "the Palestine-Israel conflict."[40]

As a final thought on the Checkpoint Conference–although I assess this conference to be anti-Semitic in some of its contents, political associations and insinuations–I do not think that its sponsors intend it to be this way. Nevertheless, my assessments included here have been shared with them by numerous people on multiple occasions. No substantial changes have occurred to the Conference's content since 2010 to the present. Not one sponsor, to my knowledge, has had the fortitude to confront anti-Semitism in their own midst, let alone in any public manner.

The reader must weigh the merits of the insights shared and decide whether they stand or fall on their own logic, truth and proof. At the same time, the Checkpoint Conference must be judged by following its logical political as well as theologically based consequences, and not solely by any of its own self-protecting, verbal claims. Nor should its religiously based language comprise our main scales of evaluation, but rather the clear messages of scripture in their own right.

I do not personally despise any of the sponsors. I feel perhaps the same way concerning them that I would have felt about John Chrysostom, Marcion or Martin Luther. Specifically, I wish that they could have found a way to express their Christianity without anti-Semitic expressions. I wish they would admit, confront and turn from its presence in their midst. Of course, the first step in doing this is admitting the presence of anti-Semitism, which the Checkpoint sponsors have heretofore not done. In keeping with the spirit of Conference Manifesto point 7, this would constitute a positive start: "Palestinian Christians must not lose the capacity for self-criticism if they wish to remain prophetic." I do not believe that the political sentiments of the Checkpoint sponsors necessarily express the majority opinion of Arab Christians. In the words of one prominent Middle Eastern cleric:

> . . . Christians often feel very removed from their spiritual leaders. Many of the ordinary Palestinian Christians talk warmly and positively about the time when their areas were controlled by Israel. . . . The really sad fact bout this is that it seems as though the evil of anti-Semitism has again reared its ugly head, though it is dressed as a call for justice and liberation for the Palestinians.[41]

This book examines the harm done by the Checkpoint Conference because its publicity has purposely been directed to the evangelical Christian world–the same world that I hope will read my words of concern and counsel.

Until there is a radical change at the Checkpoint Conferences–in the anti-Semitic messages and insinuations, the political alignment with Israel's enemies, the targeting of Israel as the source of Palestinian ills, the inferred denial of Israel's right to exist as the Jewish state, and the misinterpretation of the role of the Jewish people in the destiny of the Church–the status quo situation will not change. The consequences of that will be grave for all those within the body of Messiah.

Chapter 3

Insidious anti-Semitism in the Church— "The apartheid slander"

"It would not be impossible to prove with sufficient repetition and a psychological understanding of the people concerned that a square is in fact a circle. They are mere words, and words can be molded until they clothe ideas and disguise."

—Joseph Goebbels[1]

". . . it is well known, that when one side only of a story is heard, and often repeated, the human mind becomes impressed with it, insensibly."

—George Washington[2]

An allegation that is often repeated today calls Israel an *apartheid state.*

This, of course, is meant to accuse Israel of being akin to the apartheid regimes of South Africa in the 20th century, roughly from 1948 to 1994. Then, Black and White South Africans were forcibly segregated in order to live separate community lives under the political domination of the White minority. During that era in South Africa, Black South Africans were denied the right to vote, rights of interracial marriage, and rights to South African citizenship, as well as rights to live freely in urban areas where there were White communities. The segregation was extensive–restaurants, hospitals, and schools were included. As in the southern United States until the late 1960s, drinking fountains, toilets, and hotels all segregated Whites from Blacks.

The former apartheid treatment of the majority population in South Africa spurs emotional reaction, as it should. It does the same in the USA, where "Jim Crow" laws perpetrated segregation in certain regions of that nation. However, the fact is that Israel is not apartheid South Africa. Let us examine facts. In the following ways, the modern state of Israel shows itself to be anything *but* an *apartheid* society.

1. Arabs play in Israel's professional Premiere soccer league on Jewish teams. Four Arab athletes play on Israel's National soccer team–Beram Kayal, Moanes Dabour, Maheran Kedi, and Taleb Tawatha. As professional athletes, they have been chosen to represent the Jewish state. Two Bosnian Muslims from abroad also participated in Israel's Premier league. When I coached an Israeli national sports team in 1995, one of our athletes was Arab, and was a very welcome member of the squad, joining fully in all team and social activities. In apartheid South Africa, this would not have happened between Black and White athletes.
2. Arabs shop at the same stores where Jewish people shop. A good example is the Mamilla Mall in Jerusalem where, on any given day, many Arab families can be seen strolling their children through the area and shopping in the Jewish owned stores alongside Jewish families who are doing the

same. The workers in the stores and restaurants are both Jewish and Arab. At the Malcha Mall, also in Jerusalem, the same mix of customers can be seen. In fact, Arab shoppers can be seen daily in Jewish stores in Beersheva, Akko, Haifa, and all over Jerusalem. In apartheid South Africa, this would not have happened.

3. Arab bathers enjoy the Dead Sea and the Mediterranean Sea on many of the same beaches with Jewish bathers. There are no segregated "Jewish only" or "Arab only" beach stretches. In Israel, there are no signs forbidding anyone from any given ethnic background from bathing on beaches. In apartheid South Africa, Black and White bathers would not have shared the same stretch of beach.
4. One of Israel's recent Supreme Court justices, Salim Joubran, is an Arab. In apartheid South Africa, a Black court justice would not have been allowed to serve.
5. Israel's Eurovision song contestants in 2009 included a duo of a Jewish woman (Achinoam Nini) and an Arab woman (Mira Awad), together, representing the Jewish state. In apartheid South Africa, a White and a Black singer could not have done this.
6. Arab and Jewish doctors work side by side in Israel's hospitals, saving the lives of Jews and Arabs, Christians and Muslims. I had a surgical procedure performed by an Arab doctor who had a Jewish nurse. They both performed with professional integrity. Israel's hospitals are full of Jewish and Arab workers and patients. In apartheid South Africa, this could not have happened in most areas. Israeli MDs even performed medical procedures to save the lives

of injured Syrian militants during the current ISIS and Hezbollah invasions of Syria . . . pro bono. Obviously, this could have never happened in apartheid South Africa, but it is part and parcel of daily life in Israel.

7. Arab and Jewish students study together. One good example is at the Hadassah Technical College in Jerusalem where, on a daily basis, both Jewish and Muslim students enter and exit the building constantly. Hadassah College has at least seven Arab lecturers listed as faculty members. Neither of these scenarios would have existed in apartheid South Africa's educational system.
8. There are Arab members of Israel's Parliament, the Knesset. This is because Arab communities have the guaranteed right to vote. In apartheid South Africa, this would not have happened, as Blacks could not vote.
9. The Israeli Declaration of Independence invites Arab communities to take part in the life of the Jewish state as citizens. This has been the status quo in Israel since May 1948. In apartheid South Africa, there was no such invitation issued by the South African government to its majority Black citizenry.
10. One of Israel's recent Ambassadors to Finland, Ali Yahya, is an Arab. In apartheid South Africa, a Black diplomat of equal rank would never have been appointed.
11. Israeli Arabs, Druze and Bedouin serve in the Israeli army. They volunteer willingly to do so, with no coercion or draft compulsion. There are no "Jewish only" soldier policies in Israel. In apartheid South Africa, Blacks would not have been allowed to serve in the South African army.

12. Miss Israel in 1999 was an Israeli Arab woman, Rana Raslan. No Black South African woman could have won the title of Miss South Africa in apartheid South Africa.
13. The winner of Israel's national singing contest in 2015, "The Voice," is an Israeli Arab, Lina Makhoul. Winning a national singing title against White competition would not have happened in apartheid South Africa.
14. An estimated 4,000 Sudanese and 1,200 Darfurian refugees have fled to Israel to escape the conflicts in their birth nation. The great majority of these are Muslims, with some Christians among them. Many of these Sudanese refugees live in Tel Aviv, Israel's second largest city. This has caused a number of social problems in Israeli demographics, but Israel has been a willing host for these people until a solution is found for their situation. Apartheid South Africa would never have received Black refugees *into White cities*. The reader should ask: "Why do these people come specifically to Israel? Why not Kenya? Why not Ethiopia? Why not Lebanon? Why not Libya? Why not Somalia?" Israeli policy on taking in refugees contradicts all apartheid charges.
15. The presence of over 135,000 black-skinned Ethiopian Jewish immigrants to Israel is a clear sign of Israel's non-apartheid reality. Despite the many difficulties these immigrants had in absorbing into society, they hold all the rights of every Israeli citizen, and constitute a growing influence in the makeup of the Jewish state. Black-skinned immigrants, even if they were confessing Christians like the White population of that time, would not have been welcomed into apartheid South Africa.

16. Arab and Jewish patrons drink coffee at the same shops on a daily basis, all over Israel, and sometimes eat at the same restaurants, depending upon how strictly each family keeps their dietary traditions. There is no segregation in Jewish owned restaurants in Israel. I often drink coffee alongside Arab patrons at the Coffee Tea and Leaf coffee shop in downtown Jerusalem–an Israeli-Jewish owned and operated establishment In 36 years of living in Israel, I have never seen an Arab patron refused service in a Jewish establishment, as used to happen regularly in the United States when African Americans were refused service during the "Jim Crow" era and beyond. Blacks and Whites in apartheid South Africa would not have eaten at the same restaurants together.

17. Jews and Arabs use Israel's Ben Gurion International airport. Any given day will involve many Arab passengers who can be seen using the very same services as Israeli Jews. Flights operate between Israel and Egypt, and between Israel and Jordan. Many Palestinians fly on particularly the second route. This is not an apartheid situation.

18. The Israeli government has recently been investing funding and efforts into developing the job market for Bedouins in the Negev area, as well as around the entire country. Job concern and investment by the government for Coloureds and other minority South Africans was never a characteristic of apartheid South Africa. It *is* a characteristic of Israel, as reported in the *Jerusalem Post* daily:

> The Economy Ministry established for the Arab sector in recent years in cooperation with Joint Distribution Committee's Tevet Employment Initiative and the Prime Minister's Office . . . serve as one stop shops for the unemployed, training and guiding them regarding suitable employment. . . .
>
> A major goal of the Economy Ministry is increasing the employment rate, particularly among groups with low participation in the labor market. (One project worker noted): "They (Bedouin work-force eligible persons) don't believe in themselves and it takes a lot of energy to convince the people that they can improve their situation." This is a clear indication that the Israeli government is concerned for the welfare of this minority Arab and Muslim population group, and is making efforts to help them. This hardly would happen if Israel had an "apartheid" government. [3]

I could go on. But based just upon these 18 characterizations, alone, it is clear that Israel is no *apartheid South Africa*, and that the apartheid state in Africa has not been in any way, shape or form replicated in Israel.

It is significant that the Vanguard Leadership Organization–an association of African American university honor students in the United States–has censured the use of the word "apartheid" when applied to Israel. Those who allege such an *apartheid* slander towards Israel should pay attention to this organization's assessment of the apartheid charge. Here is the text of this prestigious group's letter:

March 2011, An Open Letter to the Students for Justice in Palestine, "Words Matter"

The use of the word "apartheid" by Students for Justice in Palestine (SJP) in its characterization of Israel is patently false and deeply offensive to all who feel a connection to the state of Israel. Your organization's campaign against Israel is spreading misinformation about its policies, fostering bias in the media, and jeopardizing prospects for a timely resolution of the Israeli-Palestinian conflict. Such irresponsibility is a blemish on your efforts.

Playing the "apartheid card" is a calculated attempt to conjure up images associated with the racist South African regimes of the 20th century. The strategy is as transparent as it is base. Beyond that, it is highly objectionable to those who know the truth about the Israeli's record on human rights and how it so clearly contrasts with South Africa's.

Under apartheid, Black South Africans could not vote and had no rights in a country in which they were the overwhelming majority of the population. SJP has chosen to manipulate rather than inform with this illegitimate analogy. Therefore, we request that you immediately stop referring to Israel as an apartheid society and to acknowledge that the Arab minority in Israel enjoys full citizenship with voting rights and representation in government. You should acknowledge that there are 14 Arab members in the Israeli Knesset, an Arab member of the Israeli governing cabinet, an Arab member of the Israeli Supreme Court, and Israeli Arabs involved in Israeli businesses, universities and the cultural life of Israel.

Decency, justice and the hope of peace and reconciliation in the Middle East compel us to demand an immediate cessation to the deliberate misappropriation of words and of the flagrant mischaracterization of Israel. Your compliance with this request will be viewed as a responsible and appropriate first step toward raising the level of discourse.

Sincerely, the 16 signatories of the organization (representing various Vanguard branches from across the United States). [4]

Ishmael Khaldi, a Bedouin Israeli diplomat who loves Israel, wrote the following:

> For those who haven't heard, the first week in March has been designated as Israel Apartheid Week by activists who are either ill-intentioned or misinformed . . . once again (they) castigate Israel as the lone responsible party for all that maligns the Middle East. . . . My perspective is unique, both as the vice consul for Israel in San Francisco, and as a Bedouin and the highest ranking Muslim representing Israel in the United States. I was born into a Bedouin tribe in Northern Israel . . . and later earned a master's degree in political science from Tel Aviv University before joining the Israel Foreign Ministry. I am a proud Israeli, along with many other non-Jewish Israelis such as Druze, Bedouin, Christians and Muslims, who live in one of the most culturally diversified societies and the only true democracy in the Middle East. Like America, Israeli society is far from perfect, but let us deal honestly. By any yardstick you choose—educational opportunity, economic development, women and gay's rights, freedom of speech and assembly, legislative representation—Israel's minorities fare far better than any

> other country in the Middle East. So I would like to share the following with organizers of Israel Apartheid week. . . . You are part of the problem, not part of the solution.[5]

To see this slander being used by members of the Church is a sad phenomenon. The World Council of Churches and the Presbyterian Church of the USA, as well as the heads of the United Church of Christ (UCC) and the Christian Church (Disciples of Christ), have joined in sympathy for the narration of those who accuse Israel of being an *apartheid* state. A danger here is that politics has become more of a priority than the clear message of the Biblical texts. [6]

One church figure who has laid the charge is Rev. Barry Morgan, the Archbishop of Wales. He noted:

> The situation resembles the apartheid system in South Africa because Gaza is next to one of the most sophisticated and modern countries in the world–Israel. Whereas Israel has excellent technology and infrastructure, in Gaza people carry goods by horse and cart. Whereas Israel has an educational system second to none, next to it children live who are denied even a basic education because their schools have been bombed. [7]

Israel is blamed because of the failures of the Hamas-run regime there to provide quality education and societal infrastructure. Yet, there is no mention that between 1993 and 2003, large sums of money were donated to the PA by Israeli taxes, by American aid, and by EU donations, for the specific purpose of building and educational and societal framework in Gaza. The funds were not used for that purpose. There would have been much improvement in this area had these designated funds, in the billions of US dollars, been used for their given purpose. Israel did not control that crucial factor. The PA did. Thus Rev. Morgan has taken a viewpoint which ignores the most salient factors in Gaza's current situation.

This participation in anti-Semitism may not be seen for what it truly is, as it is masked under the guise of participation in something politically correct and expedient, including a very strong emotional tug. This is especially true when Christian leaders like Rev. Donald Wagner and Bishop Desmond Tutu contribute to the high emotional pitch by their verbal accusation of Israel being apartheid and their support for BDS.

Reverend Pieter Grove, vice chair of the Cape Synod of the United Reformed Church in Southern Africa observed, "In my opinion the situation in Israel/Palestine is worse than it was in apartheid South Africa." [8] The problem with such a viewpoint is that making this statement does not live here. He does not hear and see the education (anti-Semitic and anti-democratic, anti-women and child abusive) that the PA and Hamas feed to their children on a daily basis, with the given goal being the destruction of the world's only Jewish state. Most South African Christians only hear and see selected things that feed into the PA's victimization narrative. This narrative touches an emotional chord with some South African Christians who experienced apartheid, and then it becomes so entwined with that emotional chord, that it is nigh to impossible to ferret out reality from deception.

For example, I have seen with my own eyes the homework assignment handed out to twelve-year old Arab students in

Hebron in 2010. That educational system is controlled by the PA. It was a poem memorization assignment. The poem called on the students to blow themselves up in a crowd of Jews, and affirmed to them that this was the purpose of their life. "If you lose life doing this, so what?" was one line. I often wonder what persons like Mr. Grove would think if he could read this assignment. Of course, it was written in Arabic, insuring that a Western audience would not likely understand it. Arab Christian parents, who were shocked by how the PA was trying to influence their son by way of this type of education, gave me this assignment to read.

In terms of an apartheid likeness, the PA's iron fisted approach to denying Jews the right to buy or own land that Arabs sell to them is noteworthy. Arabs kill other Arabs in vigilante *justice* because the victim decided, of his own free will, to sell some of his land or property to a Jew. So much for the right to do business freely in PA controlled areas:

> Palestinian Authority President Mahmoud Abbas has toughened the penalty for citizens selling property to Israelis. Abbas on Monday imposed a sentence of hard labor for life on 'anyone diverting, renting or selling land to an enemy state or one of its subjects.' Fatah's revolutionary council accused Pals, who sold their . . . properties of 'high treason', calling on the gov't and legal system to 'take the necessary steps to deter them.' . . . (and) called upon the public to 'boycott and humiliate them . . .' 'Those whose sick souls allowed them to sell their lands or homes . . . to the enemies of the Pal. people, are . . . traitors to their nation and religion. . . . They have brought shame and scorn upon themselves in this world and in the afterlife. . . . One would

> rather die . . . than betray the . . . land . . . saturated with the blood of prophets and martyrs throughout history. . . . Those traitors are destined to die a humiliating death.[9]

If apartheid kept Black South Africans from owning or purchasing "white" land, then the PA's policies resemble apartheid-era practice here. Not an ounce of human rights is being upheld in this incident. The free sale and buying of land is not allowed, and thus Jews are denied (as are Arabs) the rights to a free housing market.

> On the Mount of Olives, a large Israeli flag flies over a house where one man was possibly killed over the PA decree. "Who killed him nobody knows, but it was because of the house," said resident Abraham. Abraham's brother Mohammed was accused of selling the house to Jewish (buyers). Just days after the new residents moved in, Mohammed's dead body was found on the road between Jericho and Jerusalem.[10]

We see a similar situation described below:

> (The PA) has issued yet another warning to Palestinians against selling their . . . properties to Jews, saying those who violate the order would be accused of "high treason" – a charge that carries the death penalty. The latest warning was issued by the Chief Judge of the Palestinian Authority, Sheikh Tayseer Rajab Tamimi, who reminded the Palestinians of an existing fatwa [religious decree] that bans them from selling property to Jews. Sheikh Tamimi's warning came in response to reports that Jewish businessmen from the US had purchased 20 dunams of land from Palestinians on the Mount of Olives in Jerusalem. Warning the Palestinians against engaging in 'suspicious real estate deeds,' the

> religious leader said that according to Islamic teachings it was a 'grave sin' to sell houses and lands to Jews. He said that the ban also applies to real estate agents or middlemen who are involved in such transactions. He warned that anyone who ignores the warning would be punished in accordance with Islamic teachings and would also be ostracized by his community and family. [11]

The above describes a situation of PA sponsored coercion, and possible extortion. No human rights were practiced here. This appears to be a similar practice to the Nazi principle of outlawing business transactions between ethnic Germans and Jews.

> Farid Bashiti's bludgeoned and bound body was found Friday in . . . Ramallah. There were no condolence callers coming to pay their respects, no Koran verses being read in memory of Mr. Bashiti, who in death was declared a pariah, accused of what the Palestinian Authority last week declared a capital crime – selling land to Jews. . . . Hundreds of accused collaborators with Israel, including land dealers, were killed by Palestinian militants during a 7-year uprising.[12]

The PA's apartheid-like land policies caused suffering and death to the above-mentioned persons. As it has been stated:

> The human rights violations against . . . Christian Arabs in the disputed territories are committed by Muslims. Yet for political and economic reasons many Palestinian Christian leaders blame Israel for these crimes rather than the actual perpetrators.[13]

Oftentimes harsh critics of Israel will allege that Judea and Samaria (a.k.a. the "West Bank") are *apartheid* lands. Once again, this is a false analogy.

Yet, Judea, Samaria, the Golan Heights, Gaza and the eastern neighborhoods of Jerusalem were taken in a war *to the death* against the Jewish state. May I ask: what nations give "back" land taken in a war that was waged for survival? Perhaps before calling on Israel to give land "back"–Jordan surely would *not* want these areas "back", not in 1967 and not today–American critics of Israel should consider returning Native American land to the Native American tribes.

Of course this is a ridiculous and unrealistic challenge. Yet, this would encompass nearly the entire United States, where the great majority of that nation was taken without any defensive need, but in an expansionist settling of the USA, displacing the Native American tribes. Thus, it is quite hypocritical for the USA to call upon Israel to give "back" territory, when its own history includes Indian reservations, forced marches of Native tribes into these reservations, and discriminatory practices against Native Americans that still linger till today.

It is one thing to believe that Israel needs to improve its relationship with its Arab citizens, or that Israel needs to help up the living standards in the PA areas. I certainly would like to see this occur. But it is quite another to slander Israel by calling her *apartheid*. If Church persons participate in doing such, they do so at the risk of repeating old anti-Semitic patterns. The residents of the PA areas can only be helped by reform and cooperation *with* Israel, not by more conflict and jihad, which is what the *apartheid* charge is apt to foment.

The PA will engage in its victimization narrative, always blaming the Jews. To their own people in Arabic, they tell the jihadist narrative, encouraging the destruction of the Jews and the Jewish state. That is the bottom line.

The story of Mr. Clive Menell may be helpful. Mr. Menell, a South African Jewish businessman, was an associate of Nelson Mandela and an anti-apartheid campaigner in South Africa at the end of the last century. Menell joined Mandela in decrying the wrongs of South Africa's apartheid system. Yet, Mr. Menell was fully supportive of the Jewish state of Israel living behind firm and secure borders, and did not believe that modern Israel was in any sense *apartheid*. He knew *apartheid*, and Israel did not match that system. I met Mr. Menell, and was impressed by his love and enthusiasm for the state of Israel and its people. Mr. Mandela spoke at Mr. Menell's funeral, calling him ". . . one who labored for the cause of changing our society and upliftment of the poor." [14]

Logically, it would be difficult to imagine that Mr. Menell could have backed the state of Israel if apartheid were practiced. I don't believe his conscience would have allowed him to do such.

The foundations of apartheid South Africa were laid officially in 1948, when apartheid was enacted officially as government policy after the National Party won their election. Posters such as "To Unite and keep South Africa White" were commonplace. Yet, compare such an attitude with that of Israel, when being founded officially in that same year, 1948. The Declaration of Independence declares:

> We appeal–in the very midst of the onslaught launched against us now for months–to the Arab inhabitants of the State if Israel to return to the ways of peace and play their part in the upbuilding of the State, on the basis of full and equal citizenship and due representation in all its bodies and institutions –provisional or permanent. We extend our hand of peace and unity to all the neighboring states and their peoples, and invite them to establish bonds of cooperation and mutual help with the sovereign Jewish people settled in its own land. The State of Israel is prepared to do its share in a common effort for the advancement of the entire Middle East. [15]

Even the most superficial reading of this text from the Declaration of Independence shows forth the desire of Israel, from its inception as a modern state, to both grant full human rights to all of her inhabitants, including Arabs and Muslims, as well as work together with minority communities to build a modern Middle East. This is hardly the attitude shown by the political architects of apartheid in South Africa.

Citizenship and voting rights were denied after the 1948 elections in South Africa to its near 80% majority ethnic populations. In Israel, minority populations account for 25% of the national population. There have always been full voting rights granted to minority groups in modern Israel, and since 1949 Arabs have been getting elected to Israel's Parliament. Thus, there is no likeness here between apartheid South Africa and Israel regarding the right to vote.

One of Israel's Arab Christian leaders, Father G. Nadaff, recently wrote:

The assertion of Israel as a so-called apartheid state is complete nonsense. My successes and challenges speak loudly as to where the real problems lie for my fellow Christians. . . . All of these organizations claim that they are fighting for the weak, for the minorities who cannot stand up for themselves and demand and fight for their own rights. But ultimately, the actions of these NGOs beg the question of what rights they are really fighting for, whose interests they are protecting and what their real agenda is.

Clearly, these NGOs have no interest in seeing Christian Arabs become part of Israeli society. Much like the Arab countries that have used Palestinians in various refugee camps as pawns in fighting the State of Israel, these NGOs are content to reduce my community to cannon fodder in their efforts to de-legitimize Israel . . . the Israeli government's goal to bring them more fully into the mainstream. Doesn't the Christian community deserve the right to follow our own will and integrate, if it so chooses, into Israeli society? Not according to most of the NGOs that say they are assisting our community. . . . As Christians in Israel survey the situation of our brethren in the wider Middle East, we are appalled by the persecution that so many have experienced in Egypt, Syria and Iraq, among others. Truly, it has only been in Israel where Christians can fully practice our faith and can be productive members of society. We are not interested in misguided policies that would only bring harm and dislocation to us. Instead, we see and appreciate the opportunities to live full Christian lives in the Jewish State. It is important that Christians around the world understand that Jewish Israel has been a responsible steward for its Christians. We should be supported, and not demonized for our efforts to more fully join this benevolent society. [16]

I am familiar with a number of Israeli Christian Arabs who cannot safely give their opinions, which would be that they are satisfied living in the Jewish state, and do not wish to ever be a citizen of a PA or Hamas entity. The danger to such persons voicing this opinion publicly is not from Israel, but they risk persecution or worse by their own kinsmen for freely speaking their opinion.

Rejectionist Palestinian Christians fail to see that, after suffering for many hundreds of years as the most oppressed people in the history of mankind, Zionism was the Jewish independence movement striving to free ourselves from the domination and persecution of other peoples, and win our own human and civil rights–routinely denied to us in Europe and in the Middle East. After all, we Jews have seen how much we can rely upon the nations of the world to defend our right to exist outside of the land of Israel.

The apartheid charge is simply not true. Thus, it is a type of slander. If the worldwide Christian church does not stop engaging in spreading lies about Israel and the Jewish people, then there will be inevitable consequences. One such result is found in Genesis 12:3:

> I will give people who help you a reason to bow their knees in thanksgiving; however, those who oppose you, I will utterly curse. Through your life all peoples of the world will have reason to bow their knees in thanksgiving (to God; my translation).

This verse makes it clear that those who stand against the life, the promises and, the calling of Abraham would be found opposing God Himself! A life of curses would befall them. Indeed, subsequent chapters of Genesis confirm the veracity of this promise by revealing the fate of powers which did try to thwart Abraham.

Another consequence of spreading lies against Israel and the Jewish people is that the Church will be found participating in a possible future Holocaust against the State of Israel. False accusations against Israel of apartheid, whether overt or de facto, lay a conceptual foundation for hating and taking action against the Jewish people. This, coming on the heels of the Church's widespread complicity in the Nazi Holocaust, would signal a new height of apostasy. Can Yeshua, the Jewish Messiah who wept over his kinsmen and loved Israel with all his being, ever be pleased with such evil behavior?

Chapter 4

The Nazi Analogy: a Trip into Total Fallacy

> "The most brilliant propagandist technique will yield no success unless one fundamental principle is borne in mind constantly–it must confine itself to a few points and repeat them over and over."
>
> —Joseph Goebbels[1]

Here is a fallacy that is often repeated, with a Goebbels-like strategy of "repeat it till it is believed": "Constant attacks on Palestinians in the West Bank and Gaza signify that almost every day in Palestine is Kristallnacht."[2]

Let us look at the actual facts of what happened during *Reichskristallnacht*–which occurred on the 9th and 10th of November 1938–and see if any parallel can be drawn between that event and what occurs in the PA areas today. Let us examine the connection between *Reichskristallnacht* and Israeli policy today, to weigh the veracity of the statement about Israel's committing the same kind of actions today.

During *Reichskristallnacht,* 100 Jewish people were murdered, 30,000 Jewish men were sent to the Dachau, Buchenwald or Sachsenhausen concentration camps, Jewish businesses were put under a strictly enforced boycott, some 1,000 synagogues were burned down across Germany, and

Jewish businesses, hospitals and cemeteries were closed or destroyed. A $400 million collective fine was imposed by the Nazis on Germany's Jewish community. Never has the Palestinian population experienced this kind of atrocity–not even approaching a remote likeness–during any two-day stretch of history since modern Israel's inception. Furthermore, *Reichskristallnacht* was just the beginning of European Jewish sufferings. In my 36 years of living in Israel, never has there been a stretch of time when the *Reichskristallnacht* death toll been repeated in Palestinian communities. Never has the Israeli government embarked on a deliberate campaign of destruction against Palestinian hospitals, businesses, mosques, and never has there been a mass send-off of Palestinian men to concentration camps. The collective fines imposed by Nazi Germany upon that land's Jewish community have never been exacted from Palestinians. Never.

Reichskristallnacht spelled the deliberate and systematic destruction of some 1,000 targeted synagogues. Such actions have never occurred at the hands of Israel's government towards its Muslim population. Any claim to the contrary is a deliberate fabrication. On the contrary, Israel has been careful to preserve historic mosques inside of Israel, and has never initiated or taken part in the systematic destruction of mosques. Never. Mosques are seen in almost every Arab neighborhood in Israel, and are quite alive and well in the PA areas, undisturbed by Israel. Upon the cessation of the Six Day War, Israel gave the *Wakf* (The Muslim Religious Trust) the authority to run affairs on the Temple Mount, and Israel did not touch the Al Aksa Mosque or Mosque of Omar, found on that site. Israelis, and by virtue, Jews, respect the right of non-Jews to worship freely too much to ever systematically destroy houses of worship. This situation remains the same today on the Temple Mount. Israelis have windows of time where we can visit the Temple Mount, but it is forbidden for us by the Wakf to pray there! And we do not pray there. I hardly think that the Nazis would have had a similar arrangement with Germany's Jewish communities!

Does the alleged Palestinian *Kristallnacht* include ninety-one deaths on one day? Does it include over 1,000 mosques burning, with vandalism and looting of thousands of businesses by the Israeli population rampaging in Arab towns, all in a single day? Does it include mobs breaking into Arab homes and smashing everything in sight, beating up the residents? Were Palestinian libraries, museums and cemeteries destroyed by Israelis? Of course not. This has never happened in the PA areas, or in Arab neighborhoods in Israel's cities, nor in Arab towns in the Galilee and the Negev regions.

Here is what happened during the real *Kristallnacht*: "… (there were) more than a thousand cities, towns and villages throughout Germany in which (these) terrible events took place." [3] Synagogues, with their Torah scrolls and holy books, were burned up or destroyed in one day, in Berlin, Munich, Potsdam, Bamberg, Nuremburg, Bayreuth, Konstanz, Essen, Heilbronn, Bad Homburg, Dusseldorf, Essen, Brandenburg, Offenburg, Eberswalde, Cottbus, Mainz, Aschaffenburg, Dortmund, Wiesloch, Hoengen, Glogau, Korbach, Regensburg, Eschwege, Thalfang, Treuchtlingen Wiesbaden, Heidelberg, Zeven, Bassum, Stettin, Gustrow, Rostock and Tubingen—

again, all in one day. This is only a small listing of the many cities and towns in Germany where this occurred. In Austria, the same occurred in Linz and Vienna, among other places. Historian Martin Gilbert chronicles the eyewitness accounts of *Reichskristallnacht* in Vienna in his book, *Kristallnacht.* Rioting, mob rule, beatings, round ups to concentration camps, murders, and destruction of businesses and property, as well as that of Jewish schools and hospitals, happened nationwide-on cue-arranged by the Nazi party.

There is no evidence of such things ever being committed by Israelis, on arranged cue of a political party, towards Palestinians. Never. Any claim to the contrary lacks the evidence to support it. Thus, the use of the name *Kristallnacht* by the anti-Israeli author whom I quote–by inferring that Jews are doing these same things to Palestinians, on the same scale and severity that the Nazis carried out against Germany's Jewish community–at the very least was a mischaracterization and quite possibly was a deliberate attempt to fan the flames of anti-Semitism already prevalent in the Middle East. I consider such use of the word *Kristallnacht,* when used against Israel, to be vulgar and provocative. Christians should be careful to avoid this image, and to remember that only Jews were the victims of the historical *Reichskristallnacht.*

If even one mosque were damaged by Israelis in our day and age, international outrage would make it known. Jewish voices from within Israel would not tolerate the targeted destruction of Palestinian mosques. I know of no Israeli political party which advocates a systematic destruction of Palestinian mosques. Not one. Hitler and the Nazis not only advocated the destruction of synagogues, but they actually carried it out with their own hands. Thus, there is no valid comparison to be made here.

Contrast that, however, to when Israel voluntarily ceded its presence in the Gaza strip's Jewish towns in 2005. Upon withdrawing from Gaza, immediately gangs of Gazans, followed by the PA's bulldozers, destroyed the synagogues of Gaza. *This* is action that resembled the actions of *Reichskristallnacht*!

Have Israeli soldiers entered Palestinian villages? Certainly. Have Palestinian men been arrested and imprisoned? Certainly. Have Palestinians died while in conflict with Israeli soldiers? During both the First and Second Intifadas–rioting and armed uprisings committed by Palestinians within Israel and the PA areas from 1987-1993, and again from 2000-2005–this did occur. Yet Israeli citizens *also* suffered over 1,100 deaths and over 8,000 casualties during these same time periods. We personally suffered three terror attacks on my own family. So let us ask: is Israel engaging in a daily "*Reichskristallnacht*" against Palestinians? No. Friends, a repetition of the *Reichskristallnacht* is not happening in Palestinian cities or villages in the PA areas, nor to Israeli Arabs. Period.

Occasionally there indeed is a problem, such as a violent riot, or criminal activity occurring, or a terrorist cell is uncovered, a terrorist action has occurred, and Israeli security forces will enter an Arab village or neighborhood in a larger city, for a given mission. But there is no systematic attempt at murdering Palestinians. If there were, then we Israelis are the most inefficient and worst murderers in the history of mankind, because the Arab population in Israel *is growing*, and the Arab communities are *very alive* in our midst.[4] If an ongoing genocide were truly occurring, then the Palestinian population would have been destroyed by now. After all, we are told by a number of rejectionist, anti-Israel persons that for the past sixty-seven years, Israelis have been committing genocide against Palestinians. Sixty-seven years of genocide and no final results? *Reichskristallnacht* was all about initiating the Nazi's systematic, organized, daily plan to totally annihilate the Jewish presence in Europe, starting in Germany. No such similar initiative exists on the part of Israel towards Palestinians. The *Reichskristallnacht* likeness is, then, without foundation.

And where is any evidence of Israeli destruction of other minority groups, like the Nazis did to the Roma and Sinti (Gypsy tribes) and to the mentally handicapped? There is none. By comparison, minority groups in Israel, such as Circassians and Baha'i, quietly live productive lives, with no complaints of mistreatment. Druze communities live in Israel peacefully, and contribute to society in many ways, including the presence of Druze soldiers in the army. Indeed, a number of Lebanese Maronites–another minority group–fled to Israel for refuge after Hezbollah's takeover in south Lebanon, and remain in Israel. I have yet to hear Maronite refugees express regret about fleeing to Israel.

Any allegation that Israel treats or treated Arab communities like the Nazis treated Jewish communities is simple to refute by the numbers involved. The Nazis murdered some six million Jewish people–along with three million Poles, and were responsible for the death of over 20 million Russians, and countless other peoples in their march for conquest. How many Palestinians have been killed in conflict with Israel? Anything approaching the Holocaust numbers? Six million? No. One million? No. Not even close. 100,000? No. Already the reference to the Holocaust pales and falls away in its validity. Something is foundationally wrong with the analogy to Nazism. A review of the numbers involved quickly exposes the allegation as nothing more than anti-Semitic political rhetoric.

Let me preface this by saying that *I deem any dead persons due to war as unfortunate, in my belief that all life is sacred.* And to me, that includes Arab lives. I certainly do not rejoice over the death of the following persons that I shall now mention. Lost lives are a tragedy, no matter what their numbers. But let's more accurately examine how many Arabs have died in direct conflict with Israel, since 1987. The 1987-1993 Intifada saw 1,162 Arab casualties. The 2000-2005 Intifada saw 4,907 Arab casualties. The number of Arabs killed in Operation Cast Lead was 1,434 persons. During Operation Pillar of Defense, 158 Arab persons died, and in Operation Protective Edge, 2,100 Arab persons were killed. Thus, the total number of Arabs killed in conflict with Israel over the past twenty-five years equals a little over 9.000 persons. *What is this in comparison to six million persons*? While not meaning to compare the value of any one individual life as opposed to another, we can still draw the clear conclusion that the number of Arabs killed in all conflicts with Israel pales greatly in comparison to how many Jewish people died in the Holocaust. So clearly, there is no *Holocaust* taking place here right now. There is conflict–sometimes armed conflict–but no Holocaust.

From 1920-29, more Jews were killed in the then British Mandated area than Arabs. From 1936-1948, there were 15,000 Arab casualties, but this includes the numbers killed in Israel's War of Independence, when the armies of Egypt, Lebanon, Transjordan and Iraq, plus Syrian units, and Arab *irregulars* fought against the Jewish state. Nearly half that number of Jews, from the Mandated area alone, were killed during this same time by Arabs. The number of Arab casualties in conflict with Israel cannot even be mentioned in the same breath as the scope of the Holocaust. Additionally, most Arab casualties were as a result of actual war, with two sides firing at each other, not as a result of a one-sided genocidal operation as the Nazis carried out. No gas chambers have been used by Israel against Arab foes. No Muslims are rounded up into mosques to be burned alive, as was the custom of the SS to do in Jewish towns when the *Einsatzgruppen* invaded Eastern Europe.

An estimated one million Jews were murdered by *Einsatzgruppen* units through targeted gunfire. Much of the gunfire occurred similarly to the incident at Babi Yar in the Ukraine where at least 34,000 Jews were rounded up and routinely shot in 1941. Another four million estimated Jewish people were killed through the system of concentration and death camps, where death occurred by gassing, disease, starvation, overwork, brutal beatings and "medical" experiments.[5]

Some 125,000 Jewish persons perished in the Warsaw ghetto via starvation and disease, along with the 1943 ghetto uprising against the Nazis. Other ghettos, such as those in Lodz,

Vilna and Lvov had uncounted numbers of Jewish people die similarly as in Warsaw. Twenty thousand different Nazi work camps existed, with evidence of more European work camps being found all the time. It is uncertain how many Jewish prisoners died in some of those smaller camps. Obviously, the Nazis did not make any records of this public, and more than likely destroyed much of their paperwork as the Allied troops were in the final stages of defeating them. The bottom line is that our best estimates are that six million European Jews perished through all of the above-mentioned means.

Nothing in the Palestinian experience remotely approaches these numbers, and certainly not by the hand of Israel. How many Palestinians are starved by Israel each year? I never hear of any. Where are work camps operated by Israel which force Palestinians to work as slave laborers? There are zero such places. When does the IDF round up and shoot entire villages of innocent Palestinians on marches through Palestinian towns to enforce a policy of genocide? Even while the PA complaints of abuses, they have never shown proof of such actions by Israel.

The one time in recent history (2002) when the PA publicly cried "genocide" happened during an IDF military operation in Jenin's refugee camp to capture illegal, terrorist-serving weapons depots. The charges that Israel wiped out the entire city were found to be quite false. In a shootout between the IDF and the terrorist manufacturers of the weapons factory, some 54 Palestinians died. Israel lost 23 soldiers during this operation. It was a military operation that ended when the weapons caches were captured.

The city of Jenin had become a major terrorist center and the origin of dozens of suicide bombings. The Al Aqsa Martyrs Brigades, Hamas, and Islamic Jihad were all very active in Jenin and had carried out numerous shooting and bombing attacks. Jenin had become a terrorist headquarters complete with bomb factories. In a captured Fatah report addressed to Marwan Barghouti the Palestinians themselves call Jenin "the suiciders' capital." Defending against future attacks required Israel to move into Jenin to arrest those involved in terrorism and to confiscate their weapons.

> After the operation in Jenin, Palestinians claimed that a "massacre" had taken place and that the Israelis had killed more than five hundred people. This sparked international outrage and led to demands for a U.N. investigation. But eventually these claims were exposed as false, and the Palestinians themselves retracted them. Kadoura Mousa Kadoura, director of Yasser Arafat's Fatah movement for the northern West Bank, reported the number of Palestinian dead at fifty-six (according to another estimate it was fifty-two), which was proportional to corresponding Israeli losses (thirty-three dead). Most of the Palestinians who died were gunmen who had booby-trapped the area to inflict Israeli casualties.[6]

One senior PA official told CNN News that approximately 500 Palestinians were killed by the IDF in Jenin's refugee camp. PA Secretary Ahmed Abdel Rahman told the UPI news service that the number of Palestinian dead was in the thousands. He insinuated that Israel had kidnapped Palestinians, buried Palestinian victims in mass graves, and committed a campaign of genocide. Rumors spread that hundreds of civilians were murdered while at home. Yet, official investigations turned up no proof at all to back the allegations of "massacre" or "genocide." Thus, some of the loudest cries of "massacre" and "genocide" of recent times against Israel were found to be gross exaggerations and not true. This ought to convince Christians not to accept much that the PA claims against Israel at face value. I urge all Christians to *completely check out every charge* against Israel before joining any anti-Semitic chorus that trumpets allegations against the Jewish state.

Where are death camps like Auschwitz, Sobibor and Treblinka set up, for the purpose of gassing Palestinians the instant they arrive there? No Palestinians complain of these invisible death camps, nor is any proof every offered of this happening, because it simply does not happen. And neither does Israel use gas as a weapon against anyone. Where do medical experiments take place that are forced upon Palestinians, and end up by killing them? Where do experiments occur by Israeli MDs, performed upon Palestinian twins, such as those that were performed by Joseph Mengele? There are none.

The numbers clearly state the case and counter this most insidious claim, that there is likeness between the Nazis' actions and those of Israelis against Palestinians. There is no relation between the Holocaust and what Palestinians experience today, not from 1920 to now–and certainly not before 1920. The facts speak for themselves.

The late Holocaust scholar Robert Wistrich wrote that:

> . . . anti-Zionists' who insist on comparing Zionism and the Jews with Hitler and the Third Reich appear unmistakably to be de facto anti-Semites, even if they vehemently deny the fact! This is largely because they knowingly exploit the reality that Nazism in the postwar world has become the defining metaphor of absolute evil. For if Zionists are "Nazis" and if Sharon really is Hitler, then it becomes a moral obligation to wage war against Israel. That is the bottom line of much contemporary anti-Zionism. In practice, this has become the most potent form of contemporary anti-Semitism.[7]

Trauma psychologist Nathan Durst wrote: "When one calls everything Auschwitz, you deny the Holocaust. As everything becomes terrible, there is no absolute evil anymore. This is a great relief for the heirs of guilt."[8]

In agreement with Durst's statement, attributing the Nazis' behavior to Israel's behavior, in effect, purports that the Palestinians are in the same boat today that Europe's Jews were in in the 1930s and early 1940s. By labeling Israelis as *Nazis*, the tables of history are turned, and now the Jews can be eliminated, just like the Nazis were. Jews are turned from true victims in history to perpetrators due to the fallacy of "being modern-day Nazis." In the words of South Africa's Jewish Board of Deputies:

> Comparisons between Israel and the Nazi regime are obscene, not only because they are so grossly defamatory towards the Jewish state but because they belittle the unspeakable crimes of Nazism itself. It is self-evident that casualties resulting from a necessary and unavoidable military operation – casualties that Israel goes to considerable

> lengths to minimize – cannot be remotely equated with the systematic mass murder of millions solely on account of their being Jewish.[9]

If Christians want to show God's love to the Jewish people, joining in the chorus of those who bait Israel as being a Nazi-like entity will do *just the opposite*. It will cause Jewish people to say, "There go those anti-Semitic Christians once again, with the same allegations that they have had for 2,000 unbroken years." And I would agree with such an assessment.

The charge of Israel being *Nazi-like* is part of a worldwide anti-Semitic wave that is cresting:

> . . . official warnings have been issued to Jews in Germany, Finland, Switzerland, Ukraine, Hungary, Belgium, and Poland. Greece, Italy, France, and certain parts of Britain are following closely behind. Many have begun to make their exodus out of Europe to Israel, and Denmark is nearly Judenrein ("Jew free") now. Even the United States has seen a 127% rise from 2013 to 2014 in anti-Semitic incidents.[10]

Adding one's voice to the "Israel is a Nazi state" charge is joining that wave of anti-Semitic charges such as: Who knows one day with many such activists, the US will refuse to be exploited by its neo-Nazi blood-suckers! [11] Ironically, the author of the quote is an Arab "peace" and "rights" activist, and he refers to Israel in this quote.

Christians such as journalist Ben White repeat these images: "Pity the Palestinians, who, in the name of a 'social-democratic experiment', had to endure massacres, death-marches, and ethnic cleansing."[12]

The death marches were forced marches on which Nazi guards and soldiers forced their Jewish concentration camp inmates to go. These occurred toward the end of WWII, many in the dead of winter, for hundreds of miles, westward into Germany. Many Jewish victims died on the marches from exposure to the elements and from being shot if not able to keep up with the group's marching pace. White's invocation of this "death march" imagery is very weak, unsubstantiated by him, and again, has no connection to the point he is trying to make, since it has no basis in reality.

PA officials use comparisons to the Nazis to drum up anti-Israeli sentiment as well: (PA) official Issa Karake, who until recently served as PA Minister of Prisoners' Affairs stated: "This Hebrew state did more evil and more horrifying things than what happened in the Nazi crematoria." [13] Another anti-Semitic rant from the PA that used Nazi imagery, noted: "Netanyahu is a descendant of the Nazis, worships Hitler's ways and imitates him in all the Holocausts he has perpetrated." [14]

Jibril Rajoub, a leading official of the PA, spoke to *Awdah*, an independent Palestinian TV channel, claiming "(Israel is committing a) mass extermination as the Nazis did in Europe in the 1940s."[15] A week later, Yad Vashem stated, "Exploiting these terms from the Holocaust, in order to incite and inflame hatred, desecrates the memory of the Holocaust."[16] And then a totally insulting, atrociously inaccurate statement was issued by a PA government minister on 23 July 2014: "Israel has murdered over two million Palestinian children. . . . Jewish children murdered in the Holocaust did not exceed a million and a quarter."[17] Regardless of his intentions, this official was stoking the flames of anti-Semitism among his own populace. I can also assure the reader that the figure he issued for deaths of Palestinian children is grossly over reported–outrageously so. Yad VaShem carries the historical proof of the number of Jewish children murdered by the Nazis. No such evidence exists in the case of Palestinian children, because two million Palestinian children have not been killed by Israel.

PLO Executive Committee Member and Head of the Department for Jerusalem Affairs Ahmed Qurei claims:

> (The) Holocaust perpetrated by the Nazis is the same as is being perpetrated by the occupation against our people, [but Israel's] is even more severe, as they kidnap children, fight civilians inside their homes and places of worship, burn their crops and violate their human rights in the ugliest manner." [17]

Qurei's statements are most untrue. The scope and severity of the Nazis organized genocide against the Jewish people in no way resembles Israel's very limited, self-defensive military actions that are taken from time to time. While the death of children of all races, peoples and nations is a horrendous and unrighteous happening, Israel is not attempting any organized genocide against Palestinians, nor targeting Palestinian children. Any assertion otherwise is simply political propaganda, or highly ignorant.

Just as an example, there is a Palestinian young man in the town of Huwara today who is alive because my Jewish friends and I saved his life when he was a boy, after he had been hit by a Palestinian car, whose driver only stopped to scold the injured boy. We called an Israeli ambulance, which immediately came and brought the boy to an Israeli hospital where his life was preserved. I could see that his limbs were broken and that he was in shock. Had we been advocates of genocide against Palestinians, would we have stopped to help? I am not lauding myself. I would hope that every Israeli would stop to save a life, no matter who the victim is.

While Christian rescuers like Corrie Ten Boom and Sousa Mendes emerged in the midst of the systematic destruction of Jewish life by the Nazi's, not all share their compassion. The late American author Grace Halsell, a professed Christian, used the image of the Holocaust in a most demeaning manner describing a Jewish friend of hers: "She could focus on a holocaust of Jews while negating a modern day holocaust of Palestinians."[18] Halsell was attempting to accuse Israel of having committed a *Holocaust* against Palestinians. This is just another example of modern history being twisted to fit a political agenda–that of taking action against Israel. This progression of thought is patently anti-Semitic, and apparently Ms. Halsell's Jewish friend agreed with my assessment, as they no longer continued their friendship for long after this comment was made by Ms. Halsell.

It is absolutely mind boggling to see the incredible power of fabrications relayed through propaganda. From the PA, to the Checkpoint sponsors, to the BDS movement, to the apartheid slander, it is possible to use propaganda to infuse the minds of entire societies with totally false beliefs, based on this very propaganda. Joseph Goebbels was a master at perfecting such techniques, as indicated by this declaration:

> Propaganda is not a matter for average minds, but rather a matter for practitioners. It is not supposed to be lovely or theoretically correct . . . I speak differently in the provinces than I do in Berlin, and when I speak in Bayreuth, I say different things than I say in the Pharus Hall. That is a matter of practice, not of theory. We do not want to be a movement of a few straw brains, but rather a movement that can conquer the broad masses. Propaganda should be popular, not intellectually pleasing. It is not the task of propaganda to discover intellectual truths."[19]

Manipulating public opinion to fit the Nazi agenda was Goebbels' goal. That was his self-identified role among the evil Nazi elite. It did not bother him at all to lie, minimize or exaggerate about events to his own people, in order to carry out the Nazi political agenda. We can see the same mechanics of propaganda working in the PA and in some of the statements made by rejectionist Christians, including those who participate in the BDS movement and apartheid slander.

Denial of the truth to the public and the continuation of propagandizing them showed his lack of respect for their humanity and dignity.

Goebbels molded his words to fit the people, to use them, to make them embrace his destructive plans, when the actual flow of events began to favor the Allied powers. Denial of the truth to the public and the continuation of propagandizing them showed his lack of respect for their humanity and dignity. This is what continual propaganda does, and it is what I see as the outcome of much of the PA, BDS, apartheid slander, and rejectionist Christian platforms.

Just look at Ahlam Tamimi. Someone's continual propaganda influenced her devolution into a mass murderer of Jewish children.

Tamimi, who was jailed for life for her crimes, was released in a 1,027 to 1 prisoner exchange in 2011. She grinned on her television interview as she recalled what she did to Jewish babies through her planning of the Sbarro Pizza Café massacre in Jerusalem in 2001. As she put it with a smile: "(I murdered) Eight (of them)? Then eight it is!"[20] She was brainwashed by jihadist and anti-Semitic propaganda, then plotted an evil act of the type that the Nazis excelled at in the 1920s till 1945.

The Nazis were able to slaughter over one and a half million Jewish children under the age of 12, with no remorse, as well. Only when a culture and society dehumanize individuals can a reaction, such as Tamimi displayed, occur. This reminds me of the trial in which my father took part, as a prosecuting government official just after World War II. My father gathered evidence against a particular Nazi officer who, with his own hands, murdered four Jewish teen girls in Karlsruhe, Germany in the early 1940s. In the interview the convicted criminal gave to my father, he admitted what he had done, coldly, with no emotion. No regret was uttered. In fact, he protested his heavy sentence of a few short years in prison and the forfeiture of his assets. As I read over the transcript of my father's initial interview with him, I asked myself: "What could cause someone to feel no remorse that they brutally ended the lives of four human beings, children at that?" Tamimi displayed a like mindset. This is occurring in the PA areas. Christians worldwide must not support such brainwashing, either tacitly or covertly.

The General Conference of the United Methodist Church had an anti-Israel spokesperson who fell into the trap of publicly using the Holocaust as a PR weapon against Israel. This was the response from *Ha'aretz Daily*, a *leftist* leaning Israeli newspaper.

> What (she) did at the General Conference of the United Methodist Church – a religious institution with unequivocal emphasis on universal compassion and human rights – was to deny the Holocaust, by denying the essential humanity, and misrepresenting the essential experience, of the millions exterminated and the hundreds of thousands who survived and survive to this day. What she was saying is that their unspeakable, unhealable past is a tool to be played with and abused for the sake of a talking point. What Margaret Novak also did, as a result, was to undermine the just claims and aspirations of millions of Palestinians, by distorting and misappropriating the horror of the crimes of Nazism.[21]

Even though the papers' sponsorship may not share my own basic political positions, it is meaningful that a leftist newspaper would so strongly decry a Christian spokesperson for desecrating the meaning of the Holocaust by her misguided charges against Israel by likening the Jewish state to Nazis.

Sadly, the divestment debate among United Methodists frequently demonized Israel, with one intemperate delegate from Montana comparing the Jewish nation and the firms who do business with it to companies who facilitated the Nazi Holocaust. [22]

Another report on the 2012 United Methodist conference stated the following:

> . . . the proceedings bespoke of a monomaniacal obsession on the alleged sins of the Jewish state and absolute silence about the misdeeds of other countries in the region. (Concerning) resolutions regarding Coptic Christians in Egypt or Assyrians in Iraq . . . you will find nothing. One of the more outrageous moments of the assembly took place after it became apparent that the proposal to demand that the UMC sell stock in the three companies mentioned above was not going to pass. A woman who introduced herself as Margaret Novak said the following to the gathered assembly: 'I would just ask us all to imagine we were United Methodists back in the 1930s and 40s and that our Board of Pensions held stock in the . . . firms in Germany that . . . received the bids to manufacture the ovens for the concentration camps.
>
> The Methodist spokesperson compared Israeli policies in the West Bank to the destruction of Jews in Europe. She made this statement in front of several hundred people and the moderator of the assembly let her statement pass unchallenged. Novak's comparison between current Israeli policies and that of the Nazi regime falls under the *working definition* of anti-Semitism issued by the European Forum on Antisemitism. This definition warns against "drawing comparisons of contemporary Israeli policy to that of the Nazis."[23]

The only comfort is that full divestment from Israel was rejected at that particular conference of the United Methodist Church.

Friends, the goals that the Nazis pursued against the Jews are the logical ends of the BDS campaign, and of rejectionist Palestinian Christian political and (sometimes) theological positions. They will be more fully verbalized against Israel as time passes on. It is effective in the West because of the sad lack of memory and knowledge of history of the events leading up to WWII. It is also effective because most Christians have no idea about the Church's historical relationship with the Jewish people. Yet, I hope that the reader by now is fully persuaded that any likeness made between the Nazis and the modern state of Israel is an inaccurate, manipulative, and anti-Semitic charge.

There are no parallels to be drawn between what the Nazis carried out and Israeli policies toward Palestinians. Our detractors fling the Nazi- likeness charges when they feel it is of political benefit or gain to them.

At best, the "Nazi" charge is a sad anti-Semitic accusation. At worst, it is fertile ground for demonizing the Jewish people and further fueling the worst growth of anti-Semitism since the Nazi era! To use the Holocaust as a verbal weapon against Israel is a most insidious usage of all imagery connected to this historical event, of which the primary victims were Jews.[24] For Jews to hear the Church today misuse the memory of the Holocaust in this way is an affront to shining the light of Messiah to the Jewish people worldwide. This is especially true given the fact that the bulk of the Church in every country affected by the Holocaust was mostly silent as the Nazis butchered Jews. Christians who want to help thwart the rise of Hitlerian campaigns being conducted against Israel and the Jewish people today *must* stand against and denounce this banal usage of the Holocaust and its history by other Christians and by rejectionist Palestinian spokespersons.

In fact, the Church must learn the much needed lesson from the Holocaust before it's too late and, once again, finds itself on the wrong side of God's plans and purposes for the Jews. "(In the German Church) Protests to . . . Anti-Semitic policy . . . were few and far between. Even the Confessing church was silent at Barmen (1934) and afterwards at Stuttgart (1945)." [25] Why was this the case?

> A rise of Antisemitism is often the first seismographic reading on a serious shifting and shearing along the fault lines of bedrock Christianity. The fundamental fault line . . . is a line of false teaching about the Jewish people . . . Antisemitism serves a useful purpose to individuals insecure in their identity and to groups uncertain of their present and future prospects.[26]

I believe that Rev. Littell, quoted above, had unique insight into the "whys" behind the anti-Semitic expression that we see in the Church today, including that of rejectionist Palestinian Christians. The adoption of rejectionist, anti-Israel political doctrines in expression of Christian faith does not differ in any fundamental way from that which Rev. Littell observed. Nor does such expression differ from the early Church's same expressions of anti-Semitism, when theological anti-Semitism combined with political expediency to ostracize Jewish communities. This same pattern is occurring today in parts of the evangelical church.

The Holocaust is a truly valid reason for the Church today to identify with the State of Israel *and* the worldwide Jewish people. In the words of the former Chief Protestant Religious

Affairs Adviser to the High Command, in the de-Nazification program of the American government after WWII:

> In Christendom . . . was where the crime of the Holocaust was committed . . . for the Jews, the Christian cross is a sign of crusading slaughter, pogroms and mass murder . . . Jews . . . see the cross as something that Christians do to others.[27]

Sadly, this is how the Church has affected the Jewish people. My Christian friends, let the Holocaust speak for itself. Let the one and a half million Jewish child victims have some dignity by not furthering the decimation of their relatives–the nation of Israel. Additionally, do not use the *Nazi* slander against Israel.

I will end this chapter with a few poignant words from the book *The Crucifixion of the Jews*:

> When the Body of Christ is discovered at Auschwitz, it will be raised from among the victims, not hidden among the Protestant and Catholic guards and administrators. When the Messiah comes to consummate the longings and hopes of all mankind, he will be of the lineage of Abraham and David, not a timeless and faceless wraith, his head wreathed in abstractions. And I believe that though he tarry, yet he will come![28]

Chapter 5

Some Suggestions for "Turning it Around"

I do not deny that Palestinians have had a tough time in recent history. There has been pain suffered by Palestinian families. I wish it could have been otherwise for them. My heart goes out to them, for we, too–the Jewish people–intimately know the pain engendered by political troubles. That's been prevalent in our history for millennia.

For this, I can only hope that the Palestinians will find the answers they need to solve the problems and pain in their midst. With this in mind, I have worked with two different Israeli-Arab reconciliation movements over the past 13 years, with the goal to forge positive relationships between our peoples and procure some hope for our children.

Regarding solutions, the rejectionist Palestinian Christian *blame game* discussed in this book is no solution at all, nor does it offer any hope to its people. I desire to see the Arab peoples of the world walk in their depicted destiny as elaborated upon in Isaiah ch.19:

> On that day there will be a highway from Egypt to Ashur.
>
> Ashur will come to Egypt and Egypt to Ashur, and Egypt will worship with Ashur. On that day Isra'el will be a third partner with Egypt and Ashur, a blessing here on earth; for Adonai-Tzva'ot has blessed him: "Blessed be Egypt my people, Ashur the work of my hands and Isra'el my heritage." (Isa. 19:23-25, CJB)

Lebanon, Jordan, and Iran, among other nations, are pictured by the prophet as someday working together to bring God's kingdom to the Middle East. Partnership with Israel to this end, *specifically,* is depicted here. This prophecy has never been fulfilled in the history of mankind. It awaits a future fulfillment.

But the reader must be aware that "turning it around" for the Palestinians today will not take place and succeed, in the words of balladeer Bob Dylan, with "a noose at his (Israel's) neck and a gun at his back."[1] Until the anti-Israel propaganda and threats stop from the PA, no serious steps can be taken for "turning it around." The current conflict will continue.

In the words of Arab journalist A.K. Ajami, "We must change this narrative. Our narrative is that everyone who accepts Israel is a traitor."[2] What hope can there be when the *one* single entity in the PA areas that has the power to reverse hatred–the Church–in part espouses anti-Israel political sentiment and does nothing substantial to oppose teaching martyrdom to Palestinian children?

I will propose a positive process for Palestinians–a direction that holds promise.

First, the proverbial wheel does not have to be "reinvented". There are people on what I consider to be the best path. There are some Israeli-Palestinian reconciliation efforts which deserve the support of the Christian world–and that of the Jewish world. They are ones that bring families of Jewish, Arab, and other ethnic groups together to pray, share, befriend each other and aid in each other's work. These circles encourage each other during difficult times. They do not use the Palestinian "victimization" narrative as their script, but yearn for the fulfillment of the aforementioned promises given in Isaiah 19. They do not back violence as a political strategy. These all additionally affirm Israel's right to exist as the Jewish state behind firm and secure borders, while they love, pray for, and affirm the dignity of all Arabic speaking nations in the world. Their members come from over a dozen different nations in the Middle East. Growing these circles of prayer and friendship, as well as nourishing and supporting these groups is a worthy first step in the right direction. I do laud the efforts of the Anglican Church in Israel for having taken an active role in this. It is highly unfortunate that due to current security issues, I cannot identify these groups by name.

Second, I would affirm the worth of joint Israeli and Palestinian efforts to bring our peoples closer to each other. But this can only happen on the back of the proposed changes.

If Israelis were convinced that the PA really would live peaceably beside the Jewish state, the entire picture would change. Israel *could* and *would* work with Palestinians to build a societal infrastructure which would meet the needs of Palestinian communities. We attempted this before as part of the Oslo Accords. Throughout the world, it is often Israel that arrives with humanitarian aid first when there is a crisis. Certainly we do such in percentages that are out of proportion to our population and resources. Haiti, Thailand, the USA, Indonesia, Japan, and Turkey have been recent recipients of Israeli humanitarian aid when a natural disaster struck their populations. The power and possible success of Israel working with Palestinians in such a way would be amazing. Already, Israeli initiatives to help Palestinians exist, such as the "Save a Child's Heart" program, which has saved the lives of nearly 1,000 Palestinian child cardiac patients, *pro bono*, and has helped over 4,000 children from around the Middle East and Africa with health issues that they could not address in their home states. This program is funded and staffed by Israeli medical personnel, volunteers and funders.

As an Israeli citizen, I am sure that our nation would be eager to help build a Palestinian societal infrastructure IF we were convinced that the PA would educate and guide their proposed nation towards peace with us. But that has *not* been the case.

The failure of the Oslo Accords convinced us otherwise, and one cannot blame Israel for this fact. After all, Israel still has not seen the first step occur: an unequivocal agreement to *Israel's right to exist as the Jewish state*. Until that is attained, progress will not happen. That has not occurred.

As a third suggestion for moving matters along in a more positive direction: the Palestinian people simply must choose or form a government that will insure their basic rights, one that is willing to be fiscally responsible, as well as dedicate themselves to building a societal infrastructure. This contrasts with current thrusts that major on beating the drums of war with the Jewish people. This is where forging a future comes in. The decision must be made to build a future through meeting, planning, and drawing up business proposals for investors that do not include political rhetoric. Such a future can only hold promise if it includes tolerance for all, especially for the neighboring Jewish state.

Wholesale changes are needed in the educational curriculum of the PA's children. Anything in the subjects of social studies, civics and history that presents Jews as human beings worthy of life, and presents Israel as a neighbor, not an enemy to be dismantled, is the only way that current trends will change.

Joint educational projects are certainly possible between Israeli and PA area students, in all subjects, and in many endeavors. Joint teacher's projects have endless possibilities of creating a closeness that does not exist today. I personally took place in a number of joint student meetings between Israeli and PA area college students in the 1990s, when this was still possible. Athletic competition between schools is also a way to encourage contact between Israeli and PA area students.

I believe that joint educational projects would be warmly received by Israelis. I know that a change in the PA's educational curriculum would get such a reception.

My point is that success lays with transformation in the next generation, and educational change is foundational to any transformation. The Palestinian effort to bring this about will not be easy, because it *will* challenge the status quo and push the proverbial envelope of those wielding political and religious power amongst Palestinians today. It will take courage on the part of Palestinians to make such decisions to "turn things around". It is time to work together *with* Israel to build a future. It best starts with our children.

The Biblical model is for all nations, including Arab ones, to join with Israel in shining God's light to the world. This is envisioned by the prophet Zechariah as Gentiles firmly holding on to the *tsitsit* [6] (ritual fringes found on the clothes of a Jewish person, cf. Numbers 15:37) of Israelis in order to join in serving God. Zechariah 8:23 teaches that:

> The God of the Heavenly Armies declares, 'When that time comes, ten men from all language groups around the world will take hold of the *tsitsit* of one Jew and say, "We want to go with you, because we have heard that God is with you! (my translation).

This union is made possible by the results of Yeshua's life, and is further described by Paul in Romans 11:17-20.

Nevertheless, until every nation of the world, including Arab ones, accept, bless and love Israel in practical ways, the blessings of God will not be truly experienced. That is fact.

It is worthwhile to understand one's Christian beliefs by looking at its deep roots and foundations within the Jewish world. The unfortunate uprooting of Christianity from her Jewish world and foundations which occurred throughout history has wrought demise in both theological and political realms. Those political ramifications have spelled disaster for the Jewish people for centuries. Contemporary examples include the BDS movement and the *apartheid charge*, both of which bolster the type of anti-Semitism that leads to genocidal initiatives. There is an inherent strong connection between the Jewish world and Christianity. I encourage all readers to explore that connection as a priority, one that will greatly enrich one's faith, understanding of the Bible and appreciation of our Messiah.

The Bible must serve as the textbook for learning about Israel's role and how all nations, including Arab ones, need to relate to her. It is the only hope for moving on from the Palestinian victimization narrative, and for embracing a future that will nourish, not bury, children. This model holds out hope for Israeli *and* Palestinian children.

Unless the above changes in direction are taken, there will be more "Palestinian on Jewish" terror attacks, more dead Jews and more dead Palestinians (as a result of having to defend our very lives from these attacks). My suggestions are the only viable paths I see to improve the situation.

These are only a few general, simple suggestions, but would represent a start in the proper direction. The chances of their taking place, given today's political trends, may not be high, but it is always worth talking about it and trying to attain these ends.

Conclusion

Where will we go from here? How can another Holocaust targeting the Jewish people– this time via Israel–be prevented? Will the Church aid a future campaign to annihilate Israel? Or, will the Church stand up, defend Israel's existence as the world's only Jewish state, and help to insure the destiny of the Jewish people? These are the questions that lay before us, that is, before the Jewish people *and* the Church.

The conclusions of this book are simple. First, Israel does not relate to Palestinians or to its own Israeli Arab citizens like Nazis. There a*bsolutely* is no Israeli campaign to commit genocide against Palestinians, as the Nazis indeed did to Europe's Jews. Nor is there a single piece of evidence in socio-political experience or rhetoric that there is a parallel between Israel's relationship with the Palestinians as compared to the White domination Blacks in apartheid South Africa. Both of these allegation are completely fallacious, and ignore the many and broad efforts made by Israelis today to incorporate her Israeli Arab citizens in all facets of life, as well as philanthropic efforts to help disadvantaged Palestinians. The comparisons are flawed at their base. These are anti-Semitic accusations, constituting insult to the memory of both the six million Jewish victims of Hitler and the generations of Blacks degraded and oppressed in apartheid South Africa.

Second, the worldwide church needs to do some serious self-evaluation in order to stop anti-Semitic trends within her. Anti-Semitism continues to exist in too many Christians' expressions towards Israel, and can–even inadvertently-become a conduit for a theological, political and/or other genocidal campaign against the Jewish people by targeting the state of Israel.

Third, the Biblical texts are where we must find the purposes of God through choosing Israel. That truth, fundamentally, is that God's call to Israel and the Jewish people is irrevocable. Based on biblically mandated truth, the Church needs to become the protector and advocate for the Jewish people and the State of Israel.

Psalm 122 occupies a special place in the biblical text in this regard. In the Jewish world, it is one of the "Songs of Ascent," that is, a poetic song which was sung by Jewish pilgrims on their way to the Temple in Jerusalem during special times in the calendar year. The central message of this song ties directly into the overall picture that I have described in this book. Psalm 122 is a challenge for Christians of all denominations to love the Jewish people and to help sustain the world's only Jewish state. The Church should take particular note of the mutual benefits found in adherence to verse 6. "Pray for the peace of Jerusalem; may those who love you be secure." (Psa. 122:6, NIV) "Pray for the peace of Jerusalem: they shall prosper that love thee." (Psa. 122:6, ASV) "Diligently inquire about the well-being of Jerusalem; your lovers will be tranquil." (Psa. 122:6, my translation) If we can understand this verse in its wider context, we would find it to convey: *"Ask intently about Jerusalem's well-being. Anyone who loves her will do well."* (my translation and italics) By "intently," I mean with consistency, with energy, as a high priority, and with meaning. Verse six was written approximately 2,900 yrs. ago. Between that time and today, God's purposes for Jerusalem *have not changed*: "I am God, I have not changed. So, you, Jacob's sons, have not been annihilated." (Mal. 3:6, my translation) God's plans for Jerusalem have remained wonderfully, amazingly, consistent. He still intends for Jerusalem to be the center of the Messiah's kingdom.

At a recent conference that I attended involving Israelis and delegates from ten other Middle Eastern nations, an Anglican priest made the following statement:

> What should our response be (towards Israel)? Paul says to the church at Rome, which was getting arrogant with the attitude: "you Jews lost it; you're out, we're in," that God loves the Jewish people. If God loves the Jewish people, so should we. We can't be hateful, spiteful, or bitter towards them. Love in the New Testament is always practical. We should all stand up against anti-Semitism . . . we should all pray for Israel. We want Israel to be (a kingdom of) priests, and reach out to her neighbors. We need to pray for that.[1]

A second priest, at the same conference, also noted:

> We cannot run away from history—we have been a poor witness (to the Jewish people), allegedly based on Israel's

> sinfulness. But Israel is no more 'sinful' than the Church has been. As Christians, we must have mercy on Israel.[2]

A third delegate to this conference, from one of Israel's most virulent enemy nations, stated: "The Jewish people gave us our Bible, and they gave us our savior; for those two reasons alone they are worthy of our respect."[3]

Another Middle Eastern Christian delegate to this conference noted:

> Jesus is a Jew. He still keeps a Jewish identity. He hasn't given this up. In the book of Revelations, he identifies himself as the Lion of the Tribe of Judah. . . . If we don't understand Jesus in his Jewish context, we will fail . . . to see Jesus as he really is. . . .[4]

Whether by miseducation or malice, the separation of the Church from its Jewish roots inevitably leads to de facto anti-Semitism. For example, what response was there from local churches when, in 2009, a Ft. Lauderdale demonstration included someone engaging in clear, anti-Jewish hate speech: "Go back to the ovens. You need a big oven, that's what you need!" this person yelled at a group of Jewish and pro-Israel counter-demonstrators. Can local churches around the globe afford to remain silent, when someone in their own community publicly calls for Jews to go through the Holocaust again?

All the Jewish and Israeli blood that has been shed in the past 2,000 years surely tells us that Jewish persons have been targeted for brutality, persecution, domination and genocide simply because we are Jewish. Many people think that the human race has evolved so greatly, and reached the brink of a new international community today. We should think again. There has been no cessation today to the phenomenon of anti-Semitism. The world has had plenty of opportunities throughout ancient and modern history to hear the voice of Jewish victims cry out. The results of such opportunities, sadly enough, are quite negligible up until today. In fact, if the Church becomes party to another attempt to kill Jews on a large scale, then the blood of the victims at Auschwitz and Birkenau will have cried out, and no one will have listened.

It is one thing to discuss improving relations with Palestinians. However, to desire and/or verbalize the elimination of the Jewish state is to further the same cause that Hitler envisioned. Warring against Israel by any means is to work for the elimination of the Jewish people in the Middle East. Without our sovereign state, there would be no opportunity or chance for Jewish survival in the world.

The over-arching purpose of this book is to make an effort in preventing another Holocaust against the Jewish people. I have been compelled by my conscience to speak. Growing anti-Semitic trends in the Church have motivated me to write this treatise *now*.

As current events mix with expressed political ideologies and anti-Semitic religious thought, the "perfect storm" could occur, catapulting another Holocaust effort into action. I truly hope I am wrong, but the witness of recent anti-Jewish (not anti-Israel, in particular) events in Copenhagen, Paris, Malmo and Brussels, among many other places paint a foreboding picture of what's to come if the tide is not soon stemmed.

Psalm 122 lays out the way for Christian believers to join in an effort to avert another Holocaust–by intercession, by use of available resources, and by advocating for Jerusalem–all in pursuit of Israel carrying out and walking in her God-given destiny. The biblical text encourages everyone to give their every effort to insure that the city reaches her calling.

As a Jew, I pray that the Almighty will cause a stirring in the midst of the Christian world to act with respect and love towards the offspring of Abraham, Isaac and Jacob–Yeshua's own flesh and blood brothers–nearly half of whom today live in Israel. Without such a stirring, anti-Semitism will continue to grow and flourish by those who claim to represent the Jewish Messiah.

Appendix A

ETS Address, Summer 2000, Nashville, TN

Introductory note: The *Evangelical Theological Society* (ETS) is a society of biblical scholars; their annual conferences feature seminars presented by those in their ranks. The 2000 event featured some 400 deans, professors, scholars, and college presidents in attendance during the author's address, on the subject of, "Living in Israel through my eyes."

The content of this address touches on the issues that are included in this book, although the address was given fifteen years ago. The issues remain till today, thus, this talk is included in the book to give the reader a bit of a fifteen-year background by which to frame the issues brought up in this work.

The names of prominent involved persons have changed, but the existential threats to Israel remain the same. The positions of the Palestinian Authority (PA) remain remarkably the same over the past fifteen years. The roles of Hamas, Iran and Hezbollah are also consistent as to the time of the address given in Nashville. In fact, Iran and Hezbollah's designs on Middle Eastern politics have increased greatly in the past 15 years, as Iranian military and political influence–through its proxy army Hezbollah–now dominate Lebanon, and rob her of her full sovereignty. Syria, Iraq, Yemen and the Sudan also now are influenced strongly by the fascist, terror-sponsoring Iranian state.

It is unfortunate that things have remained relatively the same regarding Israel and the PA from the 2000 talk, quoted in full, below. In the entire Middle East, the situation has grossly worsened for Christians and other Muslim minority groups. Certainly Israel cannot be held responsible for this worsening situation across our region.

* * * *

"Ladies and gentlemen, distinguished scholars and professors, honored colleagues and friends, I am honored to address you this evening on a most difficult subject. What I say tonight I say with respect for all of you, including the distinguished plenary speakers before me. I will make my points firmly and with my full conviction, but end in an irenic manner. My points may be hard to hear, because they will not paint a pretty picture. But I believe with all my being in what I will say. I will honestly share with you my perceptions of the realpolitik of living in Israel, built upon my experiences as a long-time immigrant.

I would have liked to address you about what it is like to experience the recent Russian and Ethiopian immigrations. However, of necessity, I must comment almost solely on Israeli-Palestinian political affairs as I see them. The October events of this year have put the current states of affairs in a sad and nearly unsalvageable condition. I will share this evening on why I think these October riots occurred, and what the outcome of this behavior will lead to.

Let me say from the outset that I am not unaware of the pain undergone by Palestinians. I spent three years of my life studying Arabic, Arab history and culture while obtaining my M.A. degree in Arabic in the 1970s. In addition, I have visited three Arabic speaking countries and spoken with many Arab students, colleagues and professors regarding their feelings about my country and my people. While studying at the Hebrew University in Jerusalem, my Arab hall mate and I became fast friends, and daily discussed the politics of the Middle East. So, I don't speak this evening with an unconcerned heart toward Palestinians.

I would affirm that Palestinians should have societal and political rights in Israel. However, I also affirm that the country of Israel is a Jewish entity, and this should not be compromised by dividing up our country and our capital, or by compromising the borders of our country.

After the Israeli Defense Forces (IDF's) pullout in Lebanon, our northern border is not more stable. It is no secret that the dominant militia there, Hezbollah, with Syrian and Iranian aid, continues to stockpile weapons to war against my people. Their recent infiltration into Israel and kidnapping of three soldiers, as well as kidnapping Israeli citizens abroad, clearly shows their aims. If the PA is given sovereignty over Jerusalem, will this appease Hezbollah? No. Will it appease Saddam Hussein? No. Will it appease Syria? No. *Many Arab entities have different political agendas, and there is no coordinated political stand between them, except in demanding that Israel yield land.* At least three political entities want a geographical piece of Israel, and some still want our total destruction. The overall security situation is so bad that Prime Minister (PM) Barak, in early January, told the Israeli military brass to be prepared for a regional war in the very near future. He has never said such words before. Let's look at the picture that I see before me:

The undemocratic PA entity wants Jerusalem: according to Mr. Arafat, all of it. The dictatorial Syrian regime wants the Golan Heights, all of it. Terrorist Hezbollah, aided by Syria and Iran, want our total annihilation, as do other organizations such as the PFLP, DFLP, the Islamic Jihad and Hamas–which are all very active groups and vocal about their aims. In fact, the PFLP, the Islamic Jihad and the DFLP announced on Nov. 2nd that they will not recognize the Nov. 1st cease-fire, and the Islamic Jihad carried out their lethal terrorist strike at the Mahane Yehuda marketplace in Jerusalem that same day.

Syria, a country which often used the Golan Heights for a rocket launching pad against us prior to 1967, is continuing to build a massive arms arsenal. These weapons are not being acquired for any other purpose than to threaten Israel. Syria's armory, according to Prof. Anthony Cordesman of Georgetown University and the Center for Strategic and International Studies, includes newly acquired North Korean missiles armed with VX nerve gas warheads. Damascus *is 7 minutes* military air speed time from the Galilee. My reality, and that of my countrymen, is that Israel is a tiny nation surrounded by a sea of intolerant hatred. I personally do not think we can do anything to make peace with the greater

Arab and Muslim world outside of abdicating our country, and that will not happen.

Given our situation, our demographics cause me to doubt if what is being planned for Israel's future is positive. Friends, please understand that it will take more than words to convince the people who survived the Holocaust that the world has Israel's best interests at heart when it attempts to divide up our capital and pressures us to yield strategic land. Demographically, please understand that as our borders get smaller, we have no other place to go. As a young lady, a friend of mine from Tel Aviv, recently remarked to me, 'It feels like we're being hoarded again into a ghetto.' Israel is our only country. It takes six hours to drive the country from north to south, and some of that time would be the traffic jam one encounters while going through the Tel Aviv area. It takes less than two hours to drive the country from east to west, if we include Judea and Samaria. Without that area, which is what Israel is being pressured into ceding, it would take twenty minutes–twenty minutes, to drive the east-west axis in the center of the country. One could look out from Ben Gurion Airport, our international air terminal, and see another country just 2 miles away–a country whose pending government continues to encourage the present hostilities. Perhaps in other places of the world, this set-up could be feasible. It is for San Marino, Andorra and Monaco in Europe. But Israel is surrounded by hostility; our neighbors are not France, Spain and Italy, but Iraq, Syria and Libya. Does any other country in the world exist with such an absurd political reality being planned for it? I can't think of too many.

That's our current situation. It's a tough neighborhood to live in. Our Jewish state of five million people is surrounded by over 200 million people in some twenty-two Arab nations, many of whom are still debating whether we should have the right to live. The Palestinians claim our capital city as theirs; the Syrians claim our northern border with 33% of our water supply as theirs. The absurdity of the situation begs itself.

I would like to talk about the Israeli people and Jerusalem for a minute. Yassir Arafat has accused us of Judaizing Jerusalem. He stated:

> It is the year of Holy Jerusalem becoming our capital, our capital for eternity, whether people like it or not. Whoever doesn't like the idea can go drink the water of the Dead Sea. As far as the Holy City of Jerusalem is concerned, we refuse to accept Israeli plans to Judaize the city.

The idea of Israel Judaizing Jerusalem is absurd. Jerusalem is the capital city of the modern state of Israel. Jewish residents have inhabited the city for 3,000 years. That's when its *Judaization* occurred. Only a short period of time under Hadrianic Roman rule, and again after the Crusaders murdered Jerusalem's Jewish community in 1099, was there any break in the history of Jewish residence in Jerusalem. In more modern history–by the year 1840–there was a Jewish majority population in Jerusalem. My own experience with Jerusalem is a very intimate and personal one. I went to college there. I have lived and worked in the city; it is my home. My children graduated from its schools, and their best friends live there. My sons and I have both had the privilege of representing the city in national and international athletic competition.

I have hurt with Jerusalem, too. When terrorists blew up two city buses in 1996, my cousin was aboard. With all Israel, I wept. When suicide terrorists set off bombs on Ben Yehuda Street in 1997–thirty meters from my office–I was in shock and I wept with the city and all Israel. My work colleague dug through the body bags to see if any of our employees were dead. There is still Jewish suffering and pain in Jerusalem today. Yielding large sections of our capital city to entities which have proven themselves to be untrustworthy is not the way to eliminate the existing problems.

The nation of Israel and the Jewish people have a valid historical claim to Jerusalem, one that will not be reneged on. I do not say this out of a vengeful, hateful, nationalistic pride. Simply, I do not, nor do my countrymen, trust the world to follow through on any promises of a political offer to give up part of the city for a nebulous promise of peace. If you were in my shoes, with my people's history, you would feel the same way. The October rioting and violence punctuates this point even more. For some 2,000 years, devout Jewish communities in all the lands of the Diaspora prayed six times daily in the amidah and birkat ha-mazon prayers for their return to Jerusalem, and for the rebuilding of the city under Jewish sovereignty, as well as for the coming of the Messiah to this city. There are over 700 references to Jerusalem made in the Bible, and the Jewish men who wrote the New Testament include mention of Jerusalem in two-thirds of their writings. Jerusalem has always been, and will always be, a central focus of the Jewish consciousness, whether we speak of Israeli or Diaspora Jewry.

One of the charges you will sometimes hear is that Jerusalem needs division because Israel discriminates in allowing holy site visitations. It strikes me as rather hypocritical that from 1948-1967, there were no voices calling for the Arab world to allow Jews access to our holy sites in East Jerusalem. And a good number of our holy sites were desecrated during that time period. Yet now that Jerusalem is under Israeli sovereignty, suddenly the PA and others are screaming for UN control of Israel's holy sites, especially the Temple Mount. I can't form any opinion other than this is shameless anti-Semitism. When Jordan controlled East Jerusalem, Muslims, some Christians, and no Jews could visit the holy sites. The Western Wall–Judaism's holiest site–was shut off to Jewish pilgrims. Under Israeli sovereignty, east Jerusalem's holy sites are frequented by Jews, Muslims and Christians. There is no systematic discrimination in accessing the holy sites, such as that Israel was subjected to under Jordanian rule. But now under Israeli sovereignty, we hear, "The present situation is no good, it's not fair to the other two great faiths, the Israelis discriminate," etc., ad nauseum.

Or, we hear, "with Arab and Islamic assistance, this shall be our faithful jihad, to defend holy Jerusalem from the danger of Judaization and the Zionist plot" (Yasser Arafat). In addition, the fact is that the PA will not be satisfied with political control over part of a divided Jerusalem. I am saying this because I want you to see why I feel there is historical blindness and hypocrisy in the call to divide Jerusalem. Thus, I am quite concerned that all of our borders, including the city of Jerusalem, do not become untenable.

My father was a civil rights attorney for the Anishinabe Native American tribe, as well as the President of our local branch of the NAACP. He dedicated his life to fighting for the rights of Native and African Americans. My grandmother fought long and hard for women's rights and against anti-Semitism as the first woman and first Jewish candidate for state public office. My family has a long and distinguished history of promoting civil rights. Therefore, I cherish the concepts of life, liberty and the pursuit of happiness. With this background in mind, I have weighed what I have seen of the Palestinians' government in waiting, and I find it gravely wanting.

I realize that a future Palestinian state is an internationally sponsored fait accompli. Yet I do not feel that this is a positive development. I am warning all of us today, that a Palestinian state under the PA will not add to stability or freedom, nor help out the Palestinian Christian community. My reasons for saying this focus on the nature and character of the PA. Like it or not, friends, this is a fascist, anti-Semitic, hatred-filled organization; it has been such from its beginnings as the PLO and continues on as such. So, the PA's character and modus operandi rankle my democratic veins. Say what you want about the times Israel has not done a good job upholding civil liberties under severe and trying, pressure-cooked situations. But Israel has a democratically elected government, and citizens can, as policy–and often boisterously do–speak out our minds on every area of political life without governmental interference. I have always felt positive living in Israel in an environment like this. But this will not be the situation for our neighbors. Let me talk openly about the reality of who Yassir Arafat is, and how he will behave as the head of a state.

LAW, which is the Palestinian Society for the Protection of Human Rights, writes in their May 1998 periodical, and I quote, of . . . 'the poor human rights record of the Palestinian Authority' [unquote]. Another Palestinian organization, The Palestinian Human Rights Monitor, under its director, Bassam Eid, notes, 'The arrival of the PA in parts of Gaza and the West Bank raised hopes that . . . the mold established in human rights by other Arab regimes could be broken. This has not been the case.' Eid continues, '. . . torture is widespread and used by all the Palestinian security branches,' and adds, 'complaints of torture filed by detainees are ignored.' In fact, since 1995, according to the Palestinian Human Rights Monitor, at least eighteen Palestinians have died while under PA security forces' detention. Let us not have any illusions about the kind of government that will be on our border, or how that pending government will relate to people, including its own citizens. In early January, two alleged Palestinian collaborators with Israel were executed publicly in Gaza by PA firing squads: they had no trials. Lines of PA police opened fire on the blindfolded men, who were tied to stakes. The Reuters news photo of this incident is posted on the Israeli Ministry of Foreign Affairs website.

On January 14th, in speaking about that incident, the PA's Minister for Jerusalem Affairs, Faisal Husseini, considered a moderate, said: 'Unlike in the past, today the Palestinians are in a state of war and must expel collaborators from their midst. We had to take every possible step against those that betrayed their people.' So, now the ruling elite in the PA have taken it upon themselves to define what treason is, and are judge and jury. It is interesting that, after two days of hearing protests from the EU, Canada and Israel, the PA promised to do this no more. This is a good picture of what current human rights are like under the PA's jurisdiction. Regarding this incident, the aforementioned Mr. Eid noted, 'they (PA) were operating completely in contradiction of international fair-trial standards.'

As well, the Palestinian Rights Monitoring organization charges Mr. Arafat with interfering with freedom of the press. I quote, 'The PA has been successful in instilling a climate of fear and intimidation on the community of Palestinian journalists...' Mr. Eid further notes that every single Palestinian journalist whom he interviewed insisted on anonymity for fear that they would be harmed by one of the PA's security forces. Eid cites one editor who was imprisoned for placing a story about Mr. Arafat on the 8th page of his newspaper, not on the cover page as Arafat had ordered him to do. Press censorship and harassment has been the norm under the PA so far. I would not expect that this should change.

I sympathize with a Palestinian desire to have a government to call their own, but I am most disturbed at the quality of the organization that has been given the power to rule over them. But we have to face the facts. The PA is not a democratic, freedom-loving entity. Perhaps some of you saw the recent despicable episode of the Palestinian Broadcasting Company's children's show, called the "Children's Club," in which little children were being taught anti-Semitic slogans, such as, 'I will grow up to kill every Jew I meet,' and 'sing constantly about my life as a suicide warrior.' What is the official broadcasting authority of the PA teaching its children? It certainly does not instill confidence in me. The PA has never repudiated this hypocritical piece of virulent hatred. In fact, PBC head Radwan Abu Ayash commented that he is not allowed to broadcast pieces that promote peace with Israel. This stands in stark contrast to pieces run on Israel Television about our Arab neighbors, especially during the current peace process.

I was dismayed to read the August 3, 2000 edition of the NY Times, where an article entitled, "Palestinian Summer Camp offers Games of War" reported how 90 children's summer camps, run by PA officials, had mock kidnappings of Israeli leaders, mock attacks on Israeli military posts, and stripping down, then assembling, Kalashnikov rifles as their daily activity. Read the article and tell me if it instills doubts as to the PA's sincerity for peace with Israel in your minds. It should. Why are no Palestinian voices speaking out against such anti-Semitic and anti-Israel venom? I will tell you why: they are scared to death of retribution from one of the six security wings of the PA.

The more area that the PA controls, the more it will spread its gangland, bullying style of leadership over such areas. Mark my word on that. If anyone has succeeded in portraying to you a PA that is democratic and akin to traditional American ideals, please don't have such naivety to believe it. It is not true. It scares many of my people when we recall that the el-Husseini family, to which Mr. Arafat belongs, actively supported Adolf Hitler in WWII, and that Mr. Arafat himself supported the Soviet Union during the Cold War and Saddam Hussein in the

Persian Gulf War. Lest we forget, units of Arafat's army-in-waiting served with Saddam's forces in Iraqi-occupied Kuwait, making the PA's chairman complicit in multiple crimes. I cannot understand how the world, and how the Church, can turn a blind eye to this fact. In my opinion, for him to receive the Nobel Peace Prize is not much different than awarding one to Al Capone.

Are we to compare Mr. Arafat's life accomplishments for humanity to previous Nobel Prize winners Mother Teresa, Elie Wiesel, or to Martin Luther King? Have we forgotten who was behind the 1972 Munich Olympics massacre? Was that an honorable act? Or the 1978 hijacking and murder aboard the Achille Lauro? Mr. Arafat's closest advisor was the architect of that act. No wonder Nobel Prize committee member and confessing Christian Kaare Kristiansen of Norway resigned in protest with his famous statement, 'I would no longer be able to look at myself in the mirror if I had been a part of the committee that gave the Peace Prize to Arafat.' I applaud Mr. Kristiansen for his courage and his stand.

What is happening to moral consciousness in today's world? I am very concerned. Arafat does not have a pro-democracy track record. He has yet to publicly and finally repudiate the PLO's charter statements regarding the aim of destroying Israel. If in 1998, an American political figure had publicly stated, 'My rifle is ready to turn on the USA if it doesn't permit me to attain my political ends,' where would such a person be today? Yet, Mr. Arafat made such statements: only please substitute 'Israel' for the 'USA'. You can't talk out of both sides of your mouth and be faithful to a peace process.

True peace partners speak respectfully of one another–they try to sympathize with each other's plights. They do not engage in inflammatory rhetoric against their partner. Peace partners do not do say what Mr. Arafat did to news reporters on October 22 when he stated that PM Barak could 'go to hell' if he doesn't accept the PA's aims towards Jerusalem. Mr. Arafat, in his talk, has voiced no respectful qualities toward Israel. And that fact, ladies and gentlemen, concerns me. For all of the above-stated reasons, you can see why I do not view a neighboring PA government in a positive light. . . . A further severe problem awaits the world concerning the PA. When and if Mr. Arafat loses control of the PA, there will be a chaotic inner war to wrest control of that organization. Already, would-be leaders Jibril Rajoub and Marwan Barghouti are positioning themselves for a power struggle in such an inner war. Is the world ready for the further chaos and instability with probable internecine bloodshed that the PA will bring you? Barghouti is head of the PA's Tanzim militia, and he does not shy away from bloodshed. Rajoub is PA Preventive Security Head, a position that understands the concept of force well.

A good number of Palestinians fear their government-to-be, and with good reason! The Washington Post, on July 25, 2000 ran an article entitled, "Some Arabs Reluctant to be free of Israel." In it, they report that a good number of Arab citizens of east Jerusalem, whom their reporters polled, did not want to transfer to the PA authority. I quote from the article:

> A clear majority said they would prefer to remain under Israeli control rather than risk the economic and political uncertainties

> of Arafat's state in the making. Many said they want no part of the PA's notoriously corrupt administration, economic mismanagement and brutal, feuding police. Many expressed fear of Arafat's various security forces, whose penchant for staging gun battles with each other, shaking down unlucky citizens, and roughing up others have earned them the disdain of most Palestinians. A college student named Muhammad, who declined to give his last name, remarked, 'Our lives would change from a country that's almost democratic to a country that talks about democracy, but doesn't have any.'

Let me now be brutally honest. Palestinians have more freedom to criticize my government than their own pending one. Israeli Arabs and Palestinians can and do criticize my government in both the Palestinian and Israeli media. But they do not criticize the PA, although they know how corrupt and abusive the PA is.

Now, I speak as an Israeli who recognizes that there is a need for civil, legal and political rights for Arab residents in the Land of Israel. It is a testimony to Israel that so many Arab families freely choose to live in places like Yafo, Haifa, Ramle, Beersheva, the Galilee, and in the Negev Desert–all in the state of Israel. Such residents do possess religious freedom and full voting rights in the Jewish state. Granted, there are problems for our Arab citizens. I would like them to be addressed and solved, and I have spoken up for this. Whatever shortcomings there may be, I have observed that Israel's Arab communities enjoy the right to life, to work, to worship freely, exemption from military service, and freedom of speech. Neither Saddam Hussein, the Syrian Alawite regime, nor Yassir Arafat can have that said of their administrations. In fact it is amazing that a good number of Bedouin Arabs have freely chosen to join Israel's army and serve in it, without any legal obligation to do such.

Israel has freely elected Arab members in our Knesset. In the recent past, our ambassador to Finland, Ali Yayha, came from Israel's Arab community, and another such member served as Israel's Consul General in Atlanta. In the recent past, Nawaf Massalha served as Deputy Minister of Foreign Affairs. My point is that the facts show that there is Arab community participation in politics, voting, and government service. As well, the Israeli Court system attempts to serve its Arab citizens without ethnic deference. As Alan Dershowitz, the noted American jurist noted, 'One does not judge a democracy by the way its soldiers immediately react, young men and women under tremendous provocation. One judges a democracy by the way its courts react in the cool of judicial chambers. And the Israeli Supreme Court and other Israeli courts have reacted magnificently. For the 1st time in [modern] Middle Eastern history, there is a judiciary willing to listen to the grievances of Arabs. . . .'

Let me quote to you from my Israeli friend Elhanan, who lives in Jerusalem:

> I'm certain that this has not been reported by the media, but I am a witness to it. I taught English to a very kind Muslim father of 6 here in an Arab village in Jerusalem. When a necessary security road was to cause the destruction of his home, he took the case to the Israeli Court system, himself not an Israeli citizen; he won the case. And Israel has since constructed the road and rebuilt his lovely two story home on his own property some 20 meters away. There does exist a system of recourse in the Israeli democratic system for both Arab and Jew.

It's not a perfect legal system; there are lots of foibles. But at least we have been trying to provide our Arab citizens with legal and court services, and have done so. We are trying.

I would like to share with you, now, how I see my country in light of the teachings of the Scriptures. I will share with you what I believe the scriptures teach about sovereignty and the Land of Israel, including the city of Jerusalem. Here is what I see.

In Genesis 17:7-8 God promises to be Abraham's God, to establish his covenant with him forever, and give to him and his descendants the Land of Israel, also forever. Three times in the book of Genesis, there is a definition given as to who the descendants of Abraham are–Genesis 17:19, 21:12b and 28:3-4 make it clear that Isaac was chosen to inherit this covenant, in contradistinction to Ishmael. Now, this doesn't mean that non-Jews are inferior to the Jewish people in any way, shape or form. It does mean that the Jewish people inherit the Abrahamic covenant, which includes the Land of Israel, forever.

I have heard it said that because '. . . the Newer Testament writings are silent about the Land of Israel that we should doubt if the same statements and prophecies made by God's inspiration in the OT are relevant for us today.' Let me say this: God inspired the all of the Bible; men did not instigate this. Genesis 17:7-9, 21:12 and 28:3-4 are God's instructions to us forever.

We are instructed in the Scriptures that God has never changed–Malachi 3:6 teaches us: 'I, the Lord, have not changed. Therefore you, Jacob's sons, are not annihilated.' My understanding is that this text refers to God's character as shown in his promises to Israel. If this verse is true, and

God doesn't change, neither will his promises to Israel ever change. In fact, we are told that God's calling to and election of the Jewish people cannot be cancelled. Romans 11:29 teaches us: 'With respect to being chosen, they [the Jewish people] are loved for the Patriarch's sakes, for God's free gifts and His calling are irrevocable.'

One of God's free gifts to the Jewish people was inheriting the Land of Israel. This is called by Paul an irrevocable gift. Leviticus 26:44-46 teaches us that the Land was granted by God to Jacob's descendants unconditionally, and this grant would endure periods of covenantal failure and consequent exile.

> . . . when they are in the land of their enemies [exile], I will not reject them, nor will I abhor them as to destroy them, thereby breaking my covenant with them. For I am the Lord their God. But I will remember for them the covenant with their ancestors, whom I brought out of the land of Egypt in the sight of the nations . . . I am the Lord.

Therefore, any covenantal failure by Israel did not revoke God's covenant promises. Part of the national calling of the Jewish people is to inhabit the Land of Israel, as part of God's plans for worldwide redemption.

In addition, the Hebrew language gives us the time frame of the promises of the Land of Israel to the Jewish people. As part of my Ph.D. thesis, I did a study of the Hebrew word *'olam* which is used in the Bible to connote the concept of "forever." This word is found in our aforementioned text of Genesis 17:7-8, when God promised the Land to the Jewish people. I traced over 80 uses of this word in the Bible, and concluded that it expresses the time element of "as long as the present heaven and earth exists." The prophet Amos adds to this understanding by writing,

> I will bring back my exiled people Israel; they will rebuild the ruined cities and live in them. They will plant vineyards and drink their wine; they will make gardens and eat their fruit. I will plant Israel in their own land, *never again* to be uprooted from *the Land I have given them*, says the Lord your God. (9:14-15)

If Jewish people have been brought back by God to our homeland, then God's words that we should never again be uprooted from our Land should be most seriously considered. Politically dividing up Israel and our capital city would be to do what God says should not happen.

In addition, do Newer Testament writings in truth have nothing to say about the promises given by God to Abraham, Isaac, Jacob, Moses and all of Israel, which include the Land promises of Israel? *Yeshua Himself* commented on these promises. He stated:

> Do not think that I have come to abolish the Law of Moses and the Prophets. I have not come to do away with them, but to establish them. Remember that as long as heaven and earth last, not the least point nor the smallest detail of the Torah will be done away with—not until the end of all things (Mt. 5:17-18).

This is a clear and straightforward teaching. Yeshua has stated that Moses and the Prophets' writings are *not* to be abolished. He did not come to take away, cancel, revoke, misinterpret or wrongly teach any of the Holy Writ. Since the Land promises which give Israel to the Jewish people are found in the first five books of Moses, and in the Prophets, it is clear that until heaven and earth pass away, these promises are still intact.

Paul, Pharisaic scholar par excellence, wrote about *all* the promises of God. He taught: 'For however many promises God has made, they all find their "yes" in connection with Him [Yeshua]' (2 Cor. 1:20).

Do the Land of Israel promises given to Abraham, Isaac and Jacob, Moses and all Israel somehow not qualify as "the promises of God"? To believe not is to deny the veracity of this statement made by Paul. I need not remind us that when Paul made this statement, the Scriptures he was referring to consisted of the books Genesis to Malachi, with a *possible* dispute about two of the books found in the Writings. These thirty-nine books are where the promises of God that Paul mentions were found. In applying the principle that Paul is teaching for our discussion, we see that, in Yeshua, the promises of God to give the Land of Israel to Jacob's descendants are not nullified, but affirmed! This is because the Land is a tool of God, in his wisdom, to work for world redemption. It is where Zechariah 12:10 and 14:4 will occur, with the Jewish people being a major player in these scenarios.

Any theology that twists things in a contrary manner has to contradict Yeshua's very words in Matthew 5, as well as the entire message of the 1st thirty-nine books of the Bible concerning the Jewish people and the Land of Israel. I've never heard a contradictory theology of the Land that didn't fly in the face of the first thirty-nine books of the Bible. If you believe that the first thirty-nine books have been cancelled, you would still have to work out the great contradictions between what Yeshua and Paul taught in order to establish an anti-Israel replacement theology.

Granted, the Newer Testament writings do not devote much space to addressing the Land of Israel. But this is because all of the issues concerning the Land had *already* been addressed in the Bible. It wasn't an issue. The main reason for writing the Gospels was to tell the story of who Yeshua was. The main reason for writing the epistles was to teach and encourage young leaders and congregations on how to live their lives, as well as to explain *halakha* for certain situations that touched them. *The Land of Israel simply wasn't an issue.* If it was, then Yeshua **was** truly silent.

Yet, if it is so wrong for Israel to be in Israel, why did not Yeshua clearly say so? If it is so wrong, why didn't Peter, Paul and James tell us? I'll tell you why they didn't tell this to us—they all accepted and believed what the Scriptures taught about Israel being the Jewish homeland forever. Remember, there were no Newer Testament writings at that time. The only Bible around then taught that they had a homeland, and this homeland is where they historically lived and made their lives.

Who ultimately controls Israel? *God*, my friends. The God who sovereignly willed this Land to the descendants of Jacob. No matter how much the political situation in Israel today is not ideal, we need to take what the scriptures say about the issue of the Land of Israel seriously. It is foremost God's Land. We are taught: "It is a land which the Lord your God cares for; the eyes of the Lord your God are always upon it, from the beginning of the year to the end of the year" (Deut. 11:12).

And He has seen fit to give the Land to the descendants of Abraham, Isaac and Jacob–the Jewish people. He has a purpose in doing so: to redeem the world, and the future coming of the Messiah is the apex of *his* plan. His plans for my people are not finished yet. The prophet Zechariah, in chapter 12, verse 10 speaks of a day in which the Jewish people–*in the Land of Israel*–will see the one whom was pierced, and call on his name and believe in him, then function as ambassadors for the Messiah to the rest of the world.

You are all scholars of the texts of the Bible, and I'm sure the great majority of you are much better scholars than I am–so, I will leave off lecturing you about what the Scriptures say. Suffice it to say that I believe that the text has willed the Land to the Jewish people of today. Now, I would not hide behind my theology and say that because of the Scriptures that we in Israel can ignore the pain and desires of the Palestinian population. That would be wrong, and please know that you are *not* hearing that from me tonight.

Yet, let me also appeal to this point of history: no other people on earth has suffered as much as my people have. When I teach Jewish history, my students are shocked to see the carnage we have been through–at least 7 million Jews have been murdered and killed in the past 120 years alone. If the Church is concerned about civil rights and international justice, it would be profitable to help to rectify the conditions which have allowed so many of my people to be butchered. There have been laudable efforts to do so in many places around the world, and I am thankful for courageous men and women in the Church who have devoted their lives to this end.

They have brought out the truth that the Church is indebted to the Jewish people for sharing the Gospel in history with the nations of the world. A brave, bold decision was made in Acts 15 by Messianic Jewish leaders from Israel who opened the doors to the world to know the one true God. Each of you is a benefactor of the labor of those men and their brave decisions.

Let me address another sensitive issue–one that angers me because the world is being given one side to this story. It is a sad story, but it is two-sided, not one sided. A claim I am hearing tonight is how cruel Israel has systematically behaved toward our Arab neighbors during our continual history of conflict. Friends, to quote an ex-WWII veteran who fought against the Nazis, my father, "*You won't have civilized behavior in a war situation.*" Friends, I can tell you from my personal observation that riots almost always turn violent, and people get injured and killed. This will always be the case anywhere in the world, and that is a risk you take when you riot.

For example, the October riots of this year in Israel took on a life of their own–there is no reason why a visit to anyone's holy site by an Israeli Member of Knesset should be motivation to violently riot. I didn't care for the fact that Yassir Arafat paid a visit to Tel Aviv in September, but no one in Israel was going to disturb the civil peace due to that. No one in Israel called upon our people to riot and harm Arab communities to protest the presence of Yassir Arafat on Israeli soil. Mr. Sharon's visit, in my view, did not cause the rioting. The Chicago Sun-Times correctly noted that:

> Mr. Sharon's visit was a non-violent act. Sharon threw no stones, ignited no Molotov cocktails, fired no shots. Those came from the Palestinians. The responsibility for the killings and injuries in this terrible violence falls on Yasser Arafat. In visiting the Temple Mount, Sharon was making a statement about the importance of the holy site to Jews. Political statements inspire passions, but that is no reason to avoid [such statements].

In fact, Mr. Sharon's visit was approved by Jibril Rajoub, the head of the PA's Preventive Security service. The visit went without incident, and it was the next day when Jewish worshippers at the Western Wall were attacked from above by rock throwing, with the shouts of 'eradicate the Jews from Palestine' coming from one of the nearby mosques. Local Palestinian schools were closed, students were bussed to the Temple Mt. to participate in wider rioting while the PA's Tanzim militia were handing out Molotov cocktails. This evidence does not point at Mr. Sharon being responsible for the rioting. It is a lie and totally irresponsible to blame a non-violent visit to a holy site for what happened afterwards.

The PA has tried this type of logic on you for justifying civil unrest before now. In 1995, Mr. Arafat reported that Israel was tunneling through the underneath of the Dome of the Rock, and used this as justification for encouraging violence. Israel did not tunnel underneath the mosque–the tunneling was the opening of a historic site parallel to the mosque's foundations, and in no way threatened its structural integrity. Mr. Arafat lied to you to justify violence.

I fear that Mr. Arafat has a current plan by which Arab civil disorder in Israel and on our borders served his ends. In fact, the Palestinian Broadcasting Authority, which is controlled by Mr. Arafat, gave instructions during the October rioting to go and kill Jews because this is the only way to make sure that the El-Aksa Mosque, Jerusalem, Jaffa, Haifa and all of Palestine can be Arab again. He has been promising his people a declaration of statehood by last Sept. 13th, and it did not happen. He then promised statehood by the end of 2000. However, negotiations with PM Barak did not get him closer to that end by that date. So he has been quickly trying to get the international community involved to pressure statehood to happen. Large scale violent rioting–involving the IDF–replete with deaths, plays into his need for international sympathy. Mr. Arafat and the PA could have quelled the rioting at the outset if they had so chosen.

The PA played their violence option–*which they have consistently declared that they will play*, if negotiations did not go their way. Mr. Arafat felt violence would help Mr. Barak concede more, as well as make Israel look bad in the eyes of the international community. Now, I hate it when young Palestinians get killed in a riot. But that is what happens: riots will have tragic deaths. Innocent people will die again. You can't riot violently and not expect casualties. No such animal exists. What should that tell you? Once a riot starts, there is no respect for human life left; there is no peace possible. There is no talking to your neighbor; there is no chance for a peaceful solution to a problem. There is only a hysterical, mob-led mass attempt to injure, burn and kill whomever you can, such as was criminally done to the two Israeli soldiers who turned into

Ramallah and were butchered in a display of animal-like, mass hysteria. Every government in the world, including Israel's, will use whatever force necessary to restore social order in such circumstances.

Regarding this October's rioting, there simply has to be responsibility to behave like human beings–like real peace partners–on the side of Palestinians. Coordinated rioting at the drop of a pin is not a sign of social responsibility. An Israeli soldiers' reaction in such a situation is to preserve one's own life at all costs, and it is **not** a wrong reaction. I know; I have been in that situation. As well, contrary to some media portrayals, I can tell you from first-hand experience that such riotous crowds do not just have rocks as their weapons.

In addition, let's address the PA's encouragement of child martyrdom for a minute. The game of youths violently rioting in front of Israeli soldiers with children as their human shields, with TV cameras present, while Palestinian gunmen fire from another direction, is an excuseless scenario which happened in the October riots. The PA has been offering families $2000 for a martyr and $300 for an injury. At least forty Palestinian children have been killed, to date, as they provided cover for armed Palestinian militias who fired upon Israeli soldiers. It is time to stop using Palestinian children as human shields, and as propaganda tools against Israel.

Sweden's Queen Silvia raised her voice against this practice at the recent World Childhood Foundation meeting. She said, 'I am very worried about this. I'd like to tell them [the PA] to quit. This is very dangerous. The children should not take part. The Palestinian leaders are exploiting [the children] and risking their lives in a political fight.' Blame for this abusive practice must be put solely on the PA. They, and the parents of the children, have the power to stop this. It is time for the West to realize what this practice is: an orchestrated and deliberate attempt to have children killed and injured as a political weapon to use against Israel, with no value shown for any life–Arab or Israeli, child or adult.

When will the Palestinian people stand up to the PA's encouragement of child martyrdom, and say "no more?" No one denies that this is typical PA practice. Why does the Church condone this, and not raise its voice against the PA for this practice? As a parent and as a human being, no matter what my ethnic background is, I deplore and denounce this practice.

As a parent in Israel, I find it very hard to know how to teach my children about the Arab populous around us. I taught my children that we cannot hate Arabs, that God loves them and wants them to know his reality. Yet, children are perceptive; once my little son asked me why Arab nations pick on us. It is then that a Jewish father tells a story that has been told for many generations. It goes like this:

> We're hated. Hated because we exist. It's been that way for over 2,000 years. Witness Haman the Persian, the Seleucids, the Romans, the early Muslims, the Crusaders, the Spanish, Eastern Europeans, the Nazis and now again in the Middle East. It will continue to be the case until our Messiah comes. We are hated, not accepted, and if tolerated, rarely as equals. In Europe, in Asia, in Muslim lands, it has always been the same story. In the Middle East today, it is again our situation.

What is going to happen if Mr. Arafat thinks it is to his advantage to step things up even a little more? With 22,000 troops, 7,000 assault rifles, 150 machine guns, 44 armored personnel carriers, five helicopters and thirteen naval vessels amassed in Gaza, next time around could be an armored war [by the way, according to the Oslo Accords, half of these quantities are illegal]. No matter what problems we have, there is a supposed peace process intact, and it is up to the Palestinian *leadership and people* to behave in a responsible manner. As columnist George Will noted in his October 18th daily column, 'The PA has comprehensively violated the Oslo agreements, including the undertaking to stop anti-Semitic propaganda.' PBC television is now openly showing hooded, Koran-carrying Palestinians marching with bombs strapped to their bodies, and hailing them for their 'determination to give their lives to liberate our sacred Islamic shrines from infidel control.' The PA media is actively urging people to attack Israeli soldiers and civilians, celebrating those who die as martyrs.

In response, the American government is beginning to take some positive steps. On October 25th, Congress overwhelmingly passed a resolution condemning Palestinians for the violence. It noted, *'our solidarity with the state of Israel at this time of crisis* and condemned PA leaders for encouraging violence and 'doing so little for so long to stop it.' On October 15th, ninety-six U.S. Senators sent a strongly worded letter to President Clinton, expressing their 'solidarity with the nation of Israel, and our deep disappointment with Yassir Arafat.' It is my opinion that it is high time for the PA and the Palestinian populous to treat Israelis and the peace process with respect. Without such a change, there will be no peace.

I am not a lover of war–in fact, I marched a number of times while a student against the war in Vietnam. Nor would I ever freely choose to spend my time abusing Palestinians or withholding their civil liberties. But don't be naïve and believe that Israelis are fully responsible for perpetrating violence. Often individual Israelis, and our security forces, have been forced to defend our lives and our very existence against what I would term Palestinian brutality. Let me give you some examples–*I want you to be aware that they happen:*

While driving home one evening in 1994 as a civilian–not a soldier–I was forced to defend my life against six or so Palestinian attackers who without any provocation stopped my car, and verbally threatened my life and my family's life. They surrounded my car, and were readying to turn it over with my family inside it. My civil rights–including the right to life–were being abused. Had I not been ready to defend myself physically, I may not be here tonight. The truth that is often overlooked is that violence begets violence. That's the cycle involved. Israel and the Jewish people did not start the historical cycle of violence, nor are we to blame for it. We all have our parts in it. The irresponsible Palestinian leadership has a *major* role in it, the general Palestinian population has a role in it, and so do my people. It's a tapestry, not a 'blame Israel' situation. To blame Israel for all Palestinian suffering, for the violence in the Middle East, or for starting the problems that have plagued the Palestinian people, is to carry out the classic anti-Semitic scapegoating syndrome.

In another incident, my wife had a Molotov cocktail hurled at her, meant to take her life, as she was driving home from a doctor visit. This is abuse perpetrated on an innocent Israeli woman by a terrorist. Another evening, while driving home from teaching at King of Kings College, a brick was hurled at my windshield. It was meant to take my life. What crime had I committed? This is also abuse perpetrated on an innocent Israeli–*unless my presence in my country is to be considered a provocation deserving of death*. On another day, I was abused by Palestinian terrorists who purposely spilled oil out of the back of their truck on a rainy day. My car spun into a nearby mountainside, destroying my car; with God's protection, I only suffered bruises. But the car behind me went the other way and slipped over a cliff, and the driver was killed. This is abuse, perpetrated on innocent Israelis. So, you can see there are two sides to a story to which you are most often are presented only one side. *Palestinians also perpetrate abuse upon innocent Israelis*. My only "crime" when all of these events occurred was that I was physically in Israel.

For seven years I lived less than 1000 yards from the holy site of Joshua bin Nun's tomb. I would have liked to visit the site; it would have been meaningful. I would not have dared to do so, however. There would have been no guarantee that I would have left that site alive. A neighbor of mine, Fred Rosenfeld, of blessed memory, went to that area once for a picnic and *didn't* return. He was brutally murdered by two youths from the surrounding village. What crime had he committed? Brutality exists on the Palestinian side, my friends. Whatever the justification, brutality against Israelis remains brutality.

I want to now address how I, and many in the Messianic community, look at Israel's military presence. It is true that

Israel has a formidable military. But I do not say this as a proud fact. I am inherently sad that this has to be the situation. Violence is not a part of the Jewish ethos. If you read Jewish theological, philosophical and literary works, you will see that my people do not extol violence, nor do we enjoy taking part in it. Because of political circumstances, we have been forced to have a citizen army. No one in Israel enjoys the fact that their sons and daughters risk their lives for up to three years as young adults. No one likes to leave their family and livelihood for months each year to serve in the reserves. No one that I've met in Israel enjoys quelling riots, shooting at someone, or injuring another life. No one enjoys watching an army friend get killed. No one enjoys learning that a youngster they know has been killed while in army service. In my case, two students that I taught in the public school system were killed on our borders.

Life is sacred in Jewish thought, whether it is a Jewish life, a Palestinian life, or an American life. It is an unfortunate fact of history that we have had to learn to defend ourselves with deadly efficiency in order to survive. Israel's military can be criticized–there are occasional excesses that are committed by our soldiers, *just like there are in every other army in the world that is in a conflict situation.* There will always be such incidences *every* place in the world where there is a military conflict, period.

On the whole, I was proud of what I saw and experienced in Israel's military regarding our behavior toward others. The average Israeli soldier behaved–at least during the 1980s and 1990s when I was in the army–with restraint, in spite of what some of the international press may have wanted to portray. The international media's portrayal of Israel is a whole other story. It is worth reading a short article entitled, "Gentlemanly Anti-Semitism" by Dr. Franklin Littell, a past winner of the Religious Freedom Award. It gives a short synopsis of the slant of the international media regarding Israel. But let me give you three recent examples of such slanted media reporting:

On November 7th, an Israeli school bus, carrying children on their way to school, was attacked by Palestinian machine-gun fire. Somehow, no children were hit, but the bus was shot up. Is it acceptable to energetically report the unfortunate shooting of a 12-year old boy in Gaza, who was not a premeditated target, and not report this incident, in which we see a premeditated target of children? In fact, by November 8th, I had seen no coverage of this incident outside of our Israeli media. Why not? Is this not deplorable? In late October, the international media released an item insinuating that a Palestinian child was killed from tear gas inhalation during the course of a demonstration that the IDF dispersed. IDF examination of events showed that the child was brought early in the morning to a hospital in Hebron. Yet, the demonstrations took place later that same afternoon. This reported item was false. Since the start of the rioting, cynical use has been made of the death and wounding of Palestinian children that took place due to road accidents and other causes unrelated to rioting, showing them as if they were the result of IDF action.

In early October, an American Jewish student, Tuvia Grossman, was photographed by the Associated Press, and pictured in the N.Y. Times. He was portrayed in the paper as a Palestinian youth who had been beaten silly by Israeli forces. In fact, he was brutally beaten without provocation by Palestinian rioters, and the photographed Israeli policeman standing by him was coming to his aid, not beating him! Open letters to the Times by his family cleared up the matter, and showed us what the international media will do to portray Israel in a negative light. I once had an American Midwestern newspaper reporter tell me that he could care less about checking out the background of his Israel reports, since he had newspapers to sell, and that alone was his concern. There is a media war going on to portray Israel as at fault in our conflict with the Palestinians, and it is too often of no concern if inaccuracies abound.

I saw with my own eyes examples of Israeli soldiers helping Palestinians during the difficult times of the intifada. I particularly remember a Palestinian youth in 1990 in the village of Huwara getting run over by a neighbor's car. My army unit quickly called an Israeli army ambulance, and attended to the youngster while he laid in the street, keeping him comfortable, calming the parents, and directing traffic around him. My army unit helped save the life of a Palestinian boy. Given our circumstances, I was impressed to see 18-year-old soldiers most often act with restraint when in conflict situations when I was in the IDF.

To understand how I view the present, let me go into the past for a brief moment. Let me tell you a little bit about my people. The state of Israel was not created out of Jewish imperialist desires, as our enemies have often charged. It was not created for the end of oppressing anyone. Anyone here who has read the beginning chapters to Dr. Theodore Herzl's "Der Judenstaat" knows that the modern state was created in order to save my Jewish people from constant historical attempts at our physical annihilation. Unfortunately, the events of WWII proved that Herzl's basic assessments and assertions were true. Other early Zionist writers whose works can be read, such as Moses Hess, Leon Pinsker, Yehudah Alkalai and Zvi Hirsch, agree with Dr. Herzl's motivations–to save our people. There is a great appeal in their collective works to the humanitarian end of giving the Jewish people a chance to survive through returning to the Land of Israel. The early Zionist organizations, as the Hibbat Zion, Hovevei Zion and Bilu, envisioned settling in Israel in order to escape the anti-Semitism that plagued them, and to build a society based on their young and democratic ideals. Later American Zionist spokesmen of the 20th century–among them Supreme Court Justices Felix Frankfurter and Louis Brandeis–were motivated to support the establishment of a Jewish state due to humanitarian reasons. Each of them felt a kinship to the democratic ideals envisioned and articulated by the Zionist movement.

Not all the ideals of the early Zionist movements were realized. The hoped for peace with Arab neighbors, as articulated by Zionist thinkers Ehad Ha-Am, Martin Buber, and Israel's first President, Chaim Weizmann, did not happen. In the mid-1940s, the Holocaust forced my people to press hard to make our state a reality. It influenced the ability of our state's founding fathers to be politically 'long sighted'; but don't blame the victims for that fact. Let us remember that a sterling solution to today's problems could have been the 1947

UN Partition Plan. This plan was rejected *by the Arab world, not by the Jewish community in Israel.* My point is that, in hindsight, it is easy to see that the buildup to today's problems *could have been eased* if the Arab world could have only tolerated our existence. But it is a fact of history that the problems were exacerbated. Yet again, Israel cannot be blamed as the culprit at fault for this situation.

My friends, Israel was born out of desperation, with a time clock ticking in our ears, with the butchery and murder of a *real* genocide being perpetrated upon my parents' and grandparents' generations, and the consequences of their actions were literally life or death. My entire people were traumatized during these years, and that trauma still influences many lives in Israel today. Yet, I am continually amazed that my country has as many humanitarian hearts as we do, after all we have been through.

I am proud of the fact that Israel was the *first country in the world* to give refuge to Bosnian Muslim refugees in the recent Balkans conflict, doing so when no other Middle Eastern country made such a move. In 1994, the IDF sent a medical unit to care for refugees in the Rwandan civil war. Israel sent IDF medical and rescue-team aid to save American government personnel in the 1997 Kenyan embassy bombing, directly saving the lives of three buried victims. Presidents Clinton and Arap-moi both acknowledged this Israeli humanitarian contribution.

This year, Israel sent rescue teams to help Turkish victims of the destructive earthquakes there. In 1997 the IDF helped Turkey extinguish massive fires by sending military firefighting equipment there. Last year, the IDF sent a 70-man medical unit to Macedonia to care for Kosovan refugees. Today, Israeli physicians are active *in* the countries of Black Africa in combating the AIDs virus, helping in both research and treatment of victims. This is in contrast to the lie that PA spokesman Nabil Ramlawi told the United Nations Commission on Human Rights in 1997 when he stated that Israeli physicians had injected 300 Palestinian children with the AIDs virus during the 1980s.

For a people coming out of the trauma of the Holocaust and the trauma of constant military conflicts with a continual loss of life for fifty-two years, the aforementioned record of international aid impresses me. In an amazing act of continuing goodwill toward Muslims, my country allows Muslim pilgrims on the Hajj to Mecca to pass through Israel. In January 2001, Israelis took it upon themselves to form an organization called "to Give," and sent 22,000 tons of food and clothing to El Salvador to help the victims of that recent earthquake. On January 16, 2001, Israel's Foreign Minister announced the formation of an Israeli task force that will work on curing AIDS and malaria in Black African nations. While the intifada of the fall was in its full heat, Israel continued to give humanitarian aid in the form of medical supplies and food to the PA! I could go on. . . .

Friends, Israel is not a land of oppressive, heartless people. We are indeed a *traumatized* people–a people for whom recent world history has had a cruel reality. Twenty thousand five hundred forty-six Israeli citizens have been killed and murdered in our short history, and 79,000 Israelis are disabled as a result of military or terrorist conflicts, and are on the government's welfare roll. Two thousand one hundred seventy Israelis have been orphaned by war and terror; 3,285 widows have been created by the same. One percent of our population was killed in our War of Independence. That would correspond in percentages to roughly two and a half million Americans being killed in a conflict today. Coming on the heels of a six million person Holocaust, you can understand why I say that we are a *traumatized* people. We have been caught for the past 2,000 years in a political and historical situation that we could not determine for ourselves.

Our country represents our only chance to have a voice in our present and future. The heroic efforts of men like Menahem Begin and Yitzhak Rabin to forge peace–this represents the heart and soul of my people. During the current rioting crisis, the Israeli media did not call upon our populous to harm the Arab communities in our midst, in spite of daily PBC broadcasts that incited the Palestinian population. Provocation is not my people's heart.

The modern Israeli nation has been born–just as is foretold in the Scriptures– and deserves the support of the Church both for Biblical and humanitarian reasons. The Church can today help the Jewish people by raising your voice to give Israel a chance to live within secure borders–borders that are not defined by the PA nor any other government. I also think it is time for the Church to urge the U.S. government to recognize Jerusalem as the capital city of Israel by moving its embassy there. The National Christian Leadership Conference for Israel has pioneered this position in their May 1999 statement.

We are not a perfect nation. We can and must improve our relations with our Arab citizens and neighbors. But Israel *is* a place where the Jewish people have found a national refuge, and continue to do so. Some of the most moving moments in my life were when I listened to my Ethiopian Jewish students tell their stories of how they marched hundreds of miles on foot, fighting starvation, to get to a plane to find freedom and new life in Israel. Or when I listened to my elderly students tell their stories of how grateful they are for a homeland after enduring the hell of the European Holocaust. Israel has been God's answer to Jewish refugees from all around the world; 630,000 Jewish refugees came to Israel after being expelled *from Arab nations* around 1948, most arriving penniless. That is not a refugee story that is often told, but it is fact!

My greatest concern, expressed clearly here this evening, is that *Yassir Arafat is not a trustworthy head of state*. I know of no Messianic Jew in Israel who would disagree with such a sentiment. My historical observation is that a terrorist cannot be reformed to be *a responsible* head of state.

What will it take, in my eyes, to make peace? Israel had done a lot, risked a lot, up to October 2000. We had offered 90% of Judea and Samaria toward a Palestinian homeland. PM Barak, *much to my chagrin*, had offered the Jordan Valley and half of Jerusalem as well. We had armed the PA's forces with *our own weapons* to help make them effective in what we had hoped would be their Oslo-Accord defined roles. Israelis paid taxes which were sent to the Palestinians to help finance their state-to-be. By these actions, my country and my people extended our hand to make peace. In fact, again to my chagrin, plans were being made to give much of the Golan Heights to

Syria, as well. But how much can you give, when what you receive in return is gross irresponsible behavior? How much more Palestinian violence will we be subjected to? How many more statements to the press by Mr. Arafat will threaten my country and my people? How much longer will Syria support, finance and house Hezbollah, yet expect us to give up the Golan Heights? How much more of this despicable behavior will my people suffer before we say, "no more peace process"?

The recent behavior of the PA, in my eyes, is what has put the peace process into rampant disarray. There *may* be no hope left. To answer my own question, it will take the PA totally reversing their previous behavior and way of dealing with my country to make peace. Given Mr. Arafat's track record, I don't think the chances of that are good.

With the new administration of President Bush, I do not expect to see any quick improvements in the situation. Instead of being actively involved in brokering a peace effort, Mr. Bush is considered by political analysts to be more inclined to be involved only if absolutely needed. I think that any progress that we would see toward a supposed final peace accord will only be hurried from the side of PM Barak, as he would like to leave a final peace accord as his legacy. To fail to do this would mark the end of his political career. But all sides involved are in a waiting game now. How will the new American president react to the situation? What will the situation be like in Israel in a week's time? Will we have a new PM? Personally, I think there is no doubt that MK Ariel Sharon will defeat PM Barak in the soon upcoming elections. He leads greatly in the Israeli public opinion polls. The simple reason for that lead is that we have had enough of empty promises to stop the violence and bleeding. Israelis want it to stop without compromising the security of our people. We worry greatly about the security in and around Jerusalem, particularly if PM Barak wins the election, as he has reneged on an earlier campaign promise of not dividing the city. PM Barak understands this well, and in the current election campaign has apologized to the Israeli people for making mistakes in the peace process that led to the 44 Israeli murder casualties since September 2000. He has been pushing hard to reach a peace accord before the elections.

If Ariel Sharon becomes our PM, what scenarios does that leave us with? I cannot accurately say; however, I do feel that Mr. Sharon *will not* act the part of the warmonger that the international media has cast him in. His first concern will be to unify a government, and then his own people. His next concern will be defining his security objectives, and communicating that to his people and to the Arab nations. I can only imagine the types of extreme international pressures that he will face while he is attempting to put together a government and unify his own people. These international pressures will try to make Mr. Sharon continue on the exact same path of yielding strategic land that Mr. Barak has put our country on. These lands would include the eastern sectors of Jerusalem, the Golan Heights and all of Judea and Samaria.

So, in my analysis of the current politics, in a sense we are starting over, since two heads of state of the major players will be changing. Before I leave off, I want to address my two Palestinian colleagues who spoke before me, ironically, for a brief moment. Nothing would make me happier than to live in a peaceful environment with Palestinians and Jordanians. I want us to find peace.

To my two colleagues, I know your people and you, personally, have suffered in recent history. And you know that my people suffered greatly during the entire 20th century, and oftentimes before then. I hope you have heard some of my people's pain tonight. My hope is our peoples can learn to relate to each other without riots or international pressure, learn to talk to each other–people to people. Hear each other's pain and develop compassion for each other. I would love to see this happen. Maybe it can happen for our children, if our generation can avoid warring.

But I am afraid, doctors, that the PA leadership does not share that desire for a true peace. Given developments since October, I fear that my people will not want to take further risks. The level of trust and commitment between our peoples has dovetailed drastically in the past two months. And I honestly don't know where that leaves us; *but know that I will continue to hope and pray for a political settlement between our peoples that . . . does not threaten my people's security and existence.*

I remember some years ago when my young son, with his yarmulke on his head, wandered off at DeGaulle Airport in Paris, and sat down next to an Arab boy. My son took his toys out of his pockets, and not knowing English, he said to the other boy, 'let's play' in Hebrew. With three parents nervously watching them, play they did. I hope somehow that our grandchildren will be able to do that with each other. May God help us reach that day.

Thank you."

Appendix B

ACA's Letter to the General Public

The Aramaic Christian Association in Israel recently sponsored a general letter written to the public:

A growing number of Israeli Christians have been speaking out with a new voice and calling for integration into Israeli Jewish society. At the same time, many of us are asking for a halt to the cynical use of local Christians as pawns in the Palestinian cause or other Arab efforts to destroy Israel as a democratic Jewish state.

Like the majority of Israeli Christians, I feel that many Church leaders are betraying the Christian message and ignoring the rights of fellow Christians in the Holy Land in service to Islamic propaganda against our country, Israel.

To see Christian leaders participating in anti-Israel political conferences like "Christ at the Checkpoint" makes me feel like vomiting. I am ashamed of the duplicity of these leaders. In Israel, these Christians enjoy full rights and freedoms, even the freedom to publicly slander the state without fear. By contrast, they and their families would quickly be killed for so publicly criticizing the Palestinian Authority.

Our situation in Israel is better than any other Christian community in the entire Middle East. As we have witnessed of late, many Christians across the region have been migrating or converting to Islam by force.

What worries us as Israeli Christians is seeing fellow Christian continue in their fearful approach to the Arabs by joining with those who routinely abuse and kill our own people in order to falsely accuse Israel, the only country in the region where Christians are actually protected.

Israel will continue to be the everlasting home and safe haven of the Jews, and also of its Christian, Druze and even Arab minorities. The world needs to know these facts and to understand that the people who would cynically put Christ at the checkpoint do not represent the real Christian voice in this region, or anywhere else in the world.

We all long for peace in the Holy Land, but not a peace based on lies that can only lead to trouble for local Christians. [41]

Appendix C

"That Nasty Fence"

(Note: This segment was written in 2005, but its points remain valid today, and thus it is included in this treatise. It is my purpose to outline why this Security Fence has been an unfortunate but vital necessity. Additionally, it will be explained why the rejectionist epithet "apartheid fence" is not accurate to the purpose or use of this set of security barriers.)

Something there is that doesn't love a wall, that sends the frozen-ground-swell under it. . . . He only says, 'Good fences make good neighbors'.

. . . 'Why do they make good neighbors?

Before I built a wall I'd ask to know what I was walling in or walling out, and to whom I was like to give offence. Something there is that doesn't love a wall, that wants it down.

–Robert Frost, from his poem "The Mending Wall." [1]

American poet Robert Frost wrote the above lines, and I must admit that I feel some sympathy for his sentiments. The poem expresses, somewhat playfully, his ambivalence for the yearly ritual of repairing the wall that separated Frost's property from that of his neighbor, Napoleon Guay. Frost could not comprehend why his neighbor (or perhaps the neighbor's father) ever erected such a barrier. The poet could only repeat an extant proverb told to him by Mr. Guay, that "good fences make good neighbors." Frost, in fact, expresses some bewilderment by the content of that proverb. He seems to struggle to find a meaning to justify the existence of this wall that separates good neighbors.

Most of the world echoes a similar sentiment to a security fence that was recently erected. From afar, it could appear that the fence that separates parts of Israel from Palestinian Authority territory serves no useful purpose. I often hear such feelings expressed in no uncertain terms by members of the media. News clips such as one that I recently viewed from CNN have been broadcast to show the viewing audience that Israel's Security fence is a bad investment. It is presented as a barrier that does nothing but harm. Israel's Security Fence is seen as politically repressive, primitive and simply a measure by which to frustrate Palestinian desires to have a country.

A few years ago, an Israeli woman in her mid-30s was driving home from a doctor's visit in the Tel Aviv area. She was on a stretch of rural road, happy that her pre-diabetic condition had been caught and could be successfully treated. It was about five o'clock in the afternoon. Suddenly, with no warning, a loud boom jolted her car, and thrust it forward. The car went out of control for a second, but she was able to steer the vehicle successfully back into her lane. There were no other cars around her. Out of her rear view mirror, she saw smoke billowing upward, and could see a broken bottle lying smashed on the road behind her. No one was in sight. With her blood pressure rising and her heart beating fast, she quickly made her way for the last 5 minutes back home. When she arrived at her house, she was flushed, and quickly sat on a chair and explained to her husband what had just happened.

Piecing the story together, it was easy to see that she had been the victim of a Molotov cocktail which had been hurled at her from the ditch on the side of the road. This was a murder attempt. There was no fencing or protection for any driver on the Trans-Samaria Highway, and attacks like these were not rare then. That roadside bomb was a lethal weapon meant to take her life, and what occurred was an assault with intent to murder. I explained to my wife the mechanics of a Molotov cocktail, and she and I were both grateful that our little children still had a mother after that incident.

Having mentioned that I do not particularly care for walls and fences myself, I would make an exception for Israel's Security Fence. (In fact, for many years my family shared a back yard with my neighbors, where no lines of demarcation existed. It felt strange at first, but worked out very well, which contributed to my natural dislike for erecting barriers.) The first time I drove from Baden-Wurttemberg to Strasbourg, I rather liked the fact that there was no border check. No one stopped my car to check my passport. It felt good. Perhaps after all of these years of warring against each other, the French and German nations have progressed to the point where they do not need barriers that are always active between them. But unfortunately, the Middle East is not in that situation.

The Israel Defense Forces Spokesman's Unit has stated the reason for the erection of this fence:

> The sole purpose of the Security Fence, as stated in the Israeli government decision of July 23, 2001 is to provide security. The Security Fence is a central component in Israel's response to the horrific wave of terrorism emanating from the West Bank, resulting in suicide bombers who enter into Israel with the sole intention of killing innocent people. [2]

Living in Israel during the failure of the Oslo Accords has been an education. I am overwhelmed by the sense of how little value is placed by the critics of the Security Fence on protecting Jewish lives. Let us surmise that the erection of a Security Fence could save one child's life. Just one. Let us guess that one terrorist could be foiled by not being able to get through the Security Fence at his wanted point, and because of that, was either apprehended or gave up on his or her quest. If the reader were the parent of such a child, the Fence, at whatever cost, at whatever hardship, would be worthwhile. And let us surmise that the putting up of this Security Fence could save the life of one parent, whose children were dependent upon him or her emotionally, developmentally and economically. To such a child, the reality of a security fence gives meaning to the entire world. One may think that I am simply dabbling in the world of theory. So let us look at reality, at the numbers involved, to bring the above scenarios "home" to us.

In 2000, thirty-eight Jewish Israeli citizens were murdered in terror attacks and eighty-four others were injured. For 2001, those figures rose to 202 murdered and 1,386 injured. In 2002, those numbers read 430 and 2,100 respectively; by 2003, there were 209 murdered and 859 wounded. In 2004, 119 Jewish Israelis were murdered with another 402 injury casualties. In January and February 2005, fourteen Israelis were murdered, and sixty-six injured. The total of terrorist murders over that five-year span stands at 1,012 with another 4,902 people injured. Of course, when I speak of injuries, the great majority of them are not mere bruises. Injury casualties from a terror attack often include torn flesh, serious burns, permanent hearing disabilities, embedded glass, and long-lasting psychological trauma. [3]

I can only think that if such casualties were experienced by, let us say, the American state of Washington, that the erection of a Security Fence would be considered of prime importance. I pick Washington, as its estimated population of six million residents is close to Israel's estimated population of 6.2 million inhabitants (at the time the security fence was erected). If Washington experienced a terrorist wave that murdered over 1,000 of its citizens, and rendered another 4,000 injured, I am certain that drastic measures would be taken to prevent this from continuing. The building and maintenance of a Security Fence would be considered a rather mild way of dealing with terrorism there. [4]

Certainly the American government would not apologize to its citizens for instituting measures that are designed to save human life. If people had to endure terrorist attacks in the state's capital city of Olympia, as well as its major population and cultural center of Seattle, life would be a totally different existence than what currently exists. If the public transportation system of these cities, and autos passing by on the highways, were major targets for this terrorism, I am sure that the citizenry would pressure the government to protect them. Indeed, given Israel's current terrorist crime wave numbers, Washington State would have experienced a casualty rate of one-tenth of one percent of its population. While this might not sound like heavy numbers, it would change the way life is lived all over that state. It would be a major issue, and no other state governments would have the gall to dictate to the state of Washington how this problem should be handled.

It is interesting that Tunisia recently has approved the building of a 160 kilometer long separation barrier on its border with Libya in order to discourage the entry of terrorists into their nation. The international press as well as supposed humanitarian spokespersons has not commented upon these plans. It is once again of interest that if Israel is not involved, the voices of humanitarianism are silent. The Irish Independent noted:

> The country (Tunisia) has announced plans to build a wall along its border with Libya to counter the threat from jihadist militants. It would stretch 160 kilometers inland from the coast and be completed by the end of 2015. . . . The Tunisian army would build the wall which would have surveillance centers at certain points along it. [5]

At least one other nation in the region agrees with Israel–that erecting barriers is worth the effort if it can save lives and thwart terrorism.

An inaccurate stereotype about Israel's Security Fence is that in all places it is a tall, concrete, electrified, army-manned, solid barrier with no entrances and exits for Palestinians, and that the entire fence was built over "Palestinian farmland." Let us look at those stereotypes. Some ***95%*** of the total Security Fence is made up of wire fencing. The other ***5%*** is made up of concrete barriers. The concrete barriers have been put up at particular stretches where attacks upon Israeli traffic occurred in the past, and in particular to inhibit Palestinian shooting upon Jewish vehicles on the parallel highway. They are also effective barriers to the throwing of stones upon passing traffic. Incidentally, stones that are thrown at vehicles can and do kill and injure both passengers and drivers. This is not consistent with the situation that is often depicted, where "helpless, innocent, stone throwing youths are picked upon by Israeli security forces." Yet the truth is that rocks kill when they hit vehicles moving at high speeds–which is how highway traffic moves. The truth is that the Security Fence is in only very small measure a concrete wall. As was recently posted by the Foundation for the Defense of Democracies:

> While the barrier (Israel's Security Fence) is monotonously called a wall by Palestinian advocates, almost all of it will be a chain-link fence—much like the one the UN has recently announced its intention to build to protect its Manhattan headquarters. Exceptions are 30-foot-high concrete sections, totaling about fifteen of the barrier's 400 miles (or less than 4 percent), being built to block three areas where Palestinian snipers have shot at cars traveling on the trans-Israel highway. Comparison with the Berlin Wall is risible in any event. The fence separates distinct peoples—Israelis and Palestinians—in the manner of fences installed by the U.S. at parts of its border with Mexico or by Israel at its borders with Lebanon, Syria, and Jordan. In most places, the fence's "footprint" is only about 160 feet wide, less than

> the distance covered by a runner moving from first to third base on a ball field; accommodated within this space are underground and long-range sensors, trenches, land-mines, and guard paths. [6]

Being that Jerusalem has been a major target of Palestinian terrorism, we would expect that all of these above listed stereotypes, if they were true, would be seen along this particular stretch of that "Nasty Fence." Yet this is not the case whatsoever. If the reader were to visit Israel he or she would see, this stretch of the Fence consists of wire, the same type that one would find along highways in many countries of the world. The top part of the wire fencing turns at an angle, to repel any objects that may be thrown at passing automobiles. However, it is clearly seen that anyone older than a child can easily throw a rock, a brick or an explosive device over this part of the Fence. At best, it is a partial deterrent.

Further north along the Fence, there is a stretch of approximately three quarters of a kilometer of a low concrete barrier. This constitutes a minority of the area of the Fence in its more than seven and a half kilometer length along this road. I have seen similar concrete wall stretches on highways, for example, the one that runs along a highway in Scottsdale, Arizona. The Arizona concrete wall is higher than the concrete area of Israel's Security Fence, and there is no particular terror problem in Scottsdale at this time to be concerned about. So why is it there? I suppose it is there to muffle highway noise, to keep pedestrians from entering the highway, and to decorate the view, as the barrier displays modern art designs on at least one of its sides.

Try telling the bleeding, cut-up German Christian tourists whom I found stunned on the shoulder of the road. I tried to comfort them a few moments after their vehicle was hailed on by a rock salvo. Their faces did not relay joy, nor did they feel much sympathy for the Palestinian youths who assaulted them. Their faces did relay horror, shock, fear and injury. There was no Security Fence along the stretch of highway where they were assaulted. I would imagine they wished there had been one there. When the three quarters of a kilometer length of concrete wall ends, the Israeli Security Fence again turns into an approximately six foot high wire fence with curved tops. It continues on as such, and then ends abruptly before a road going to Ramallah intersects the end of the highway.

In fact, the Israeli Supreme Court, under international pressure (and some national pressure), refused to allow the Security Fence to be continued along the Modi'in Road. So every time that road is used, motorists risk being victims of what can be lethal rock attacks. The continuation of the Security Fence could have provided a sound barrier from any possible assault. But world opinion is that Israelis do not deserve the best barriers from possible terrorism. Even with the Holocaust in the shadows of modern history, Jewish blood remains cheap in the eyes of much of world opinion.

The World Daily Net ran an interesting article–the story of a Palestinian who was the victim of a Palestinian terror attack. His suffering made him change his mind on the validity of Israel's Security Fence:

> Sammi Masrawa, a 29-year old Arab Israeli wounded in yesterday's Tel Aviv bus bombing, told reporters from his hospital bed that he now supports the West Bank security fence that the International Court of Justice claims is "illegal." "A month ago I went to protest the fence," Sammi said, "Now I believe it can only strengthen us. These terrorists don't differentiate between Jews and Arabs, they just want to kill." [7]

It may be true that most of the Arab villagers in towns along the roads I have been describing are happy enough to live side by side in peace with Jewish Israelis. However, there is still a good percentage of the Palestinian youth who are encouraged by the Palestinian Authority, its media and its educational institutions, as well as by the terror organizations in their midst, to kill Jews. With such encouragement and education, deadly anti-Semitic assaults continue. What makes the situation further sad is that terrorism can be indiscriminate terrorism.

As Sammi Masrawa mentioned in the above article, there are also Arab victims of Arab terror, such as 20-year old Hebrew University student George Khoury. While jogging in Jerusalem, Khoury was felled by an Arab terrorist's bullet. The Fatah Organization (which was Mr. Arafat's political party, and is that of Mahmoud Abbas, directly connected to the Palestinian Authority) later apologized to the family of the student. A Fatah gunman slew Khoury "mistakenly." Oops. The murderer thought Mr. Khoury was a Jew! What an excellent excuse to carry out a murder. In fact, George was the son of a prominent Palestinian attorney. Attempting to institute futile damage control, Mr. Arafat promised the Khoury family that

George would be considered, and I quote, "a martyr." This is quite a promise from a Nobel Peace Prize winner. I was purposely listening for voices from abroad that would censure the Fatah organization for this act, and I heard none.

The further inability or unwillingness of PA President Mahmoud Abbas and his forces to stop Palestinian terror organizations is another reason that the Security Fence is crucial to cutting down the number of terror incidents in Israel.

On April 24, 2005, incidents such as these were still being reported:

> Israel Defense Forces troops at the Beit Farik checkpoint in the West Bank arrested a Palestinian youth on Friday who was carrying four pipe bombs ready for use. Earlier Friday, troops detained a Palestinian trying to smuggle bullets in a videocassette at the Hawara checkpoint. In the past month, Palestinians have tried eight times to smuggle weapons or explosives through checkpoints in the Nablus region. [8]

I would hate to think what may have happened if our military checkpoints and Security Fence in those areas did not exist. With incidents like these occurring, any call to weaken Israel's domestic defense ability is ridiculous. The Jerusalem Post of 27 April 2005 documented another good reason for employing a security fence. It stated:

> In the fourth attempt in recent months to use children or teenagers to perpetrate terror attacks, two Palestinian 'boy bombers'–aged 15 and 16–were arrested at the Jalama checkpoint near Jenin in the West Bank on Wednesday. In their possession, IDF troops found 11 explosive devices, including several pipe bombs. A homemade gun was also

> discovered. A local military commander told *The Jerusalem Post* that the two had been paid NIS 100 each to detonate the bombs near soldiers manning the checkpoint. The youths said they were asked to bring the weapons into Israel and were intending to make another trip with more weapons. Also Wednesday, Jerusalem police went on a heightened state of alert following intelligence warnings, which indicated that a Palestinian terrorist may try to carry out a suicide bombing in the center of the city, police said. [9]

The results of nearly five years of pre-planned, virulent, anti-Israeli campaigns in the PA controlled media and educational institutions have created a "monster." The PA continues to give its tacit support to acts of terrorism, despite its claims to the contrary. Encouraging hatred towards Jews is their bottom line. Below are some very brief examples of such, spoken by a prominent Palestinian cleric. Given that years of this "education" have influenced the rank and file of the population, it is far better for Israel to err on the side of caution to protect our citizens than err on the side of ignorance. Thus, the Security Fence is necessary, due to the direction that the PA has purposefully led its population in the past ten years. To undo this "education"–if it is even possible–will take years of sustained effort. I venture the guess that this is not a priority in the PA's plans for the near future. The following quotes are as reported by the Palestinian Media Watch organization. A Palestinian Authority sponsored TV broadcast on 4 February 2005 aired this:

> We might return to the 1967 borders by diplomacy, but we shall not return to the 1948 borders by diplomacy. No one

> on this earth recognizes [our right to] the 1948 borders. Therefore, we shall return to the 1967 borders, but it does not mean that we have given up on Jerusalem, and Haifa, Jaffa, Lod, Ramle, Netanya and Tel Aviv. Never... Your father's blood was shed there, at the villages, at Ashqelon, Ashdod, Hirbia [Kibbutz Zikim] and hundreds of villages and towns that demand it from us. [Their blood] shall curse anyone who will concede a grain of earth of those villages. The land of Palestine will demand the Palestinians return . . . as a conqueror.[10]

As a further example of typical PA sponsored "domestic" education and propaganda, the following shows a point that has been stressed in this effort:

> The Muslim remembers how the Jews corrupted the land... Oh Muslims! The Jews are Jews. Their character and custom are the corruption and destruction of this land. We keep warning you: the Jews are a cancer that spreads inside the body of the Islamic and Arab nation.... They invest in the East Asian countries, which were destroyed [by the Tsunami] because of the Jewish and American corruption and destruction." [11]

For too long the Western world has either ignored such quotes, or looked at them as akin to children's words of threatening—not real death threats, just the hot tempered musings of frustration. Israel cannot afford to listen to such words and not take them seriously, for this is what is being taught to Palestinian children, *still*. It is post-Oslo Agreement and post-Yassir Arafat's dictatorial reign. The Palestinian Media Watch has documented many incidents of Palestinian Authority media, government, and clerical incitement against Israel's population. I refer the reader to his website (www.pmw.org.il). Having been raised in the post-Holocaust world, such publicly broadcast threats bear too much of a resemblance to those of Joseph Goebbels and Adolf Hitler to warrant being ignored.

At the end of 2003, the PA Broadcasting Company was airing words as these:

> (President) Bush said that Israel is a Jewish state, which is a cause for our concern. This should not have been said . . . What is the meaning of the concept of a Jewish state... Does this mean that this is Shi'ite, this is Sunni, that one is Alawite, this is Christian? [12]

Again, the Palestinian Media Watch organization noted in December 2003:

> . . . the Chairman of the PA Public Library, and Arafat's Advisor on Education, Dr. Jarir Al-Kidwah, again taught (the) de-legitimization of Israel's existence with significant elaboration and detail. Using the denial of Jewish nationhood as a starting point, they taught that modern Jews have no connection to the Land of Israel, and the early Zionists were therefore not interested in returning to Israel. [13]

The famous anti-Semitic document "The Protocols of the Elders of Zion" was cited publicly at the same time as a valid purveyor of international Jewish intentions. The PMW organization again noted that in December 2003, yet another Palestinian "authority" on Jewish history, Dr. Sisalem, publicly taught that:

> The Jews lived in isolated areas, in ghettos in Poland and in Russia. They were the remains of the Khazars . . . with

> no connection to our land and the history of our land [Palestine]... and even those who made this name have no history or connection to this land. [14]

There is only one reason why Dr. Sisalem would state such a thing—to try to de-legitimatize the State of Israel. Archaeology and history can guarantee the reader that the connection between the Jewish people and the Land of Israel is a historically based one. No one needs a graduate degree to know this information! One wonders from which textbooks Dr. Sisalem learned his Jewish history. But, that is a side issue.

Former anti-Soviet activist, Prisoner of Zion, and Israeli cabinet minister, Natan Sharansky, summarized the current atmosphere in the PA areas as follows:

> As in Nazi Germany, there is an entire 'culture of hatred' in Palestinian society today, from textbooks to crossword puzzles, from day camps to TV music videos," Sharansky said, "Calling for the murder of Jews, as Jews, is the end result." [15]

Sharansky was Israel's Minister of Diaspora Affairs. Having battled the fascist and anti-Semitic political system in the USSR during his residence there, it should concern all people that a person of his stature and experience said the above words.

He has been, throughout his career, a fighter and advocate for human rights. He knows dangerous political programs when he sees them. Indeed, the PA's educational programs for its children are alarming. An educational program by the PMW Organization, which I attended, brought out the following situations:

> Since 2006, sporting events in the PA areas have been named after terrorists who murdered Israelis. The PA's Ministry of Education sponsors such. One example is the Basah al-Deh soccer tournament. Al-Deh murdered 31 Israelis who were celebrating a religious ceremony (Passover) in the city of Netanya. Al-Deh's brother distributed the trophies of the tournament. The PMW organization brought out that the lesson for the Palestinian children taking part in the tournament is that Abdel-Basset Odeh is their role model par excellence. He is known only for murdering 30, mostly elderly, Jews at a Jewish religious celebration. A table tennis tourney in 2014 was sponsored by the PA, and was named after Ahmed abu-Sukr, who was the terrorist who blew up a refrigerator bomb at Zion Square in Jerusalem in 1975, which murdered 15 Israelis. Again, what is the lesson for the youths who participated in this tourney? Abu Sukr is their role model par excellence, and he is known only for murdering Jews. The message of the PA to its children and youth is this—in the words of the PMW Organization: ". . . if you murder Israeli civilians, it is heroic. It is sport." [16]

One can hear many Palestinian objections to the Security Fence. Let us look at some of them, and assess their merit.

One web site objected to the existence of our security fence with the assertion that:

> (The Security Fence) is the enforcement of an apartheid-like system by physically keeping the two communities apart. The Wall's stated purpose of security, of preventing Palestinian suicide bombers from entering Israel and killing innocent Israelis, has been undermined by the actual route of the Wall. [17]

First of all, the status of Israel's Arab/Palestinian communities is a far cry from that of Black Africans in apartheid South Africa. Arab communities have the right, and do, work in Israel, shop in Israel, attend movies and theatres in Israel, and eat in restaurants in Israel. There are no signs anywhere that forbid Arab residents from taking part in daily life in Israel. Walk along Jaffa Road, Nevi'im Street or Ben Yehuda Street in Jerusalem, and you will see that Palestinians walk alongside Israelis, Arabs besides Jews, with no apartheid laws. Go to the Dead Sea beaches, and you will see women with Muslim head coverings holding their children, standing beside Israeli women who are doing the same. The beaches do not read, "Arabs not allowed." There are no armed guards who enforce a "no entry" law. This is because apartheid laws do not exist, and any assertion to the contrary is a politically induced fabrication.

On a sadder note, the fact that above mentioned George Khoury was murdered in a Jewish neighborhood is because *he lived there*. He was not a victim of apartheid. Arab communities vote and elect candidates who represent their own political parties. Arab Knesset members are allowed, as part of our democratic system, to argue against the very foundations of the Jewish state. Yet, since there is no apartheid, *they have the right to do this*. The IDF employs Arab Bedouin trackers, who are pleased for the opportunity to be employed in the defense of the state. Yes, there are major problems. But no, there is no apartheid. Examine Israel's Declaration of Independence, and you will see a section that calls upon Israel's Arab communities to live *side by side* with the new Jewish state, in peace. This is not akin to the situation in the former apartheid South Africa.

In the summer of 2004, terrorist attacks hit a reduced level, and thus more than sixty military and police roadblocks and checkpoints were removed in Judea and Samaria. It benefits the Palestinian community when there is no terror, and Israel's stated intention to return to normalization with the PA took a small step forward at that objective. However, this, in itself, will not lead to the removal of the Security Fence.

Perhaps with a fuller security fence, terrorists would not have murdered Tehilla Natanson, of blessed memory, who was 3 years old, or Shmuel Taubenfeld, of blessed memory, who was all of 3 months old, nor Shmuel Zargari, of blessed memory, who was 11 months old, in a horrific bus bombing on August 19, 2003 in Jerusalem. The Israeli press reported that the MDs who tried to treat other children injured in that blast needed psychological counseling afterwards. I do not mean to use the lives of these children as political cannon fodder, and my apologies go out to their families if it appears that way. However, I do mean to emphasize and illustrate the point that this is the type of horrendous attack that Israelis have been made to suffer at the hands of Palestinian terrorists. The Security Fence is hardly an issue if it prevents this from happening just once again in the present or future. In fact, if opponents of the fence claim that it is not in the best interests of humanitarianism to have a security fence, I would argue that it is not humanitarian to withhold taking security measures against groups who vow to slaughter our children.

There is a common argument against the Fence that puts more value on saving time than saving lives. It goes as follows: "The stresses resulting from increased security procedures often result in long waiting lines at border crossing points." [18]

I would not deny this situation. Yes, the lines are long and more cumbersome than they were prior to the start of the 2000 *intifada* (armed uprising and assaults) and its waves of terrorism. But should not due consideration be given to the stresses that result to Israelis from casualties due to suicide bombers? What about the stresses that have happened to the victims in numbers listed above? Advocating for the human rights of these victims of Arab terror *would include preventing this from ever happening to them or their people again.* What human being would not think it worthwhile to temporarily stall Palestinian traffic coming into Israel if the process of close and efficient security checks could save the life of but *one* child? This more efficient checking process is what the Security Fence enables to occur. Why is it that we never read of a Fence critic stating that Israeli citizens have the right to be free from Palestinian terror? Where is the value on human life in this criticism listed above? I, for one, am happy to delay the traffic of my neighbor if it saves but one innocent life. *I, too, am delayed by halts in traffic due to security checks.* I once waited for 2 hours in my car as a gun battle between terrorists and Israeli security forces took place around me. Bomb threats and threats of terrorist activities delay traffic and business quite often in Israel's urban centers. All Israelis have lived with this situation for years. Yet, not too many media voices seem to care about *these* delays.

I hope the reader can sense the hypocrisy that I am addressing here. The presence of terrorism causes road delays in order to insure adequate security is taken to prevent murders. Until Palestinian terrorism and the educational effort leading up to it stop, the inevitable road delays are a small price to pay for saving lives. Let the terror and the anti-Semitic education cease permanently, and then I cannot help to think that Israel would take our security barriers down. We, too, like Robert Frost, are not the biggest fans in the world of fences.

Throughout the era of the Oslo Accords, the PA's corruption was a huge factor in the failure of political integrity for the Palestinian population. Yet, of course, Israel was to be blamed: ". . . the Israeli policy of enforced hunger will make voluntary emigration the only viable option to an unsustainable existence." [19]

Perhaps the above quoted author should thank prior PA Chairman Yassir Arafat for "mis-placing" large sums of money that should have been used to help feed the Palestinian population. Large donations of funds from international sources disappeared during Mr. Arafat's dictatorial chairmanship. These monies were given to the PA (some of it by Israel!) in order to build governmental and societal infrastructures. As author Jonathan Schanzer, a former US government employee and a counterterrorism expert, put it: "Under Arafat, in fact, the PA funneled untold amounts of international donor funding to a select group of insiders and did little to forge economic solutions that would create jobs or new opportunities for Palestinians . . ."[20]

Most normally, a government that is concerned about its citizens will earmark and use such funds to insure that methods of feeding its people are put into place. Blaming Israel for "enforced hunger" is a purposeful political "misdirection," and a very misguided charge. Israel did not cause Palestinian hunger. In fact, during the 2000-2003 *intifada*, and during Operation Protective Edge in 2014, Israel continued to send foodstuffs into the PA territories to provide relief for already existing Palestinian hunger. Of course, the PA would never claim that they were financially responsible for what happened with the above-mentioned donations. But let the reader put one plus one together. In its report entitled "Corruption and Exploitation of the Population in the Palestinian Authority", the Intelligence and Terrorism Information Center for Special Studies states its case in agreeing with my assessment of Mr. Arafat's use of donated funds in order to finance terrorism. I refer the reader to their report, found at: http://www.intelligence.org.il/eng/ corruption.htm.

The International Monetary Fund found that former PA dictator Mr. Arafat embezzled or misappropriated 900 million dollars of funding. Think of how much food that money, or even a good portion of it, could have bought for Palestinians.

Thus, it is doubtful that the security fencing is the major cause for any hunger in the PA territories. That is simply an excuse to again blame Israelis, when the true background of that situation is *mired in PA corruption and PA apathy about its own residents.* I am all for trying to eliminate hunger in the PA territories. Where and if hunger exists, it should be beaten by a cooperative effort at providing aid. But to blame Israel for this problem is sheer anti-Semitism–period–and based on hatred instead of looking at the entire picture, *or* at any viable solution.

I am very impressed by the wealth displayed by a Palestinian village on a road near to Jerusalem. New, modern apartment buildings have risen in that village during the past three years, and rival anything that I have seen in Jewish areas for beauty and elegance. Whoever lives in those buildings is not suffering from poverty.

The reader should not think that all Palestinians are hungry and in dire need. This is simply not the case. The reader should not think that all Palestinians are hungry and in dire need. I recommend the best-selling book "Catch the Jew" by Tuvia Tennenbom (published 2015) for a description of what he encountered when he visited the PA areas—the areas were hardly 100% poverty-stricken!

However, according to our city officials 30% of Jerusalem's Jewish children go to bed hungry every night. So hunger is a social problem that exists among Jews in Israel.

Now, let us address the issue of "voluntary emigration." Perhaps the most prominent area where that has occurred in the PA areas is in the city of Bethlehem. The mass exodus of the Arab Christian population from Bethlehem often is blamed on Israel (and now, upon the Security Fence). Joseph Farah, a prominent Arab American media figure, addresses the cause of this "exodus":

> Now, ask yourself a question: Why would the security fence dispropor-tionately affect Christians? If the security fence were contributing to the exodus, it should be causing an exodus of Muslims as well, right? .... Four years ago, when this exodus began, the Israelis had not even started construction of the security fence. . . . If the Israelis contributed in any way to the exodus of Christians it was by withdrawing from Bethlehem and the so-called "Palestinian territories"

> in the West Bank. Since they left, the Palestinian Authority has waged a jihad against the Christian community–raping women, extorting businessmen, lynching "collaborators," and seizing homes.... That's why the Christians have left and continue to leave. They enjoyed life while their towns were under the control of Israel. Once they were turned over to the terrorists, there wasn't much left to keep them in the areas in which their families lived for generations. [21]

The PA's own policies have driven the Christian population to leave. Granted, there may be some other reasons, as well. However, why was there no such "exodus" from 1967-2000, *during Israeli administrative control of Bethlehem*?

> . . . Yasser Arafat determined the policy that led up to this demographic shift . . . Arafat's motivation for the change was to ensure a Muslim majority in any elections to be held in the area. [22]

One could see these very machinations at work during the early part of the second *intifada*, Zohair Hamdan, the Palestinian *mukhtar* (mayor) of a Jerusalem suburb close to Bethlehem, publicly opposed the *intifada.* He also verbally attacked Yassir Arafat for causing problems for the Palestinian community. The PA's answer to his criticism was an armed attempt at assassinating him, which he survived:

> An outspoken and vociferous critic of the PA and Arafat, and a champion of peaceful coexistence with Israel, Hamdan was shot by suspected Palestinian assailants outside his village home on the night of October 5th. When Jerusalem Arab neighborhoods were slated to fall under PA control under

> former Prime Minister Ehud Barak's peace plan, Hamdan publicly criticized the idea. He declared that he would prefer to under Israeli sovereignty and was not interested in coming under Arafat's rule. In an unprecedented move for a Jerusalem Arab, he started a petition campaign and collected more than 10,000 signatures of Jerusalem Arabs against any change in their status. Threats started coming from the PA, and Hamdan's name was placed on the PA's wanted list. [23]

I could understand it if Christian residents would prefer to leave an area where this could be expected, rather than live with this. In my personal conversations with a Palestinian Christian academic who worked in Bethlehem in 1997, I asked him point blank why he would choose to support the PA's policies. Did he not expect persecution against him as a non-Muslim who was active in his church and in trying to spread the message of Christianity? His answer was, "I give to Muslim charities, and participate in helping local Muslim youth organizations. As long as I do that, there will be no problems." I asked him what will happen when his Western source for his charity donations dries up. He was not happy to face this question, nor could he answer it honestly for me.

The issue of Israel's Security Fence needs to be seen in the light of the international problem with terrorism. If our Fence is isolated as an issue unto itself, then global terror will have won a small propaganda victory. If the American government is correct in its calculations, and I have no reason to doubt its figures, then the world better learn a lesson from what is occurring here in Israel. Instead of weakening any given nation's ability to thwart terror, the international community ought to be backing every nation's attempt to quell this worldwide threat.

The issue of the Security Fence should be seen in the broader context of yet another struggle: that of Israel to survive in the midst of the hatred and rejection of the Middle Eastern realpolitik. The political context of the Security Fence must keep in mind that six million Jewish people are trying to build our lives in the midst of a continent filled with anti-Semitism, and where the efforts of the PA to control Palestinian terrorism are halfhearted at best. Put radical, Israel-hating governments like Iran into the mix, and it is easily understandable why my nation wants to take every possible measure to protect itself.

In true pro-Communist, 1960s style, "revolutionary" language, the security fence is described as: . . . an attempt (at) . . . colonial expansionist plans. . . .[24] All of this, of course, is part of ". . . the Apartheid system that Israel is creating."[25].

In good propaganda lingo, the authors of this site are attempting to equate Israel's Security Fence with, again, South Africa's past apartheid policies. As a side note, it is interesting to see the large South African Jewish number who actively opposed the apartheid policies of South Africa. In fact, it was stated by a Black South African politician in 2002:

> That people of Jewish descent should be so prominent in the (South African) liberation movement says something fundamental about the compassion of Judaism. Many Jewish immigrants who arrived in our shores in abject poverty, laying claim to little but their rich commitment to humanitarian and egalitarian ideals. These commitments were sometimes rooted in traditional Jewish teaching. They

> sometimes emerged from traditions of socialism. Whatever the case, Jewish compassion is the fruit of empathy, rather than sympathy. It is the fruit of struggle over many millennia, against racism and persecution.[26]

Should not a post-Oslo world strongly censure such a public broadcast? One could hardly think that this was carried out in the spirit of the Oslo Accords. Should not moderate Muslims put their foot down, and say "enough is enough, stop with the Jew hatred and poisoning of our people?"

The 1956 Treason Trials saw 14 of 26 defendants come from South Africa's Jewish community, and they all risked their lives to battle apartheid. The anti-apartheid journal, *Africa South*, was founded by a Jewish South African. My point is that these Jewish South Africans did not equate Israel with an apartheid state. Since they opposed apartheid with their very lives, it is very hard to imagine that they would have kept silent if they had believed Israel to be an apartheid state.

Using the best "catch phrase" she can think of, the *Sabeel's Newsletter*'s Elizabeth Campbell labels Israeli housing construction as "Zionist colonization." This newsletter complains how Israel's policies cause Palestinians to have to emigrate from Jerusalem. Maybe I could take this newsletter a little more seriously if it included another side to the story . . . why do they not complain that Arab anti-Semitic policies caused wholesale Jewish emigration from Iraq, Syria, Lebanon, Egypt, Tunisia, Algeria, Morocco, Libya and the Yemen just a generation and a half ago? The *entire* Jewish communities of these countries were forced to leave. I wonder if the newsletter's staff is even aware of this fact. I am not aware of any Jewish person living in Saudi Arabia. It is against the law. Dear friends at the *Sabeel Newsletter*, do the concept of civil liberties a favor and complain to the Saudi government about *that* human rights violation. See how far you get. Yet no one from *Sabeel* says a word about this situation. A double standard is being applied to Israel, and to Jewish people. The reader needs to ask, "Why is a double standard applied to Israel and Jewish people?"

The *Sabeel Newsletter* harps on another "catch phrase", that of "Palestinian ethnic cleansing." Maybe their staff never goes to Jerusalem and sees Palestinians eating and shopping alongside Israelis. Perhaps they have never seen the Arab neighborhoods of Bet Safafa or Bet Hanina in Jerusalem, where Muslims freely worship at mosques. Maybe they think that a nation trying to build a Security Fence in order to protect itself from terrorism equals ethnic cleansing.

Obviously, they do not comprehend that ethnic cleansing means to *physically exterminate a people*, as happened to my people in Europe during the Holocaust; and as happened to Armenians in Turkey. That constituted forcible expulsion, and much worse. When a Security Fence is built for protection, it constitutes a physical move to avoid terror. It is not ethnic cleansing by any means of the phrase's definition.

The *Sabeel Newsletter* states:

> Stage four (of "Israel's plan for ethnic cleansing!") ensures that no Palestinian is even allowed to enter Jerusalem – not even for a single hour. The closure has culminated in the fourth stage of ethnic cleansing, where Palestinian

> businessmen of all types are forced to leave the city in order to survive economically. [27]

The Newsletter's author has apparently and secretly discovered that Israel is scheming to bar every Palestinian from Jerusalem. I hope the reader will check out the truth of this accusation. It is patently false. *Let the reader be aware that there is no such closure as she mentions, and no such barring of Palestinians from Jerusalem. She scares up anti-Semitic and anti-Israeli sentiment, and states it as if it were a fact. It simply is not!* Certain Palestinians, who have criminal or terrorist organization affiliations or backgrounds are indeed barred from entering Jerusalem, with good reason! Would you want such persons roaming freely in your neighborhood? I sincerely doubt it. And the checkpoints along the security barrier in Israel allow Israel to distinguish between those who enter the city for peaceful purposes, and those who would enter to cause problems, or worse. This takes a checking of IDs, sometimes questioning, occasionally inspection of vehicles to insure there is no contraband, drugs, or illegal weapons in the car. The alternative is to drop this process, and allow an open door for trouble.

Certain times may see a temporary quota on the number of Arabs allowed in a certain area. But this is always temporary, and again, one sees that the normal traffic in any given day in Jerusalem includes a high number of Arab citizens and residents. The typical Jerusalem situation today for Arab residents is a better situation than the one that existed for Jews during the Jordanian rule over Jewish holy sites in Jerusalem (when Jews were barred from entry, and Jewish holy sites were indeed abused).

I am always grateful for the insights of Joseph Farah about our Security Fence:

> Israel is doing just what we do in our own personal lives to protect ourselves. It is building fences to protect its civilians from hostile neighbors and it is punishing mass murderers with execution. It's the right of any nation to defend itself and that is what Israel is doing. Israel is militarily capable of destroying its enemies – all of them. But it does not. It shows restraint – even in the face of murderous provocation. [28]

The reader has seen that the Security Fence is crucial to Israel's defense system as a means of thwarting terrorist attacks. The decrease in incidents of terrorism over the past ten years can be attributed, in part, to the presence of the Fence. The reasons typically cited for opposing the existence of the Fence are built upon blaming Israel for social problems that have beset the Palestinian community before the arrival of the Security Fence. Although the Fence will indeed delay traffic and make travel more difficult for Palestinians in affected areas, the positive outcome of saving lives must be seen as more important than the inevitable time delays that occur.

The real solution, if the fence is to be dismantled, entails a sincere effort by the PA to end its Israel-hating education efforts and to stop all aiding, encouraging and abetting of terror acts against Israel. If this does not occur–*and it has not happened to date*–then the Security Fence will not be dismantled. Instead, it will continue to contribute to the defense of Israel's civilian population, as it already does. Israel's Security Fence is a test case for the world on the issue of terrorism. Standing up to terrorism by supporting Israel's right to defend herself will be respected as a sign of strength in the warped world and mindset of terrorist organizations. Opposing Israel's Security Fence will be looked at as an act of weakness. When terror organizations sense weaknesses and openings, they begin to try to spread their influence in those areas. This is a fact that most Israelis understand very well.

Over the past years, I have met a number of Palestinians whom I consider as highest quality people. It is a tragedy that their political leadership has *not* been responsible, and I fault *them,* as well as his predecessors–Haj Amin al-Husseini, being one of them–for the predicaments that Palestinian society experiences today.

Faraj Shalhoub, an expert on Palestinian affairs... explained that:

> 'Palestinians aren't blowing themselves up out of frustration with the occupation or because of poor living conditions; rather the willingness to become a 'martyr' originates from a deep religious conviction instilled in the Palestinians by their spiritual leaders. The level of faith among a wide sector of the young believers instills in them the concept of jihad. . . . They are committed even before they reach the fighting stage. . . .' said Shalhoub. [29]

In light of all that has been noted, the various security barriers that are found in our nation do not comprise an "apartheid wall" (sic). It is simply a physical attempt to thwart terrorism, insure physical security, deter jihadism, and administer the flow of traffic, so that there is an orderly and supervised procedure to it.

This is the tough neighborhood that we live in. It is a neighborhood where one has to learn how to defend one's self. Therefore, the issue of the Security Fence is really just one small issue in a much bigger picture: that of the right of the State of Israel to exist as the Jewish state in the midst of a hostile and threatening environment.

If the presence of the security barrier has saved the life of *just one* baby or child, Jewish or Arab (and I assure the reader it has done so), it was worth the money invested, the waiting in lines, the slower traffic, and the longer routes that we all have had to endure. "... whoever saves a life, it is considered as if he saved an entire world." (Mishna Sanhedrin 4:1, T. Yerushalmi).

Appendix D

The Christ at the Checkpoint Manifesto

1. The Kingdom of God has come. Evangelicals must reclaim the prophetic role in bringing peace, justice and reconciliation in Palestine and Israel.
2. Reconciliation recognizes God's image in one another.
3. Racial ethnicity alone does not guarantee the benefits of the Abraham Covenant (sic).
4. The church in the land of the Holy One has borne witness to Christ since the days of Pentecost. It must be empowered to continue to be light and salt in the region, if there is to be hope in the midst of conflict.
5. All forms of violence must be refuted unequivocally.
6. Any exclusive claim to the land of the Bible in the name of God is not in line with the teaching of scripture.
7. Palestinian Christians must not lose the capacity for self-criticism if they wish to remain prophetic.

8. There are real injustices taking place in the Palestinian territories, and the suffering of the Palestinian people can no longer be ignored. Any solution must respect the equity and rights of Israeli and Palestinian communities.
9. For Palestinian Christians, the occupation is the core issue of the conflict.
10. Any challenge to the injustices taking place in the Holy Land must be done in Christian love. Criticism of Israel and the occupation cannot be confused with anti-Semitism and the delegitimization of the State of Israel.
11. Respectful dialogue between Palestinian and Messianic believers must continue. Though we may disagree on secondary matters of theology, the gospel of Jesus and his ethical teaching take precedence.
12. Christians must understand the global context for the rise of extremist Islam. We challenge stereotyping of all faith forms that betray God's commandment to love our neighbors and enemies.

Taken from: http://christatthecheckpoint.com/new/index.php/en/catc4-manifesto

End Notes

Introduction

1. Then Israeli Prime Minister Ariel Sharon was being referred to in this inscription.
2. http://tabletmag.com/jewish-news-and-politics/96146/swedens-damn-jew problem.
3. http://linguaspectrum.com.
4. http://www.theguardian.com/society/2014/aug/07/antisemitism-rise-europe-worst-since-nazis.
5. http://www.israelnationalnews.com/Articles/Article.aspx/13856

Chapter One

1. Kruger, 6.
2. Ibid.
3. Rector S. Stanton, public address, London, England. June 2015.
4. http://www.jpost.com/Middle-East/Abbas-wants-not-a-single-Israeli-in-future-Palestinian-state-321470
5. White, 113-115.
6. This category of person is written about in the following excellent essay: Patrice Fischer, "Modern-Day Godfearers: A Biblical Model for Gentile Participation in Messianic Congregations," in John Fischer, ed., *The Enduring Paradox: Exploratory Essays in Messianic Judaism* (Baltimore: Lederer, 2000), pp. 178-180.

7. www.sabeel.org/pdfs/2001%20Easter%20Message.htm.

8. Quoted from "The Church at Christ's Checkpoint", 5. The Church has had its eras of unfaithfulness towards God, as well, in this author's opinion. If God would withdraw His love and calling from the Church due to its failures, there would be no future for Christians. It would be hypocritical for the Church to constantly harp that Israel has failed God, and thus God has withdrawn His calling to Israel, given both the messages at the end of Romans 11 (cf. v. 29), *and* the history of the Church.

9. http://www.jewishvirtuallibrary.org/jsource/anti-semitism/Luther_on_Jews.html

10. Ibid.

11. In spite of the fact that Marcion was excommunicated from the early Church, his theologically based ideas about the Jewish people lived on, and still live on today.

12. Kershaw, 134.

13. http://www.markdankof.com/get_off_the_pot.htm

14. A. Avi-Hai, "How I almost became a Catholic, and why I am angry with the Catholic Church," *The Jerusalem Post,* August 14, 2015, p. 21

Chapter Two

1. http://www.jpost.com/Magazine/Features/Spotlight-on-modern-loathing.

2. http://www.jpost.com/Jewish-World/Jewish-News/Nirenstein-Classical-anti-Semitism-is-no-longer-the-primary-threat-334372.

3. Littell, 19.

4. http://www.israelnationalnews.com/Articles/Article.aspx/17042

5. See the actual report, found at: https://www.freedomhouse.org/sites/default/ files/FIW%202013%20Booklet_0.pdf

6. http://research.calvin.edu/german-propaganda-archive/goeb1.htm.

7. Brown and Penner, 56.

8. Ibid. 61.

9. https://ukmediawatch.org/in-their-own-words/ben-white/

10. https://seismicshock.wordpress.com/2011/07/
11. https://seismicshock.files.wordpress.com/2011/11/antisemitism-and-christ-at-the-checkpoint-2012.pdf
12. Marcus, 49.
13. http://roshpinaproject.com/tag/christ-at-the-checkpoint-2014/.
14. http://www.wnd.com/2015/06/isis-threatens-ancient-monastery-filled-with-christians/#svpqkxEDf2QpKvo4.99
15. http://english.alarabiya.net/en/News/middle-east/2015/06/28/ISIS-executes-over-3-000-in-Syria-in-year-long-caliphate-.html.
16. http.//www.memri.org/report/en/0/0/0/0/0/0/8622.htm.
17. Taken from a private on-line discussion, June 2015.
18. http://www.breakingisraelnews.com/12745/new-anti-semitism-tailored-evangelicals/?fb_comment_id=223717771151586_415901#0xjhG4mxYyOEQ7OC.97
19. https://www.gatestoneinstitute.org/4230/christ-at-the-checkpoint
20. https://samiawad.wordpress.com/2007/01/23/non-violent resistance-wake-up-every-day-and-ask-yourself-what-you-can-do-to-resist-the-occupation)
21. White, 114.
22. http://www.algemeiner.com/2014/03/12/ngo-monitor-u-s-u-k-netherlands-fund-anti-israel-%E2%80%98christ-at-the-checkpoint%E2%80%99-conference/
23. https://seismicshock.files.wordpress.com/2011/11/antisemitism-and-christ-at-the-checkpoint-2012.pdf.
24. http://www.algemeiner.com/2014/03/12/ngo-monitor-u-s-u-k-netherlands-fund-anti-israel-%E2%80%98christ-at-the-checkpoint %E2%80%99-conference/
25. Littell, 19.
26. http://www.bnaibrith.org/press-releases/bnai-brith-world-center-dismayed-at-vanleer-institute-for-cooperating-with-upcoming-anti-israel-conference
27. http://www.jpost.com/Jewish-World/Jewish-Features/Christians-angry-over-anti-Semitic-parley.

28. https: www.gatestoneinstitute.org/4230/christ-at-the-checkpoint
29. https://www.foreigntranslations.com/languages/arabic-translation/arabic-language-history/).
30. http://jcpa.org/article/palestinian-crimes-against-christian-arabs-and-their-manipulation-against-israel/
31. Brown and Penner, 66-67.
32. http://blogs.timesofisrael.com/dean-of-evangelical-school-in-israel-has-a-problem-with-jews-and-their-state/
33. "Replacement theology", a.k.a. "supercessionism", claims that Israel has had our national covenants (as in Genesis 12, 15, 17, 21 and as found in the entire book of Deuteronomy, cancelled, and that the promises in them are inherited by Christians only).
34. Littell, 97.
35. http://www.camera.org/index.asp?x_context=2&x_outlet=118&x_article=2221
36. http://www.palwatch.org/site/modules/print/preview.aspx?fi=157&doc_id=4109
37. http://roshpinaproject.com/tag/manfred-kohl/.
38. Ibid.
39. http://blogs.timesofisrael.com/bethlehem-bible-college-and-christ-at-the-checkpoint-a-different-message-for-a-different-audience/ #.Vbxrgz7vF3EE. email.
40. http://www.jpost.com/Opinion/Op-Ed-Contributors/Why-Jews-dont-attend-the-Christ-at-the-Checkpoint-conference-345912.
41. White, 115.

Chapter Three

1. http://www.goodreads.com/author/quotes/281832.Joseph_Goebbels.
2. Ellis, 214.
3. http://www.jpost.com/Israel-News/Bringing-the-jobs-to-Beduin-women-410837.
4. http://sophia.smith.edu/blog/jerusalem/2011/05/30/words-matter/.

5. Ishmael Khaldi in *The San Francisco Chronicle*, 4 March 2009 http://www.israeliapartheidweek.com/content/notable_quotes.asp.
6. *Peshat* is the Hebrew word for the simple, literal-historical meaning of the biblical text. In order to arrive at the conclusions that undergrid the theological thought that is behind the "Israel is like the Nazis" charges, scripture is twisted, taken out of context, divorced from its history, and totally removed out of the culture and people from which they came. Logic is ignored, and little attention is paid to the Hebrew language in which the scriptures were written. Terms and words are redefined to match the political aims of the readers. The above mentioned, rejected items are *always necessary* in understanding *all of Scripture.*
7. http://www.bbc.com/news/uk-wales-11421019.
8. http://electronicintifada.net/blogs/ali-abunimah/south-african-church-leaders-endorse-israeli-apartheid-week.
9. http://www.timesofisrael.com/abbas-toughens-law-against-palestinians-selling-land-to-jews/.
10. http://www.cbn.com/cbnews/insideisrael/2011/July/PA-Law-Selling-Land-to-Jews-Punishable-by-Death/.
11. http://www.jpost.com/Middle-East/PA-Death-penalty-for-those-who-sell-land-to-Jews.
12. http://www.nytimes.com/1997/05/12/world/arab-s-death-and-the-selling-of-land-to-jews.html.
13. "Palestinian Crimes against Christian Arabs and Their Manipulation against Israel", Interview with J. R. Weiner, Jerusalem Center for Public Affairs, No. 72, Sept. 2009.
14. http://www.anc.org.za/show.php?id=3332
15. http://www.brijnet.org/israel50/decl-eng.htm
16. http://observer.com/2015/its-hard-to-be-a-christian-arab-in-israel-but-not-because-of-jews/#ixzz3b96Fwxb.

Chapter Four

1. http://thinkexist.com/quotation'if_you_tell_a_lie_big_enough_and_keep_repeating/345877.html
2. http://www.alternativeinsight.com/israel_Faces_Detractors.html.

3. Gilbert, 30.
4. http://www.alternativeinsight.com/israel_Faces_Detractors.html. A recent landmark study entitled "Human Rights of Christians in Palestinian Society" discusses *why* the Christian population of Bethlehem has recently declined, and does *not* blame Israel whatsoever. It identifies these worsening conditions for Christians as being the result of deliberate actions by Islamists. This situation is not as simple as "blame those Jews" once again. But "blame the Jews" is what we hear from Israel-hating spokespersons from the Middle East, Europe and the Americas. The effect of blaming Israel for lessening the Christian population is to focus attention off of the real reasons for the declining Christian population, which reasons are fingered in the above mentioned study. I refer the reader to this very helpful book.
5. This figure is based on the estimate of the US Holocaust Museum, found at http://www.ushmm.org/wlc/en/article.php?ModuleId=10005144.
6. http://www.peacewithrealism.org/pdc/jenin.htm
7. http://www.jcpa.org/phas/phas-wistrich-f04.htm
8. http://jcpa.org/article/holocaust-inversion-the-portraying-of-israel-and-jews-asnazis/
9. http://www.jpost.com/Jewish-World/Jewish-Features/ANC-comparison-of-Israel-to-Nazis-riles-South-African-Jews-362289.
10. http://www.israelsvoice.org/what-we-do/antisemitism-monitor/
11. http://newagebd.net/31269/israels-nazi-like-criminal-campaign-in-gaza/#sthash.6cxcTIJe.dpuf.
12. http://www.palestinechronicle.com/ben-white-boycott-the-backlash/?print=pdf.
13. http://unitedwithisrael.org/palestinian-authority-slanders-israel-as-nazi-state-pmw-reveals/
14. http://www.palwatch.org/site/modules/print/preview.aspx?fi=157&doc_ id=12680.
15. http://unitedwithisrael.org/palestinian-authority-slanders-israel-as-nazi-state-pmw-reveals/.

16. Ibid. Yad VaShem is the Israeli Museum of the Holocaust, located in Jerusalem. It contains archives and photographic displays of the history of the Holocaust, and ongoing research offices with memorials at various places on its grounds. The author has donated some original papers that testify first-hand of murders of Jewish residents of Baden-Wurttemberg during the Holocaust, and that testify to the incitement of the local clergy that contributed to the anti-Semitism present then.
17. http://unitedwithisrael.org/palestinian-authority-slanders-israel-as-nazi-state-pmw-reveals/
18. http://www.ihr.org/leaflets/what_christians.shtml
19. Lochner, 533.
20. Tamimi's statement can be viewed on a television interview found at: https://www.youtube.com/watch?v=wkAuvIQTzWU
21. http:/www.haaretz.com/blogs/a-special-place-in-hell/the-progressive-who-paints-israel-as-a-genocidal-nazi-state.premium-1.429999.
22. http://frontpagemag.com/2012/mark-d-tooley/united-methodists-reject-divestment/
23. http://blog.camera.org/archives/2012/05/antisemitic_rant_passeswithou. html.
24. I recognize, sadly, that over 20 million Russians were also killed, and over three million or more Poles, as well as many Roma, mentally handicapped, homosexual and other targeted groups, along with Europe's Jewish communities. Yet, it was the Nazi's declared intent to commit genocide against European Jewry. The overwhelming majority of the victims of the gas chambers were targeted Jewish persons.
25. Littell, 109. Barmen and Stuttgart were the locations of two Church confessional conferences where nothing happened to oppose anti-Semitism (Barmen), nor the genocide (1945) against the Jewish people. At Barmen, the evangelical Church did not directly address anti-Semitism, though it broke from the state Church. Later in Stuttgart, a new evangelical Church was formed in Germany, but nothing addressed its complicity in the genocide against Jewish people. Littell's excellent essay on these two conferences is found at: https://www.jstor.org/stable/23913120?seq=1#page_scan_tab_contents
26. Ibid. 109.
27. Ibid. 130.
28. Ibid. 131.

Chapter Five

1. From "Neighborhood Bully" by Bob Dylan.
2. A.K. Ajami, private lecture, 14 May 2015, Jerusalem, Israel.
3. *Tsitsit* (cf. Nu. 15.37) are string-like fringes worn by Jewish men, to remind us to carry out the Biblical instructions. *Tefillin* (cf. Deut. 6. 8) are leather straps tied around the arm and put on the forehead of Jewish men, to remind us to think about and carry out God's instructions.

Conclusion

1. A British Muslim pro-Israel advocate, wrote this sentence. His story is told at: http://www.frontpagemag.com/2014/joseph-puder/kasim-hafeez-a-story-of-a-miraculous-transformation/
2. D. Williamson, private lecture, London, England, June 2015.
3. R. McKinnon, private lecture, London, England, June 2015.
4. The biblical Hebrew alphabet has no punctuation mark akin to an exclamation mark. However, the poetry and rhythm of the text can take on the role of what an exclamation mark does in any given text.
5. As a matter of interest, the solution to this given situation would undoubtedly be to abstain from fasting, in Jewish jurisprudence (halakhic thought). Preserving lfe is always the highest goal. If the elderly person's medical care provider and family agree, and the person very much wants to do so, perhaps a limited fast (e.g., liquids) could be tried. But if life is ever under threat, the fasting would be prohibited. Thus, children, the chronically ill (e.g., diabetics and pregnant women often will abstain from fasting on Yom Kippur.

Appendix C: That Nasty Fence

1. The "Mending Wall" is found at: http://www.poets.org/poetsorg/poem/ mending-wall
2. http://www.securityfence.mod.gov.il/Pages/ENG/purpose.htm.
3. These statistics are taken from: http://www.johnstonsarchive.net/terrorism/terrisraelsum.html.
4. These population figures were found at: http://quickfacts.census.gov/ qfd/states/53000.html and http://www.cia.gov/cia/publications/factbook/ rankorder/2119rank.html.

5. R. Culvert, "Tunisia ramps up security in face of further terror attacks", *The Irish Independent*, July 9, 2015, p. 25.
6. Taken from "The End of the Right of Self-Defense? Israel, the World Court, and the War on Terror" by Andrew McCarthy, found at: Error! Hyperlink reference not valid.
7. "Arab Bomb Victim Backs Security Barrier" by Aaron Klein, July 12, 2004, *World Daily Net*.
8. dailyowner@dailyalert.org
9. http://www.jpost.com/servlet/Satellite?pagename=JPost/JPArticle/ ShowFull&cid=1114568594963&p=1078027574097.
10. http://www.pmw.org.il/. This was Palestinian Authority Television show from January 7, 2005, quoting a leading Palestinian cleric.
11. http://palwatch.org/main.aspx?fi=764&doc_id=796.
12. This was spoken by then PA Prime Minister Ahmad Qurei, quoted by the PMW Organization, taken from http://www.pmw.org.il/.
13. From, "PA Promotion of Racism and Anti-Semitism" by Itamar Marcus, taken from http://www.pmw.org.il/.
14. Dr. Isam Sisalem, Senior Historian and PA Television host, quoted in "The Protocols of the Elders of Zion and Denying Israel's Right to Exist," by I. Marcus, taken from http://www.pmw.org.il/.
15. Taken from http://redtigers.tblog,com.
16. From a lecture by P. Hurwitz, PMW Organization, give in Jerusalem, Israel, 11/2014.
17. Taken from www.wfp.org.
18. Ibid.
19. Ibid.
20. Schanzer, 9.
21. http://www.wnd.com/2004/12/28255/.
22. J. R. Weiner, *Palestinian Crimes against Christian Arabs and Their Manipulation against Israel*, p. 3.
23. http://www.freerepublic.com/focus/f-news/1328745/posts.
24. http://stopthewall.org/maps/860.shtml.

25. Ibid.
26. http://www.maurice-ostroff.org/
27. http://www.sabeel.org/old/news/newslt15/campbell.htm.
28. "Israel Fights Back" by J. Farah, May 19, 2004, taken from http://www.worldnetdaily.com/news/article.asp?ARTICLE_ID=38556.
29. http://www.wnd.com/2004/07/25472/

Glossary

Adonai: one of the Hebrew words used for "God" in the Bible.

Amidah: the "standing prayer"–a set of 18 blessings recited by Jewish worshippers.

al-Nakba: the Arabic rejectionist term, meaning "the disaster," referring to the birth of the State of Israel in May 1948.

Anti-Semitism: beliefs and/or actions, as well as prejudices that belittle, demean or minimize the value of Jewish people; as well, any effort given to harm Jewish people or their only state, Israel, can be assessed as anti-Semitic. The US Holocaust Memorial Museum defines "anti-Semitism" as "prejudice against or hatred of Jews."

Apartheid: the system of society which was legislated into existence in South Africa from 1948-1994, which divided and privileged the minority white South Africans from all other ethnic groups.

BDS: the boycott, divestment and sanctions political movement that targets the nation of Israel.

Birkat HaMazon: one of the Jewish thanksgiving prayers, this one is recited after eating meals.

Birobidzhan: an area of Russia close to China, located 5,000 miles from Moscow, where Joseph Stalin attempted to settle many Russian Jews, and turn it into the "Jewish Autonomous Region." This attempt fell short of Stalin's plan.

Chrislam: The nickname given to the movement that promotes unification between the Christian and Muslim worlds, focusing on joint theological understandings and dialogues.

Dhimmi: This is the Arabic word for the status of being an ethnic or religious minority needing to pay the *jizya* (a special community tax) to garner Muslim protection, and to live in various ways as less privileged citizens than the Muslim majority. The quality of community life depended in large part upon the local Muslim political powers.

Einsatzgruppen: The wing of the SS whose mission it was to find and destroy Jewish communities in Eastern Europe during the Nazi invasion of the Soviet Union. Typically this was carried out by mass shootings of Jewish civilians.

Geulah b'eto: Literally, "redemption in its time." This is the rabbinic teaching that Israel will be redeemed step-by-step, slowly, in stages, in real time.

Holocaust: The deliberate, planned genocide of Jewish communities in Europe by the Nazis and their allies, carried out from 1939-1945. Some six million Jewish persons were murdered in this campaign, including one and a half million Jewish children.

Intifada: Arabic for an "uprising," referring to the two periods of time when Israel was subject to violence, terrorism and riots inside her borders by various rejectionist Arab groups and individuals.

Jim Crow: The term used to refer to local laws in the southern part of the USA that remained in force till 1965. These laws and customs were prejudicial against African Americans, upholding racial inequality.

Judenrein: German for "without Jews", meaning an area that does not allow Jewish people to live there, or is otherwise lacking any Jewish population.

Koine: the name for the particular dialect or style of Greek used in the Newer Testament writings.

Kristallnacht (more correctly, *Reichskristallnacht*)**:** Literally, "national night of glass," refers to November 9-10, 1938, when the Nazis destroyed chosen synagogues and Jewish owned shops in Germany, carrying out a nation-wide pogrom.

NAACP: The National Association for the Advancement of Colored People–an organization with which the author's father worked in the 1960s.

PA: The Palestinian Authority, which is fractured into two rival governing organizations–Fatah and Hamas–and are based in two different locations (Fatah in the city of Ramallah and Hamas in the Gaza strip).

Peshat: Hebrew for the simple meaning of a text, based on its logical, straight forward context.

Rejectionist: Used to describe Christians who reject the right of Israel to be the Jewish state, and who do not support Israel's right to live behind firm and secure borders.

Roma and Sintis: The Gypsy tribes that the Nazis attempted to annihilate.

Shavuot: The Hebrew name for the holy time of Weeks (see Leviticus chapter 23).

Sukkot: The Hebrew name for the holy week of Tabernacles or Booths (see Leviticus chapter 23).

Supersessionism: The theological belief that Christians have replaced the Jewish people as the recipients of all promises in the Bible that were given to Abraham, Isaac and Jacob.

Talmud: A compendium of Jewish rabbinical writings that discuss and summarize the development of jurisprudence and Biblical analyses, spanning an approximate 700 year time period.

Tefillin: Leather straps used by Jewish men during morning prayer. They symbolize, among other things, the use of mind and body in the service of God.

Tsitsit: Ritual fringes that are worn by Jewish men, in obedience to what is written in Numbers 15:37 of the Bible.

Wakf: The Jerusalem Islamic Wakf is the committee which controls the Temple Mount in Jerusalem regarding religious affairs, visiting rights and practices.

This word also is the political concept that once a land has been, in history, under a Muslim ruler or ownership, that it is to be considered forever as a Muslim property.

Yad VaShem: From a verse in the Bible, this Hebrew name means "a memorial and a name", and refers to the Israeli Holocaust Museum in Jerusalem, dedicated to explaining, displaying, researching and teaching the history of the Holocaust.

Yeshua: Jesus's original Hebrew name.

Bibliography

Bernovsky, Yael. “aliya mad’igah b’antisemiut b’germania, britania ve’artsot haberit” *Israel Hayyom* Daily, June 24, 2015, p. 13.

Brackman, Harold and Breitbarth, Aaron. “Holocaust Denial’s Assault on Memory: Precursor to Twenty-First Century Genocide?” Wiesenthal Center: Los Angeles, CA, 2007.

Brown, W. and Penner, P., editors. *Christian Perspectives on the Israeli-Palestinian Conflict.* Neufeld-Verlag: Schwarzenfeld, Germany, 2008.

Carroll, James. *Constantine’s Sword*. Mariner Books: New York, N.Y., 2001.

Culvert, Richard. “Tunisia ramps up security in face of further terror attacks”, *The Irish Independent*, July 9, 2015, p. 25

DelGado, J. D. “The Cultivated Olive and Wild Olive.” Unpublished essay. Jerusalem, Israel, 2013.

Ditters, E. and Motzki, H. Approaches to Arabic Linguistics. Brill Publishers: Leiden, The Netherlands, 2009.

Eidar, Dror. “Zekuyot ‘adam hashuvot raq ‘im ma’ashimim et yisra’el”, *Israel Hayyom*, June 26, 2015, pp. 6-7.

Ellis, Joseph. *His Excellency, George Washington*. Vintage Books: New York,, N.Y., 2004.

Gilbert, Martin. *Kristallnacht.* Harper-Collins Publishers: New York, N.Y., 2006.

Goldberg, Jonah. *Liberal Fascism.* Doubleday Books: New York, N.Y., 2007.

Gray, Ena. *Healing the Past Catholic Anti-Semitism: Roots and Redemption*. Veritas Publications: Dublin, Ireland, 2009.

Hirsch, Yoni. "Obama meshaneh medini'ut: mutar l'shalem kofer l'irgunay teror", *Israel Hayyom*, June 24, 2015, p. 13.

Holy Bible: New American Standard Bible. 1995. LaHabra, CA: The Lockman Foundation.

Kershaw, Alex. *To Save A People*. Arrow: London, England, 2010.

Kristof, Nicholas. "A rain of bombs in the Nuba Mountains." *The N.Y. Times,* June 22, 2015, p. 7.

Kruger, S. Joela. "From Ridicule to Respect". ESM: Darmstadt, Germany, 2015.

Littell, Franklin. *The Crucifixion of the Jews*. Mercer University Press: Macon, GA., Lochner, Louis. *The Goebbels Diaries.* Doubleday Books: N.Y., N.Y., 1948.

Marcus, Itamar and Zilberdik, N. J. *Deception: Betraying the Peace Process*. PMW: Jerusalem, Israel, 2012.

McBrearty, Danny. "Altering Meaning of words won't change facts on the ground." *The Irish News.* July 6, 2015: p. 19.

Naveh, Joseph. *Origins of the Alphabet.* Palphot, Ltd.: Herzliyya, Israel, 1994.

NGO Monitor, publishers. *Christ at the Checkpoint*. NGO Monitor: Jerusalem, Israel, 2014.

Oder, Werner. *Battling Nazi Demons*. Onward and Upwards: West Horsley, Surrey, UK: 2011.

Schanzer, Jonathan. *State of Failure.* Palgrave MacMillan Books, New York, N.Y: 2013.

Schrauger, Brian. "Anti-Semitism's Global Comeback". *Dispatch from Jerusalem, Vol. 40, No.4.* August 2015. BFP: Jerusalem, Israel.

Senor, Dan and Singer, Saul. *Start Up Nation*. Hatchette Book Group: New York, N.Y., 2009.

Stern, David, translator. *Complete Jewish Bible.* Jewish New Testament Publications, Clarksville, MD, 1998.

Va'ad HaYeshivot, editors and publishers. *Maseket Sanhedrin min Talmud Bavli.* Va'ad HaYeshivot: Jerusalem, Israel, 1987.

White, Andrew. *Father, Forgive. Reflections on Peacemaking.* Monarch Books, Oxford, UK, 2013.

Wilkinson, Paul. *The Church at Christ's Checkpoint.* Unpublished essay, no date given.

Williamson, D. Private lecture. London, England, June 2015.

Wistrich, Robert. "Anti-Zionism and Anti-Semitism". *Jewish Political Studies Review* 16:3-4 (Fall 2004), accessed on 5/17/2015 from: http://www.jcpa.org/phas/phas-wistrich-f04.htm

Electronic

http://dailyowner@dailyalert.org

http://www.adl.org/israel-international/israel-middle-east/content/AG/inaccuracy-Arabs-anti-semitic.html

http://www.algemeiner.com/2014/03/12/ngo-monitor-u-s-u-k-netherlands-fund-anti-israel-%E2%80%98christ-at-the-checkpoint%E2%80%99-conference/

http://www.alternativeinsight.com/israel_Faces_Detractors.html

http://www.anc.org.za/show.php?id=3332

http://www.answering-christianity.com/anti_semites.htm

http://www.antisemitism.org.il/eng/Chapter%203%3A%20The%20beginnings%20of%20Christian%20Anti-Semitism%20-%20Judeophob

http://archive.frontpagemag.com/readArticle.aspx?ARTID=5835

http://archive.org/stream/paulJosephGoebbelsWritingsAndEssays/Goebbels_wri-tings_essays_djvu.txt

http://www.bbc.com/news/uk-wales-11421019

http://www.bdsmovement.net/bdsintro#sthash.5xDESezJ.dpuf

http://www.biblebelievers.org.au/jesusjew.htm

http://blog.camera.org/archives/2012/05/antisemitic_rant_passes_withou.html

http://blogs.wsj.com/law/2015/05/19/illinois-lawmakers-pass-divestment-bill-to-counter-israel-boycotts/

http://blogs.timesofisrael.com/bethlehem-bible-college-and-christ-at-the-checkpoint-a-different-message-for-a-different-audience/#.Vbxrgz7vF3EE.email

http://www.bobdylan.com/us/songs/neighborhood-bully

http://www.brijnet.org/israel50/decl-eng.htm

http://www.buergervereinigung-landsberg.de/geschichte/orginalfilm.htm

http://www.camera.org/index.asp?x_context=2&x_outlet=118&x_article=2221

http://www.cbn.com/cbnnews/insideisrael/2011/July/PA-Law-Selling-Land-to-Jews-Punishable-by-Death/

http://www.cia.gov/cia/publications/factbook/rankorder/2119rank.html

http://www.dailymail.co.uk/news/article-2325502/Map-shows-worlds-racist-countries-answers-surprise-you.html

http://www.dailywritingtips.com/are-anti-semitic-arabs-self-haters/

https://danutm.files.wordpress.com/2012/03/colinchapman-a-christian-response-to-radical-islam.pdf

http://jcpa.org/article/holocaust-inversion-the-portraying-of-israel-and-jews-as-nazis/#sthash.3CG60zcK.dpuf

http://www.dailyalert.org/Mobile/mobile.html

http://www.defenddemocracy.org/in_the_media/in_the_media_show.htm?doc_id=245738)

http://docstalk.blogspot.ae/2008/09/palestinian-crimes-against-christian.html

http://english.alarabiya.net/en/News/middle-east/2015/06/28/ISIS-executes-over-3-000-in-Syria-in-year-long-caliphate-.html

http://english.al-akhbar.com/node/7418

http://www.frontpagemag.com/2014/joseph-puder/kasim-hafeez-a-story-of-a-miraculous-transformation/

http://electronicintifada.net/blogs/ali-abunimah/south-african-church-leaders-endorse-israeli-apartheid-week

http://www.european-forum-on-antisemitism.org

http://www.freerepublic.com/focus/f-news/986307/posts

http://www.frontpagemag.com/2015/ben-shapiro/is-israel-the-problem-or-are-jews-the-problem/

http://www.frontpagemag.com/2012/mark-d-tooley/united-methodists-reject-divestment/

http://germanhistorydocs.ghi-dc.org/sub_image.cfm?image_id=1940

http://www.goodreads.com/author/quotes/281832.Joseph_Goebbels

http://www.haaretz.com/blogs/a-special-place-in-hell/the-progressive-who-paints-israel-as-a-genocidal-nazi-state.premium-1.429999

http://www.hadassah-med.com/doctor-search.aspx

http://www.ihr.org/leaflets/what_christians.shtml

http://inconvenienthistory.com/archive/2010/volume_2/number_1/goebbels_on_the_jews.php

http://www.independentsentinel.com/what-we-can-learn-from-joseph-goebbels/

http://www.infoisrael.net/cgi-local/text.pl?source=4/b/viii/070420051.

http://www.israeliapartheidweek.com/content/notable_quotes.asp

http://www.israelnationalnews.com/Articles/Article.aspx/16253#.VVcbGc4lbG4

http://www.israelsvoice.org/what-we-do/antisemitism-monitor/

https://www.jewishvirtuallibrary.org/jsource/biography/Suha_Arafat.html.

https://www.jewishvirtuallibrary.org/jsource/biography/WilhelmMarr.htl

http://www.jewishjournal.com/opinion/article/president_obama_vs._the_la_times_on_anti_semitism

http://www.jns.org/latest-articles/2015/4/27/israelis-who-hate-israeland-the-christians-who-fund-them#.VWMYqGAlbG4=

http://www.johnstonsarchive.net/terrorism/terrisraelsum.html

http://www.jpost.com/Middle-East/Abbas-wants-not-a-single-Israeli-in-future-Palestinian-state-321470

http://www.jpost.com/Arab-Israeli-Conflict/Dershowitz-lambastes-BDS-movement-for-ignoring-human-rights-offenses-around-the-world-405442

www.jpost.com/Arab-Israeli-Conflict/Initial-report-Stabbing-attack-in-Pisgat-Zev-third-of-day-in-Jerusalem-423719

http://www.jpost.com/Arab-Israeli-Conflict/PLO-ambassador-endorses-Protocols-of-the-Elders-of-Zion-408250

http://www.jpost.com/Israel-News/Bringing-the-jobs-to-Beduin-women-410837

http://www.jpost.com/Christian-News/Christian-groups-battle-anti-Semitism-at-the-UN-411915

http://www.jpost.com/JewishWorld/JewishFeatures/Article.aspx?id=261103

http://www.jpost.com/Jewish-World/Jewish-Features/ANC-comparison-of-Israel-to-Nazis-riles-South-African-Jews-362289

http://www.jpost.com/Jewish-World/Jewish-News/Nirenstein-Classical-anti-Semitism-is-no-longer-the-primary-threat-334372

http://www.jpost.com/Magazine/Features/Spotlight-on-modern-loathing

http://www.jpost.com/Middle-East/PA-Death-penalty-for-those-who-sell-land-to-Jews

http://www.jpost.com/Opinion/Op-Ed-Contributors/Why-Jews-dont-attend-the-Christ-at-the-Checkpoint-conference-345912

http://www.jpost.com/servlet/Satellite?pagename=JPost/JPArticle/ShowFull&cid=1114568594963&p=1078027574097).

http://www.knesset.gov.il/docs/eng/megilat_eng.htm

http://linguaspectrum.com/English-quotations/English-quotations-by-author-name.php?id=Joseph%20Goebbels

http://www.markdankof.com/get_off_the_pot.htm

http://www.maurice-ostroff.org

http://members.xoom.virgilio.it/

http://www.merriam-webster.com/dictionary/ethnic%20cleansing

http://newagebd.net/31269/israels-nazi-like-criminal-campaign-in-gaza/#sthash.6cxcTlJe.dpuf

http://ngomonitor.org/article/ngo_leadership_in_boycott_and_divestment_campaigns

http://ngo-monitor.org/articles.php?cat_id=48

http://www.nytimes.com/1997/05/12/world/arab-s-death-and-the-selling-of-land-to-jews.html

http://observer.com/2015/03/its-hard-to-be-a-christian-arab-in-israel-but-not-because-of-jews/#ixzz3b96F5wxb

http://pages.pomona.edu/~vis04747/h124/readings/Barak_failure_of_peace_process.pdf

http://palwatch.org/main.aspx?fi=157&doc_id=832.

http://palwatch.org/main.aspx?fi=472&fld_id=474&doc_id=5873

http://www.palestinechronicle.com/ben-white-boycott-the-backlash/?print=pdf

http://www.palwatch.org/main.aspx?fi=844

http://www.palwatch.org/main.aspx?fi=157&doc_id=14898

http://palwatch.org/main.aspx?fi=472&fld_id=474&doc_id=5873

http://www.peacewithrealism.org/pdc/jenin.htm

http://research.calvin.edu/german-propaganda-archive/goeb1.htm

http://www.palwatch.org/site/modules/print/preview.aspx?fi=157&doc_id=12680

http://www.peacewithrealism.org/pdc/jenin.htm

http://www.poets.org/poetsorg/poem/mending-wall

http://quickfacts.census.gov/qfd/states/53000.html

http://research.calvin.edu/german-propaganda-archive/goeb1.htm

http://roskam.house.gov/media-center/press-releases/roskam-anti-bds-provisions-headed-to-presidents-desk

http://www.wfp.org.

http://www.sabeel.org/old/news/newslt15/campbell.htm

http://www.sandrawilliams.org/ANTI/anti-semitism.html

http://www.securityfence.mod.gov.il/Pages/ENG/purpose.htm

https://seismicshock.files.wordpress.com/2011/11/antisemitism-and-christ-at-the-checkpoint-2012.pdf

http://sophia.smith.edu/blog/jerusalem/2011/05/30/words-matter/.

http://www.startribune.com/lawyers-for-minnesota-terror-suspects-argue-isil-not-a-terrorist-organization/321094901/

http://stopthewall.org/maps/860.shtml)

http://www.sullivan-county.com/identity/jew_haters.htm

http://www.texemarrs.com/042013/jews_not_descendants_of_abraham.htm

http://www.thecommentator.com/article/4723/christians_against_bds_in_the_heart_of_london

http://www.tertullian.org/fathers/chrysostom_adversus_judaeos_01_homily1.htm

http://thinkexist.com/quotation/if_you_tell_a_lie_big_enough_and_keep_repeating/345877.html

www.timesofisrael.com/abbas-accuses-israel-of-executing-teen-pisgat-zeev-stabber/

http://www.timesofisrael.com/abbas-toughens-law-against-palestinians-selling-land-to-jews/

http://unitedwithisrael.org/palestinian-authority-slanders-israel-as-nazi-state-pmw-reveals/

http://www.ushmm.org/wlc/en/article.php?ModuleId=10005144

http://www.wildolive.co.uk/CATC2014.htm

http://www.wnd.com/2015/06/isis-threatens-ancient-monastery-filled-with-christians/#svpqkxEDf2QpKvo4.99

http://www.worldnetdaily.com/news/article.asp?ARTICLE_ID=38556).

http://www.wymaninstitute.org/articles/2003-03-denier.php

http://www.yashanet.com/library/fathers.htm

Disclaimer: the author assumes no responsibility for the cited websites being active on the date of this book's publication, or afterwards.

Other Related Resources

Available at Messianic Jewish Resources Int'l. • www.messianicjewish.net
1-800-410-7367

(Check our website for current discounts and promotions)

First Time in History!

General Editor: Rabbi Barry Rubin
Theological Editor: Dr. John Fischer

The Complete Jewish Study Bible

Insights for Jews and Christians

—Dr. David H. Stern

A One-of-a-Kind Study Bible that illuminates the Jewish background and context of God's word so it is more fully understandable. Uses the updated *Complete Jewish Bible* text by David H. Stern, including notes from the *Jewish New Testament Commentary* and contributions from Scholars listed below. 1990 pages.

Hardback	978-1619708679	$49.95
Flexisoft	978-1619708693	$79.95
Leather	978-1619708709	$139.95

< Hardcover Edition

Leather Edition w/color gift box

Flexisoft Edition w/color sleeve

CONTRIBUTORS & SCHOLARS

Rabbi Dr. Glenn Blank	Rabbi Dr. David Friedman	Rabbi Elliot Klayman	Dr. Michael Rydelnik
Dr. Michael Brown	Dr. Arnold Fruchtenbaum	Jordan Gayle Levy	Dr. Jeffrey Seif
Rabbi Steven Bernstein	Dr. John Garr	Dr. Ronald Moseley	Rabbi Tzahi Shapira
Rabbi Joshua Brumbach	Pastor David Harris	Rabbi Dr. Rich Nichol	Dr. David H. Stern
Rabbi Ron Corbett	Benjamin Juster	Rabbi Mark J. Rantz	Dr. Bruce Stokes
Pastor Ralph Finley	Rabbi Dr. Daniel Juster	Rabbi Russ Resnik	Dr. Tom Tribelhorn
Rabbi Dr. John Fischer	Dr. Walter C. Kaiser	Dr. Richard Robinson	Dr. Forrest Weiland
Dr. Patrice Fischer	Rabbi Barney Kasdan	Rabbi Dr. Jacob Rosenberg	Dr. Marvin Wilson
Rebbitzen Malkah Forbes	Dr. Craig S. Keener	Rabbi Isaac Roussel	

QUOTES BY CURRENT JEWISH SCHOLARS & ANCIENT JEWISH SAGES

Dr. Daniel Boyarin	Rabbi Gamaliel	Rabbi Akiva
Dr. Amy-Jill Levine	Rabbi Hillel	Maimonides
Rabbi Jonathan Sacks	Rabbi Shammai	and many more

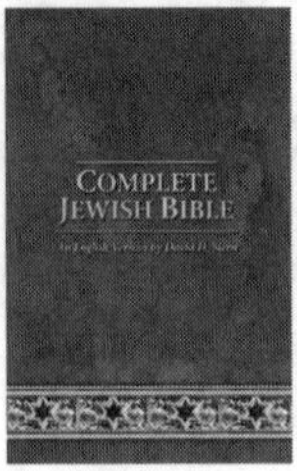

Complete Jewish Bible: *An English Version*

—Dr. David H. Stern (Available March 2017)

Now, the most widely used Messianic Jewish Bible around the world, has updated text with introductions added to each book, written from a biblically Jewish perspective. The CJB is a unified Jewish book, a version for Jews and non-Jews alike; to connect Jews with the Jewishness of the Messiah, and non-Jews with their Jewish roots. Names and terms are returned to their original Hebrew and presented in easy-to-understand transliterations, enabling the reader to say them the way *Yeshua* (Jesus) did! 1728 pages.

Paperback	978-1936716845	$29.95
Hardcover	978-1936716852	$34.95
Flexisoft Cover	978-1936716869	$49.95

Jewish New Testament

—Dr. David H. Stern

The New Testament is a Jewish book, written by Jews, initially for Jews. Its central figure was a Jew. His followers were all Jews; yet no other version really communicates its original, essential Jewishness. Uses neutral terms and Hebrew names. Highlights Jewish references and corrects mistranslations. Freshly translated into English from Greek, this is a must read to learn about first-century faith. 436 pages

Hardback	978-9653590069	**JB02**	$19.99
Paperback	978-9653590038	**JB01**	$14.99
Spanish	978-1936716272	**JB17**	$24.99

Also available in French, German, Polish, Portuguese and Russian.

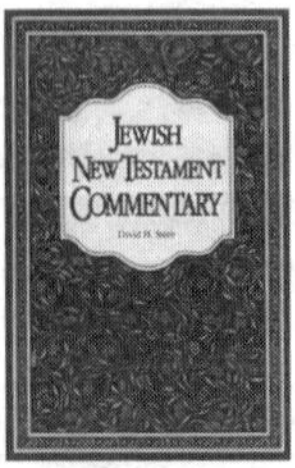

Jewish New Testament Commentary

—Dr. David H. Stern

This companion to the *Jewish New Testament* enhances Bible study. Passages and expressions are explained in their original cultural context. 15 years of research. 960 pages.

Hardback	978-9653590083	**JB06**	$34.99
Paperback	978-9653590113	**JB10**	$29.99

Psalms & Proverbs *Tehillim* תְהִלִּים-*Mishlei* מִשְׁלֵי

—Translated by Dr. David Stern

Contemplate the power in these words anytime, anywhere: Psalms-*Tehillim* offers uplifting words of praise and gratitude, keeping us focused with the right attitude; Proverbs-*Mishlei* gives us the wisdom for daily living, renewing our minds by leading us to examine our actions, to discern good from evil, and to decide freely to do the good. Makes a wonderful and meaningful gift. Softcover, 224 pages.

978-1936716692 LB90 $9.99

Messianic Judaism *A Modern Movement With an Ancient Past*

—David H. Stern

An updated discussion of the history, ideology, theology and program for Messianic Judaism. A challenge to both Jews and non-Jews who honor Yeshua to catch the vision of Messianic Judaism. 312 pages

978-1880226339 **LB62** $17.99

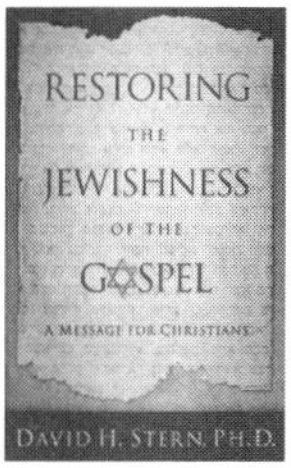

Restoring the Jewishness of the Gospel

A Message for Christians

—David H. Stern

Introduces Christians to the Jewish roots of their faith, challenges some conventional ideas, and raises some neglected questions: How are both the Jews and "the Church" God's people? Is the Law of Moses in force today? Filled with insight! Endorsed by Dr. Darrell L. Bock. 110 pages

English	978-1880226667	**LB70**	$9.99
Spanish	978-9653590175	**JB14**	$9.99

Come and Worship *Ways to Worship from the Hebrew Scriptures*

—Compiled by Barbara D. Malda

We were created to worship. God has graciously given us many ways to express our praise to him. Each way fits a different situation or moment in life, yet all are intended to bring honor and glory to him. When we believe that he is who he says he is [see *His Names are Wonderful!*] and that his Word is true, worship flows naturally from our hearts to his. Softcover, 128 pages.

978-1936716678 **LB88** $9.99

His Names Are Wonderful

Getting to Know God Through His Hebrew Names

—Elizabeth L. Vander Meulen and Barbara D. Malda

In Hebrew thought, names did more than identify people; they revealed their nature. God's identity is expressed not in one name, but in many. This book will help readers know God better as they uncover the truths in his Hebrew names. 160 pages.

978-1880226308 **LB58** $9.99

The Return of the Kosher Pig *The Divine Messiah in Jewish Thought*

—Rabbi Tzahi Shapira

The subject of Messiah fills many pages of rabbinic writings. Hidden in those pages is a little known concept that the Messiah has the same authority given to God. Based on the Scriptures and traditional rabbinic writings, this book shows the deity of Yeshua from a new perspective. You will see that the rabbis of old expected the Messiah to be divine. Softcover, 352 pages.

"One of the most interesting and learned tomes I have ever read. Contained within its pages is much with which I agree, some with which I disagree, and much about which I never thought. Rabbi Shapria's remarkable book cannot be ignored."

—Dr. Paige Patterson, President, Southwest Baptist Theological Seminary

978-1936716456 **LB81** $ 39.99

Proverbial Wisdom & Common Sense

A Messianic Commentary

—Derek Leman

A Messianic Jewish Approach to Today's Issues from the Proverbs
A devotional style commentary, divided into chapters suitable for daily reading. An encyclopedia of practical advice on topics relevant to everyone. 248 pages

Paperback 978-1880226780 **LB98** $19.99

Matthew Presents Yeshua, King Messiah *A Messianic Commentary*

—Rabbi Barney Kasdan

Few commentators are able to truly present Yeshua in his Jewish context. Most don't understand his background, his family, even his religion, and consequently really don't understand who he truly is. This commentator is well versed with first-century Jewish practices and thought, as well as the historical and cultural setting of the day, and the 'traditions of the Elders' that Yeshua so often spoke about. Get to know Yeshua, the King, through the writing of another rabbi, Barney Kasdan. 448 pages

978-1936716265 **LB76** $29.99

Rabbi Paul Enlightens the Ephesians on Walking with Messiah Yeshua

A Messianic Commentary

—Rabbi Barney Kasdan

The Ephesian were a diverse group of Jews and Gentiles, united together in Messiah. They definitely had an impact on the first century world in which they lived. But the Rabbi was not just writing to that local group. What is Paul saying to us? 160 pages.

Paperback 978-11936716821 **LB99** $17.99

James the Just Presents Application of Torah

A Messianic Commentary

—Dr. David Friedman

James (Jacob) one of the Epistles written to first century Jewish followers of Yeshua. Dr. David Friedman, a former Professor of the Israel Bible Institute has shed new light for Christians from this very important letter.

978-1936716449 **LB82** $14.99

Jude On Faith and the Destructive Influence of Heresy

A Messianic Commentary

—Rabbi Joshua Brumbach

Almost no other canonical book has been as neglected and overlooked as the Epistle of Jude. This little book may be small, but it has a big message that is even more relevant today as when it was originally written.

978-1-936716-78-4 **LB97** $14.99

At the Feet of Rabbi Gamaliel

Rabbinic Influence in Paul's Teachings

—David Friedman, Ph.D.

Paul (Shaul) was on the "fast track" to becoming a sage and Sanhedrin judge, describing himself as passionate for the Torah and the traditions of the fathers, typical for an aspiring Pharisee: "…trained at the feet of Gamaliel in every detail of the Torah of our forefathers. I was a zealot for God, as all of you are today" (Acts 22.3, CJB). Did Shaul's teachings reflect Rabbi Gamaliel's instructions? Did Paul continue to value the Torah and Pharisaic tradition? Did Paul create a 'New' Theology? The results of the research within these pages and its conclusion may surprise you. Softcover, 100 pages.

978-1936716753 **LB95** $8.99

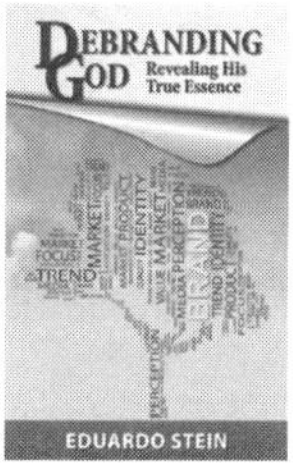

Debranding God *Revealing His True Essence*

—Eduardo Stein

The process of 'debranding' God is to remove all the labels and fads that prompt us to understand him as a supplier and ourselves as the most demanding of customers. Changing our perception of God also changes our perception of ourselves. In knowing who we are in relationship to God, we discover his, and our, true essence. Softcover, 252 pages.

978-1936716708 **LB91** $16.99

Under the Fig Tree *Messianic Thought Through the Hebrew Calendar*

—Patrick Gabriel Lumbroso

Take a daily devotional journey into the Word of God through the Hebrew Calendar and the Biblical Feasts. Learn deeper meaning of the Scriptures through Hebraic thought. Beautifully written and a source for inspiration to draw closer to Adonai every day. Softcover, 407 pages.

978-1936716760 **LB96** $25.99

Under the Vine *Messianic Thought Through the Hebrew Calendar*

—Patrick Gabriel Lumbroso

Journey daily through the Hebrew Calendar and Biblical Feasts into the B'rit Hadashah (New Testament) Scriptures as they are put in their rightful context, bringing Judaism alive in it's full beauty. Messianic faith was the motor and what gave substance to Abraham's new beliefs, hope to Job, trust to Isaac, vision to Jacob, resilience to Joseph, courage to David, wisdom to Solomon, knowledge to Daniel, and divine Messianic authority to Yeshua. Softcover, 412 pages.

978-1936716654 **LB87** $25.99

The Revolt of Rabbi Morris Cohen

Exploring the Passion & Piety of a Modern-day Pharisee
—Anthony Cardinale

A brilliant school psychologist, Rabbi Morris Cohen went on a one-man strike to protest the systematic mislabeling of slow learning pupils as "Learning Disabled" (to extract special education money from the state). His disciplinary hearing, based on the transcript, is a hilarious read! This effusive, garrulous man with an irresistible sense of humor lost his job, but achieved a major historic victory causing the reform of the billion-dollar special education program. Enter into the mind of an eighth-generation Orthodox rabbi to see how he deals spiritually with the loss of everything, even the love of his children. This modern-day Pharisee discovered a trusted friend in the author (a born again believer in Jesus) with whom he could openly struggle over Rabbinic Judaism as well as the concept of Jesus (Yeshua) as Messiah. Softcover, 320 pages.

978-1936716722 **LB92** $19.99

Stories of Yeshua

—Jim Reimann, Illustrator Julia Filipone-Erez

Children's Bible Storybook with four stories about Yeshua (Jesus). *Yeshua is Born: The Bethlehem Story* based on Lk 1:26-35 & 2:1-20; *Yeshua and Nicodemus in Jerusalem* based on Jn 3:1-16; *Yeshua Loves the Little Children of the World* based on Matthew 18:1–6 & 19:13–15; *Yeshua is Alive-The Empty Tomb in Jerusalem* based on Matthew 26:17-56, Jn 19:16-20:18, Lk 24:50-53. Ages 3-7, Softcover, 48 pages.

978-1936716685 **LB89** $14.99

To the Ends of the Earth – How the First Jewish Followers of Yeshua Transformed the Ancient World

— Dr. Jeffrey Seif

Everyone knows that the first followers of Yeshua were Jews, and that Christianity was very Jewish for the first 50 to 100 years. It's a known fact that there were many congregations made up mostly of Jews, although the false perception today is, that in the second century they disappeared. Dr. Seif reveals the truth of what happened to them and how these early Messianic Jews influenced and transformed the behavior of the known world at that time.

978-1936716463 **LB83** $17.99

Passion for Israel: *A Short History of the Evangelical Church's Support of Israel and the Jewish People*

—Dan Juster

History reveals a special commitment of Christians to the Jews as God's still elect people, but the terrible atrocities committed against the Jews by so-called Christians have overshadowed the many good deeds that have been performed. This important history needs to be told to help heal the wounds and to inspire more Christians to stand together in support of Israel.

978-1936716401 **LB78** $9.99

Jewish Roots and Foundations of the Scriptures I & II

—John Fischer, Th.D, Ph.D.

An outstanding evangelical leader once said: "There is something shallow about a Christianity that has lost its Jewish roots." A beautiful painting is a careful interweaving of a number of elements. Among other things, there are the background, the foreground and the subject. Discovering the roots of your faith is a little like appreciating the various parts of a painting. In the background is the panorama of preparation and pictures found in the Old Testament. In the foreground is the landscape and light of the first century Jewish setting. All of this is intricately connected with and highlights the subject—which becomes the flowering of all these aspects—the coming of God to earth and what that means for us. Discovering and appreciating your roots in this way broadens, deepens and enriches your faith and your understanding of Scripture. This audio is 32 hours of live class instruction - audio is clear and easy to understand.

9781936716623 **LCD03 / LCD04** $49.99 each

The Gospels in their Jewish Context

—John Fischer, Th.D, Ph.D.

An examination of the Jewish background and nature of the Gospels in their contemporary political, cultural and historical settings, emphasizing each gospel's special literary presentation of Yeshua, and highlighting the cultural and religious contexts necessary for understanding each of the gospels. 32 hours of audio/video instruction on MP3-DVD and pdf of syllabus.

978-1936716241 **LCD01** $49.99

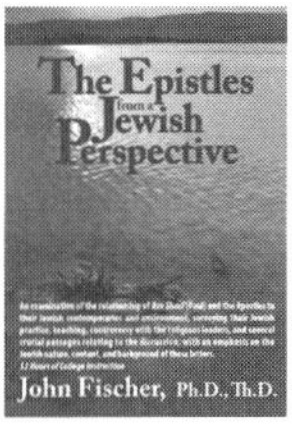

The Epistles from a Jewish Perspective

—John Fischer, Th.D, Ph.D.

An examination of the relationship of Rabbi Shaul (the Apostle Paul) and the Apostles to their Jewish contemporaries and environment; surveys their Jewish practices, teaching, controversy with the religious leaders, and many critical passages, with emphasis on the Jewish nature, content, and background of these letters. 32 hours of audio/video instruction on MP3-DVD and pdf of syllabus.

978-1936716258 **LCD02** $49.99

The Red Heifer *A Jewish Cry for Messiah*

—Anthony Cardinale

Award-winning journalist and playwright Anthony Cardinale has traveled extensively in Israel, and recounts here his interviews with Orthodox rabbis, secular Israelis, and Palestinian Arabs about the current search for a red heifer by Jewish radicals wishing to rebuild the Temple and bring the Messiah. These real-life interviews are interwoven within an engaging and dramatic fictional portrayal of the diverse people of Israel and how they would react should that red heifer be found. Readers will find themselves in the Land, where they can hear learned rabbis and ordinary Israelis talking about the red heifer and dealing with all the related issues and the imminent coming and identity of Messiah.

978-1936716470 LB79 $19.99

The Borough Park Papers

—Multiple Authors

As you read the New Testament, you "overhear" debates first-century Messianic Jews had about critical issues, e.g. Gentiles being "allowed" into the Messianic kingdom (Acts 15). Similarly, you're now invited to "listen in" as leading twenty-first century Messianic Jewish theologians discuss critical issues facing us today. Some ideas may not fit into your previously held pre-suppositions or pre-conceptions. Indeed, you may find some paradigm shifting in your thinking. We want to share the thoughts of these thinkers with you, our family in the Messiah.

Symposium I:

The Gospel and the Jewish People

248 pages

978-1936716593 LB84 $39.95

Symposium II:

The Deity of Messiah and the Mystery of God

211 pages

978-1936716609 LB85 $39.95

Symposium III:

How Jewish Should the Messianic Community Be?

978-1936716616 LB86 $39.95

On The Way to Emmaus: *Searching the Messianic Prophecies*

—Dr. Jacques Doukhan

An outstanding compilation of the most critical Messianic prophecies by a renowned conservative Christian Scholar, drawing on material from the Bible, Rabbinic sources, Dead Sea Scrolls, and more.

978-1936716432 LB80 $14.99

Yeshua *A Guide to the Real Jesus and the Original Church*

—Dr. Ron Moseley

Opens up the history of the Jewish roots of the Christian faith. Illuminates the Jewish background of Yeshua and the Church and never flinches from showing "Jesus was a Jew, who was born, lived, and died, within first century Judaism." Explains idioms in the New Testament. Endorsed by Dr. Brad Young and Dr. Marvin Wilson. 213 pages.

978-1880226681 **LB29** $12.99

Gateways to Torah *Joining the Ancient Conversation on the Weekly Portion*

—Rabbi Russell Resnik

From before the days of Messiah until today, Jewish people have read from and discussed a prescribed portion of the Pentateuch each week. Now, a Messianic Jewish Rabbi, Russell Resnik, brings another perspective on the Torah, that of a Messianic Jew. 246 pages.

978-1880226889 **LB42** $15.99

Creation to Completion *A Guide to Life's Journey from the Five Books of Moses*

—Rabbi Russell Resnik

Endorsed by Coach Bill McCartney, Founder of Promise Keepers & Road to Jerusalem: "Paul urged Timothy to study the Scriptures (2 Tim. 3:16), advising him to apply its teachings to all aspects of his life. Since there was no New Testament then, this rabbi/apostle was convinced that his disciple would profit from studying the Torah, the Five Books of Moses, and the Old Testament. Now, Rabbi Resnik has written a warm devotional commentary that will help you understand and apply the Law of Moses to your life in a practical way." 256 pages

978-1880226322 **LB61** $14.99

Walk Genesis! Walk Exodus! Walk Leviticus! Walk Numbers! Walk Deuteronomy!

Messianic Jewish Devotional Commentaries

—Jeffrey Enoch Feinberg, Ph.D.

Using the weekly synagogue readings, Dr. Jeffrey Feinberg has put together some very valuable material in his "Walk" series. Each section includes a short Hebrew lesson (for the non-Hebrew speaker), key concepts, an excellent overview of the portion, and some practical applications. Can be used as a daily devotional as well as a Bible study tool.

Walk Genesis!	238 pages	978-1880226759	**LB34**	$12.99
Walk Exodus!	224 pages	978-1880226872	**LB40**	$12.99
Walk Leviticus!	208 pages	978-1880226926	**LB45**	$12.99
Walk Numbers!	211 pages	978-1880226995	**LB48**	$12.99
Walk Deuteronomy!	231 pages	978-1880226186	**LB51**	$12.99
SPECIAL! Five-book Walk!		5 Book Set **Save $10**	**LK28**	$54.99

Good News According To Matthew

—Dr. Henry Einspruch

English translation with quotations from the Tanakh (Old Testament) capitalized and printed in Hebrew. Helpful notations are included. Lovely black and white illustrations throughout the book. 86 pages.

978-1880226025 **LB03** $4.99

Also available in Yiddish. **LB02** $4.99

They Loved the Torah *What Yeshua's First Followers Really Thought About the Law*

—Dr. David Friedman

Although many Jews believe that Paul taught against the Law, this book disproves that notion. An excellent case for his premise that all the first followers of the Messiah were not only Torah-observant, but also desired to spread their love for God's entire Word to the gentiles to whom they preached. 144 pages. Endorsed by Dr. David Stern, Ariel Berkowitz, Rabbi Dr. Stuart Dauermann & Dr. John Fischer.

978-1880226940 **LB47** $9.99

The Distortion *2000 Years of Misrepresenting the Relationship Between Jesus the Messiah and the Jewish People*

—Dr. John Fischer & Dr. Patrice Fischer

Did the Jews kill Jesus? Did they really reject him? With the rise of global anti–Semitism, it is important to understand what the Gospels teach about the relationship between Jewish people and their Messiah. 2000 years of distortion have made this difficult. Learn how the distortion began and continues to this day and what you can do to change it. 126 pages. Endorsed by Dr. Ruth Fleischer, Rabbi Russell Resnik, Dr. Daniel C. Juster, Dr. Michael Rydelnik.

978-1880226254 **LB54** $11.99

eBooks Now Available!

All books are available as ebooks for your favorite reader

Visit www.messianicjewish.net for direct links to these readers for each available eBook.

God's Appointed Times *A Practical Guide to Understanding and Celebrating the Biblical Holidays* – **New Edition.**

—Rabbi Barney Kasdan

The Biblical Holy Days teach us about the nature of God and his plan for mankind, and can be a source of God's blessing for all believers–Jews and Gentiles–today. Includes historical background, traditional Jewish observance, New Testament relevance, and prophetic significance, plus music, crafts and holiday recipes. 145 pages.

English	978-1880226353	**LB63**	$12.99
Spanish	978-1880226391	**LB59**	$12.99

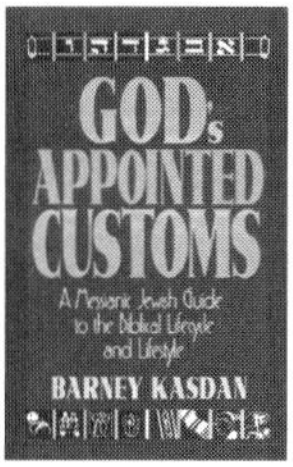

God's Appointed Customs *A Messianic Jewish Guide to the Biblical Lifecycle and Lifestyle*

— Rabbi Barney Kasdan

Explains how biblical customs are often the missing key to unlocking the depths of Scripture. Discusses circumcision, the Jewish wedding, and many more customs mentioned in the New Testament. Companion to *God's Appointed Times*. 170 pages.

English	978-1880226636	**LB26**	$12.99
Spanish	978-1880226551	**LB60**	$12.99

Celebrations of the Bible *A Messianic Children's Curriculum*

Did you know that each Old Testament feast or festival finds its fulfillment in the New? They enrich the lives of people who experience and enjoy them. Our popular curriculum for children is in a brand new, user-friendly format. The lay-flat at binding allows you to easily reproduce handouts and worksheets. Celebrations of the Bible has been used by congregations, Sunday schools, ministries, homeschoolers, and individuals to teach children about the biblical festivals. Each of these holidays are presented for Preschool (2-K), Primary (Grades 1-3), Junior (Grades 4-6), and Children's Worship/Special Services. 208 pages.

978-1880226261 **LB55** $24.99

Passover: *The Key That Unlocks the Book of Revelation*

—Daniel C. Juster, Th.D.

Is there any more enigmatic book of the Bible than Revelation? Controversy concerning its meaning has surrounded it back to the first century. Today, the arguments continue. Yet, Dan Juster has given us the key that unlocks the entire book—the events and circumstances of the Passover/Exodus. By interpreting Revelation through the lens of Exodus, Dan Juster provides a unified overview that helps us read Revelation as it was always meant to be read, as a drama of spiritual conflict, deliverance, and above all, worship. He also shows how this final drama, fulfilled in Messiah, resonates with the Torah and all of God's Word. — Russ Resnik, Executive Director, Union of Messianic Jewish Congregations.

978-1936716210 **LB74** $10.99

The Messianic Passover Haggadah

Revised and Updated

—Rabbi Barry Rubin and Steffi Rubin.

Guides you through the traditional Passover seder dinner, step-by-step. Not only does this observance remind us of our rescue from Egyptian bondage, but, we remember Messiah's last supper, a Passover seder. The theme of redemption is seen throughout the evening. What's so unique about our Haggadah is the focus on Yeshua (Jesus) the Messiah and his teaching, especially on his last night in the upper room. 36 pages.

English	978-1880226292	**LB57**	$4.99
Spanish	978-1880226599	**LBSP01**	$4.99

The Messianic Passover Seder Preparation Guide

Includes recipes, blessings and songs. 19 pages.

English	978-1880226247	**LB10**	$2.99
Spanish	978-1880226728	**LBSP02**	$2.99

The Sabbath *Entering God's Rest*

—Barry Rubin & Steffi Rubin

Even if you've never celebrated Shabbat before, this book will guide you into the rest God has for all who would enter in—Jews and non-Jews. Contains prayers, music, recipes; in short, everything you need to enjoy the Sabbath, even how to observe havdalah, the closing ceremony of the Sabbath. Also discusses the Saturday or Sunday controversy. 48 pages.

978-1880226742 **LB32** $6.99

Havdalah *The Ceremony that Completes the Sabbath*

—Dr. Neal & Jamie Lash

The Sabbath ends with this short, yet equally sweet ceremony called havdalah (separation). This ceremony reminds us to be a light and a sweet fragrance in this world of darkness as we carry the peace, rest, joy and love of the Sabbath into the work week. 28 pages.

978-1880226605 **LB69** $4.99

Dedicate and Celebrate!

A Messianic Jewish Guide to Hanukkah

—Barry Rubin & Family

Hanukkah means "dedication" — a theme of significance for Jews and Christians. Discussing its historical background, its modern-day customs, deep meaning for all of God's people, this little book covers all the how-tos! Recipes, music, and prayers for lighting the menorah, all included! 32 pages.

978-1880226834 **LB36** $4.99

The Conversation

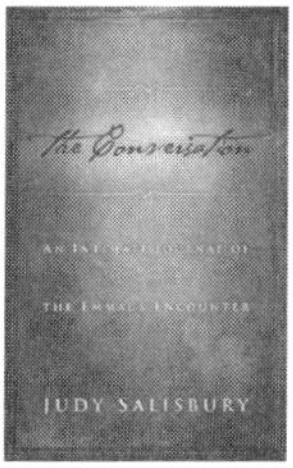

An Intimate Journal of the Emmaus Encounter

—Judy Salisbury

"Then beginning with Moses and with all the prophets, He explained to them the things concerning Himself in all the Scriptures." Luke 24:27

If you've ever wondered what that conversation must have been like, this captivating book takes you there.

"The Conversation brings to life that famous encounter between the two disciples and our Lord Jesus on the road to Emmaus. While it is based in part on an imaginative reconstruction, it is filled with the throbbing pulse of the excitement of the sensational impact that our Lord's resurrection should have on all of our lives." ~ Dr. Walter Kaiser President Emeritus Gordon-Conwell Theological Seminary. Hardcover 120 pages.

Hardcover	978-1936716173	**LB73**	$14.99
Paperback	978-1936716364	**LB77**	$9.99

Growing to Maturity

A Messianic Jewish Discipleship Guide

—Daniel C. Juster, Th.D.

This discipleship series presents first steps of understanding and spiritual practice, tailored for the Jewish believer. It's purpose is to aid the believer in living according to Yeshua's will as a disciple, one who has learned the example of his teacher. The course is structured according to recent advances in individualized educational instruction. Discipleship is serious business and the material is geared for serious study and reflection. Each chapter is divided into short sections followed by study questions. 256 pages.

978-1936716227 **LB75** $19.99

Growing to Maturity Primer: *A Messianic Jewish Discipleship Workbook*

—Daniel C. Juster, Th.D.

A basic book of material in question and answer form. Usable by everyone. 60 pages.

978-0961455507 **TB16** $7.99

Conveying Our Heritage A Messianic Jewish Guide to Home Practice

—Daniel C. Juster, Th.D. Patricia A. Juster

Throughout history the heritage of faith has been conveyed within the family and the congregation. The first institution in the Bible is the family and only the family can raise children with an adequate appreciation of our faith and heritage. This guide exists to help families learn how to pass on the heritage of spiritual Messianic Jewish life. Softcover, 86 pages

978-1936716739 **LB93** $8.99

That They May Be One *A Brief Review of Church Restoration Movements and Their Connection to the Jewish People*

—Daniel Juster, Th.D

Something prophetic and momentous is happening. The Church is finally fully grasping its relationship to Israel and the Jewish people. Author describes the restoration movements in Church history and how they connected to Israel and the Jewish people. Each one contributed in some way—some more, some less—toward the ultimate unity between Jews and Gentiles. Predicted in the Old Testament and fulfilled in the New, Juster believes this plan of God finds its full expression in Messianic Judaism. He may be right. See what you think as you read *That They May Be One*. 100 pages.

978-1880226711 **LB71** $9.99

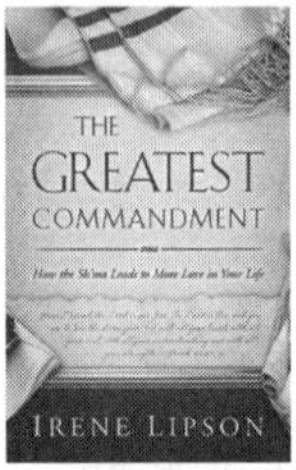

The Greatest Commandment

How the Sh'ma Leads to More Love in Your Life

—Irene Lipson

"What is the greatest commandment?" Yeshua was asked. His reply—"Hear, O Israel, the Lord our God, the Lord is one, and you are to love Adonai your God with all your heart, with all your soul, with all your understanding, and all your strength." A superb book explaining each word so the meaning can be fully grasped and lived. Endorsed by Elliot Klayman, Susan Perlman, & Robert Stearns. 175 pages.

978-1880226360 **LB65** $12.99

Blessing the King of the Universe

Transforming Your Life Through the Practice of Biblical Praise

—Irene Lipson

Insights into the ancient biblical practice of blessing God are offered clearly and practically. With examples from Scripture and Jewish tradition, this book teaches the biblical formula used by men and women of the Bible, including the Messiah; points to new ways and reasons to praise the Lord; and explains more about the Jewish roots of the faith. Endorsed by Rabbi Barney Kasdan, Dr. Mitch Glaser, & Rabbi Dr. Dan Cohn-Sherbok. 144 pages.

978-1880226797 **LB53** $11.99

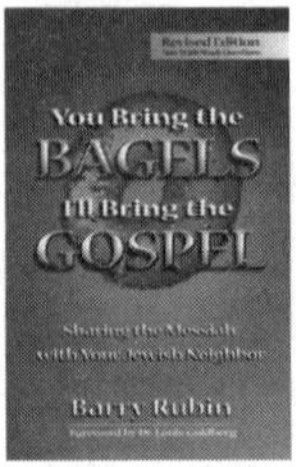

You Bring the Bagels, I'll Bring the Gospel

Sharing the Messiah with Your Jewish Neighbor

Revised Edition—Now with Study Questions

—Rabbi Barry Rubin

This "how-to-witness-to-Jewish-people" book is an orderly presentation of everything you need to share the Messiah with a Jewish friend. Includes Messianic prophecies, Jewish objections to believing, sensitivities in your witness, words to avoid. A "must read" for all who care about the Jewish people. Good for individual or group study. Used in Bible schools. Endorsed by Harold A. Sevener, Dr. Walter C. Kaiser, Dr. Erwin J. Kolb and Dr. Arthur F. Glasser. 253 pages.

English	978-1880226650	**LB13**	$12.99
Te Tengo Buenas Noticias	978-0829724103	**OBSP02**	$14.99

Making Eye Contact With God

A Weekly Devotional for Women

—Terri Gillespie

What kind of eyes do you have? Are they downcast and sad? Are they full of God's joy and passion? See yourself through the eyes of God. Using real life anecdotes, combined with scripture, the author reveals God's heart for women everywhere, as she softly speaks of the ways in which women see God. Endorsed by prominent authors: Dr. Angela Hunt, Wanda Dyson and Kathryn Mackel. 247 pages, hardcover.

978-1880226513 **LB68** $19.99

Divine Reversal

The Transforming Ethics of Jesus

—Rabbi Russell Resnik

In the Old Testament, God often reversed the plans of man. Yeshua's ethics continue this theme. Following his path transforms one's life from within, revealing the source of true happiness, forgiveness, reconciliation, fidelity and love. From the introduction, "As a Jewish teacher, Jesus doesn't separate matters of theology from practice. His teaching is consistently practical, ethical, and applicable to real life, even two thousand years after it was originally given." Endorsed by Jonathan Bernis, Dr. Daniel C. Juster, Dr. Jeffrey L. Seif, and Dr Darrell Bock. 206 pages

978-1880226803 **LB72** $12.99

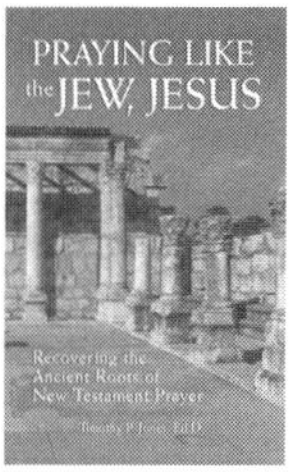

Praying Like the Jew, Jesus

Recovering the Ancient Roots of New Testament Prayer

—Dr. Timothy P. Jones

This eye-opening book reveals the Jewish background of many of Yeshua's prayers. Historical vignettes "transport" you to the times of Yeshua so you can grasp the full meaning of Messiah's prayers. Unique devotional thoughts and meditations, presented in down-to-earth language, provide inspiration for a more meaningful prayer life and help you draw closer to God. Endorsed by Mark Galli, James W. Goll, Rev. Robert Stearns, James F. Strange, and Dr. John Fischer. 144 pages.

978-1880226285 **LB56** $9.99

Growing Your Olive Tree Marriage *A Guide for Couples from Two Traditions*

—David J. Rudolph

One partner is Jewish; the other is Christian. Do they celebrate Hanukkah, Christmas or both? Do they worship in a church or a synagogue? How will the children be raised? This is the first book from a biblical perspective that addresses the concerns of intermarried couples, offering a godly solution. Includes highlights of interviews with intermarried couples. Endorsed by Walter C. Kaiser, Jr., Rabbi Dan Cohn-Sherbok, Jonathan Settel, Dr. Mitchell Glaser & Natalie Sirota. 224 pages.

978-1880226179 **LB50** $12.99

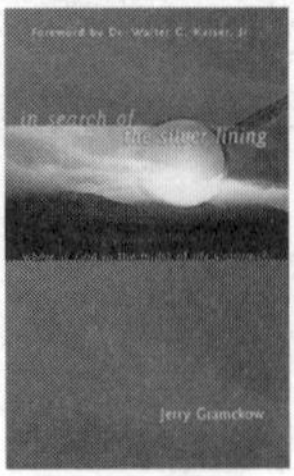

In Search of the Silver Lining *Where is God in the Midst of Life's Storms?*

—Jerry Gramckow

When faced with suffering, what are your choices? Storms have always raged. And people have either perished in their wake or risen above the tempests, shaping history by their responses…new storms are on the horizon. How will we deal with them? How will we shape history or those who follow us? The answer lies in how we view God in the midst of the storms. Endorsed by Joseph C. Aldrich, Ray Beeson, Dr. Daniel Juster. 176 pages.

978-1880226865 **LB39** $10.99

The Voice of the Lord *Messianic Jewish Daily Devotional*

—Edited by David J. Rudolph

Brings insight into the Jewish Scriptures—both Old and New Testaments. Twenty-two prominent Messianic contributors provide practical ways to apply biblical truth. Start your day with this unique resource. Explanatory notes. Perfect companion to the Complete Jewish Bible (see page 2). Endorsed by Edith Schaeffer, Dr. Arthur F. Glaser, Dr. Michael L. Brown, Mitch Glaser and Moishe Rosen. 416 pages.

9781880226704 **LB31** $19.99

Kingdom Relationships *God's Laws for the Community of Faith*

—Dr. Ron Moseley

Dr. Ron Moseley`s Yeshua: A Guide to the Real Jesus and the Original Church has taught thousands of people about the Jewishness of not only Yeshua, but of the first followers of the Messiah.

In this work, Moseley focuses on the teaching of Torah -- the Five Books of Moses -- tapping into truths that greatly help modern-day members of the community of faith. 64 pages.

978-1880226841 **LB37** $8.99

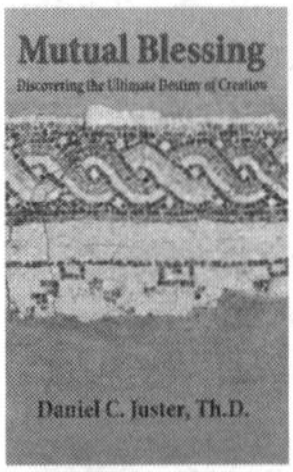

Mutual Blessing *Discovering the Ultimate Destiny of Creation*

—Daniel C. Juster

To truly love as God loves is to see the wonder and richness of the distinct differences in all of creation and his natural order of interdependence. This is the way to mutual blessing and the discovery of the ultimate destiny of creation. Learn how to become enriched and blessed as you enrich and bless others and all that is around you! Softcover, 135 pages.

978-1936716746 **LB94** $9.99

Train Up A Child *Successful Parenting For The Next Generation*

—Dr. Daniel L. Switzer

The author, former principal of Ets Chaiyim Messianic Jewish Day School, and father of four, combines solid biblical teaching with Jewish sources on child raising, focusing on the biblical holy days, giving fresh insight into fulfilling the role of parent. 188 pages. Endorsed by Dr. David J. Rudolph, Paul Lieberman, and Dr. David H. Stern.

978-1880226377 **LB64** $12.99

Fire on the Mountain - *Past Renewals, Present Revivals and the Coming Return of Israel*

—Dr. Louis Goldberg

The term "revival" is often used to describe a person or congregation turning to God. Is this something that "just happens," or can it be brought about? Dr. Louis Goldberg, author and former professor of Hebrew and Jewish Studies at Moody Bible Institute, examines real revivals that took place in Bible times and applies them to today. 268 pages.

978-1880226858 **LB38** $15.99

Voices of Messianic Judaism *Confronting Critical Issues Facing a Maturing Movement*

—General Editor Rabbi Dan Cohn-Sherbok

Many of the best minds of the Messianic Jewish movement contributed their thoughts to this collection of 29 substantive articles. Challenging questions are debated: The involvement of Gentiles in Messianic Judaism? How should outreach be accomplished? Liturgy or not? Intermarriage? 256 pages.

978-1880226933 **LB46** $15.99

The Enduring Paradox *Exploratory Essays in Messianic Judaism*

—General Editor Dr. John Fischer

Yeshua and his Jewish followers began a new movement—Messianic Judaism—2,000 years ago. In the 20th century, it was reborn. Now, at the beginning of the 21st century, it is maturing. Twelve essays from top contributors to the theology of this vital movement of God, including: Dr. Walter C. Kaiser, Dr. David H. Stern, and Dr. John Fischer. 196 pages.

978-1880226902 **LB43** $13.99

The World To Come *A Portal to Heaven on Earth*

—Derek Leman

An insightful book, exposing fallacies and false teachings surrounding this extremely important subject... paints a hopeful picture of the future and dispels many non-biblical notions. Intriguing chapters: Magic and Desire, The Vision of the Prophets, Hints of Heaven, Horrors of Hell, The Drama of the Coming Ages. Offers a fresh, but old, perspective on the world to come, as it interacts with the prophets of Israel and the Bible. 110 pages.

978-1880226049 **LB67** .$9.99

Hebrews Through a Hebrew's Eyes

—Dr. Stuart Sacks

Written to first-century Messianic Jews, this epistle, understood through Jewish eyes, edifies and encourages all. 119 pages. Endorsed by Dr. R.C. Sproul and James M. Boice.

978-1880226612 **LB23** $10.99

The Irrevocable Calling *Israel's Role As A Light To The Nations*

—Daniel C. Juster, Th.D.

Referring to the chosen-ness of the Jewish people, Paul, the Apostle, wrote "For God's free gifts and his calling are irrevocable" (Rom. 11:29). This messenger to the Gentiles understood the unique calling of his people, Israel. So does Dr. Daniel Juster, President of Tikkun Ministries Int'l. In *The Irrevocable Calling*, he expands Paul's words, showing how Israel was uniquely chosen to bless the world and how these blessings can be enjoyed today. Endorsed by Dr. Jack Hayford, Mike Bickle and Don Finto. 64 pages.

978-1880226346 **LB66** $8.99

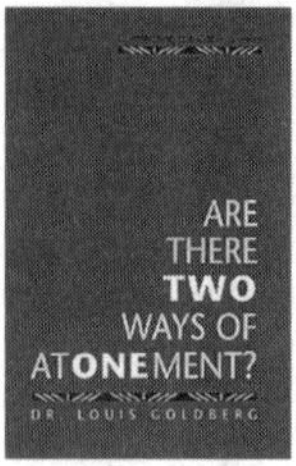

Are There Two Ways of Atonement?

—Dr. Louis Goldberg

Here Dr. Louis Goldberg, long-time professor of Jewish Studies at Moody Bible Institute, exposes the dangerous doctrine of Two-Covenant Theology. 32 pages.

978-1880226056 **LB12** $ 4.99

Awakening *Articles and Stories About Jews and Yeshua*

—Arranged by Anna Portnov

Articles, testimonies, and stories about Jewish people and their relationship with God, Israel, and the Messiah. Includes the effective tract, "The Most Famous Jew of All." One of our best anthologies for witnessing to Jewish people. Let this book witness for you! Russian version also available. 110 pages.

English 978-1880226094 **LB15** $ 6.99
Russian 978-1880226018 **LB14** $ 6.99

The Unpromised Land *The Struggle of Messianic Jews Gary and Shirley Beresford*

—Linda Alexander

They felt God calling them to live in Israel, the Promised Land. Wanting nothing more than to live quietly and grow old together in the country of refuge for all Jewish people, little did they suspect what events would follow to try their faith. The fight to make *aliyah*, to claim their rightful inheritance in the Promised Land, became a battle waged not only for themselves, but also for Messianic Jews all over the world that wish to return to the Jewish homeland. Here is the true saga of the Beresford`s journey to the land of their forefathers. 216 pages.

978-1880226568 **LB19** $ 9.99

Death of Messiah *Twenty fascinating articles that address a subject of grief, hope, and ultimate triumph.*

—Edited by Kai Kjaer-Hansen

This compilation, written by well-known Jewish believers, addresses the issue of Messiah and offers proof that Yeshua—the true Messiah—not only died, but also was resurrected! 160 pages.

978-1880226582 **LB20** $ 8.99

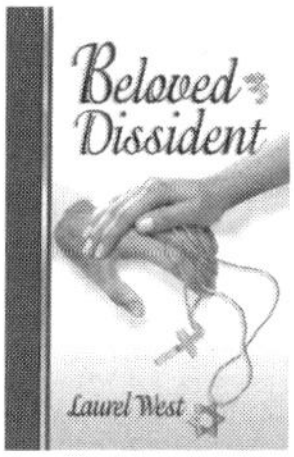

Beloved Dissident *(A Novel)*

—Laurel West

A gripping story of human relationships, passionate love, faith, and spiritual testing. Set in the world of high finance, intrigue, and international terrorism, the lives of David, Jonathan, and Leah intermingle on many levels--especially their relationships with one another and with God. As the two men tangle with each other in a rising whirlwind of excitement and danger, each hopes to win the fight for Leah's love. One of these rivals will move Leah to a level of commitment and love she has never imagined--or dared to dream. Whom will she choose? 256 pages.

978-1880226766 **LB33** $ 9.99

Sudden Terror

—Dr. David Friedman

Exposes the hidden agenda of militant Islam. The author, a former member of the Israel Defense Forces, provides eye-opening information needed in today's dangerous world.

Dr. David Friedman recounts his experiences confronting terrorism; analyzes the biblical roots of the conflict between Israel and Islam; provides an overview of early Islam; demonstrates how the United States and Israel are bound together by a common enemy; and shows how to cope with terrorism and conquer fear. The culmination of many years of research and personal experiences. This expose will prepare you for what's to come! 160 pages.

978-1880226155 **LB49** $ 9.99

It is Good! *Growing Up in a Messianic Family*

—Steffi Rubin

Growing up in a Messianic Jewish family. Meet Tovah! Tovah (Hebrew for "Good") is growing up in a Messianic Jewish home, learning the meaning of God`s special days. Ideal for young children, it teaches the biblical holidays and celebrates faith in Yeshua. 32 pages to read & color.

978-1880226063 **LB11** $ 4.99
